TRANSFORMATIVE PATHWAYS TO SUSTAINABILITY

Transformations to sustainability are increasingly the focus of research and policy discussions around the Sustainable Development Goals. However, the different roles played by transdisciplinary research in contributing to social transformations across diverse settings have been neglected in the literature. *Transformative Pathways to Sustainability* responds to this gap by presenting a set of coherent, theoretically informed and methodologically innovative experiments from around the world that offer important insights for this growing field.

The book draws on content and cases from across the 'Pathways' Transformative Knowledge Network, an international group of six regional hubs working on sustainability challenges in their own local or national contexts. Each of these hubs reports on their experiences of 'transformation laboratory' processes in the following areas: sustainable agricultural and food systems for healthy livelihoods, with a focus on sustainable agri-food systems in the UK and open-source seeds in Argentina; low carbon energy and industrial transformations, focussing on mobile-enabled solar home systems in Kenya and social aspects of the green transformation in China; and water and waste for sustainable cities, looking at Xochimilco wetland in Mexico and Gurgaon in India. The book combines new empirical data from these processes with a novel analysis that represents both theoretical and methodological contributions. It is especially international in its scope, drawing inputs from North and South, mirroring the universality of the Sustainable Development Goals.

The book is of vital interest to academics, action researchers and funders, policy makers and civil-society organisations working on transformations to sustainability.

The Pathways Network conducts action research into transformations to sustainability in six hubs across the world. Since 2015, it has been co-led (with Anabel Marin) by the editor, Adrian Ely, a Reader in Technology and Sustainability at SPRU and the STEPS Centre, University of Sussex, UK.

Pathways to Sustainability Series

This book series addresses core challenges around linking science and technology and environmental sustainability with poverty reduction and social justice. It is based on the work of the Social, Technological and Environmental Pathways to Sustainability (STEPS) Centre, a major investment of the UK Economic and Social Research Council (ESRC). The STEPS Centre brings together researchers at the Institute of Development Studies (IDS) and SPRU (Science Policy Research Unit) at the University of Sussex with a set of partner institutions in Africa, Asia and Latin America.

The Water–Food–Energy Nexus
Power, Politics and Justice
Jeremy Allouche, Carl Middleton and Dipak Gyawali

The Circular Economy and the Global South
Sustainable Lifestyles and Green Industrial Development
Edited by Patrick Schröder, Manisha Anantharaman, Kartika Anggraeni and Tim Foxon

Water for Food Security, Nutrition and Social Justice
Lyla Mehta, Theib Oweis, Claudia Ringler, Barbara Schreiner and Shiney Varghese

The Politics of Uncertainty
Challenges of Transformation
Edited by Ian Scoones and Andy Stirling

Transformative Pathways to Sustainability
Learning Across Disciplines, Cultures and Contexts
The Pathways Network

For more information about this series, please visit: www.routledge.com/Pathways-to-Sustainability/book-series/ECPSS

This book – over five years in the making – clearly illustrates the powerful potential of internationally-networked, transdisciplinary research. It marks an important step forward in the study of social transformations for sustainability, and is a key resource for those who concern themselves with today's important challenge of transforming science.

— *Heide Hackmann, PhD, Chief Executive Officer, International Science Council (ISC)*

There is a proliferation of studies about the Sustainable Development Goals (SDGs), but this well written and structured book goes to the heart of the debate: the necessary transformations for addressing the SDGs. What emerges is an important tapestry of theories and rich selection of local experiences that can be used to understand transformations and work with stakeholders using Transformation-Lab methodologies. It is an exemplary and compelling account of an exciting collective and global transdisciplinary research adventure. A must-read for anyone, academic and practitioners, engaged with the deep challenges of our time.

— *Johan Schot, Professor of Global History and Sustainability Transitions at the Utrecht University Centre for Global Challenges and Academic Director of the Transformative Innovation Policy Consortium (TIPC)*

Transformation requires collective wisdom. Once this is forged by connecting and communicating across boundaries, it creates a bigger coherence that unites and steers us all, whatever our location, speciality or profession. This book describes how collective wisdom can be created to support transformative action.

— *Oliver Greenfield, Convenor, Green Economy Coalition*

The best way to shape the future is to imagine it, and the best way to imagine it is to learn from pioneering examples. This book provides the examples and the theory that explains them. Fantastic reading for practitioners, scholars and dreamers!

— *Carlota Perez, Honorary Professor at the Institute for Innovation and Public Purpose IIPP-UCL*

In this potentially decisive decade for human well-being and planetary health, the question of how systemic or transformative change happens remains critical. How do we transition to social and economic pathways that ensure prosperity for all without cataclysmic environmental and climatic consequences? What role can transdisciplinary research play in identifying and helping to resolve structural barriers to transformative change? In this moment of unusual opportunities and challenges, this mould-breaking book tackles these questions head on. It is a timely and welcome challenge to the global development, research and policy communities to think and act differently.

— *Dr. Cosmas Milton Obote Ochieng, Global Director, Governance, Poverty and Equity, World Resources Institute*

This book offers rich insight into how transformative change happens. It is the output of an established global community of researchers and practitioners working to enhance the ways in which research and innovation improves the lives of those facing critical social, economic and environmental challenges. It is a hugely valuable resource for others in that growing community who share the ambitions and motivations of the authors.

— *Prof Joanna Chataway, Head of Department of Science, Technology, Engineering and Public Policy (UCL STEaPP), University College London*

TRANSFORMATIVE PATHWAYS TO SUSTAINABILITY

Learning Across Disciplines, Cultures and Contexts

Produced by the Pathways Network

Routledge
Taylor & Francis Group
LONDON AND NEW YORK

First published 2022
by Routledge
2 Park Square, Milton Park, Abingdon, Oxon OX14 4RN

and by Routledge
605 Third Avenue, New York, NY 10158

Routledge is an imprint of the Taylor & Francis Group, an informa business

British Library Cataloguing-in-Publication Data

A catalogue record for this book is available from the British Library

Library of Congress Cataloging-in-Publication Data
Names: Pathways Network (Project)
Title: Transformative pathways to sustainability : learning across disciplines, cultures and contexts / The Pathways Network.
Description: Abingdon, Oxon ; New York, NY : Routledge, 2022. | Series: Pathways to sustainability | Includes bibliographical references and index.
Identifiers: LCCN 2021020005 (print) | LCCN 2021020006 (ebook)
Subjects: LCSH: Sustainable development.
Classification: LCC HC79.E5 T73539 2022 (print) | LCC HC79.E5 (ebook) | DDC 338.9/27—dc23
LC record available at https://lccn.loc.gov/2021020005
LC ebook record available at https://lccn.loc.gov/2021020006

ISBN: 978-0-367-35522-7 (hbk)
ISBN: 978-0-367-35523-4 (pbk)
ISBN: 978-0-429-33193-0 (ebk)

DOI: 10.4324/9780429331930

Typeset in Bembo
by codeMantra

CONTENTS

ACKNOWLEDGEMENTS

We would collectively like to thank the key funders that have supported our collaborative work. The STEPS Centre was funded between 2006 and 2021 by the UK Economic and Social Research Council (ESRC). The 'Pathways' TKN was supported by the Transformations to Sustainability Programme, which was coordinated by the International Social Science Council (ISSC, now ISC – the International Science Council), funded by the Swedish International Development Cooperation Agency (SIDA), and implemented in partnership with the National Research Foundation of South Africa (Grant Number SSC2015-TKN150224114426).

We would like to thank the STEPS Centre directors and other colleagues from across all hubs in the Pathways Transformative Knowledge Network who were involved in the earlier stages of conceiving this project but were not able to continue their engagement to the point of publication of this book.

Special thanks go to Becky Ayre for the cover artwork and Rowan Davis for initial compilation of raw data for Chapters 5–10, and contribution to the analysis that features in Table 5.1 and Figures 5.3, 7.1 and 8.1.

The lead authors of the following specific chapters would also like to thank:

1 This chapter, like the book as a whole, drew upon the knowledge, wisdom and inspiration provided by the wider 'Pathways' network. The editor wishes to thank all the contributors for their ongoing solidarity, patience and support over the years since this book project was initiated. In particular, he is grateful for the discussions in Santiago (2019) including suggestions from Robert Walker, which led to a re-configuration of the chapters, in line with the open access format in which the book will appear.

2 We thank the former STEPS Centre directors Melissa Leach, Andy Stirling and Ian Scoones (who was principal investigator of the seed funding grant),

as well as Xiulan Zhang, Braven Zhang, Per Olsson, Ed Hackett, Hallie Eakin, Cosmas Ochieng, Pranav Desai, Ritu Priya and Dinesh Abrol for their key roles in the establishment of the 'Pathways to Sustainability' consortium and the TKN. Harriet Dudley and Becky Ayre also provided vital support during the early days.

3 This chapter drew upon work from across the consortium and I am particularly grateful for the contributions made by Lakshmi Charli-Joseph (who led the cross-hub exploration of different theories and methods with help from Patrick Van Zwanenberg) and Hallie Eakin and Ed Hackett (whose initial ideas around learning significantly shaped our approach). The details in Figure 3.5 reflect the discussions of all those present at the workshop in Dundee in 2017, captured in note-form by Harriet Dudley. Marina Apgar's writing on monitoring and evaluation was also drawn upon.

4 We would like to acknowledge the inputs of all those involved with and who attended the T-Lab workshops in South Africa that were a precursor to those discussed here. In particular, the Center for Complex Systems in Transition and the Southern Africa Food Lab that hosted the process. This work was supported by the Guidance for Resilience in the Anthropocene: Investments for Development (GRAID) project funded by the Swedish International Development Agency (SIDA), and in part by the National Research Foundation of South Africa (Grant 115300).

5 We would like to acknowledge the inputs of all those who attended the T-Lab workshops, gave their time for interviews and discussions, and contributed to the implementation of some of the ideas that emerged. In particular we would like to thank the Sussex Sustainability Research Programme for co-funding the first T-Lab workshops and the Brighton & Hove Food Partnership for their invaluable work in the city.

6 We would like to thank the many individuals who gave up their time, knowledge and opinions to collaborate in a series of T-Lab workshops in Argentina on the topic of seed systems and sustainability. We have also been extremely lucky to have been accompanied by a great group of people working hard to make Bioleft happen, thanks to all of you too numerous to mention individually here. We also want to acknowledge the support of the Conservation, Food and Health Foundation who provided follow-on funding to Bioleft

7 Much appreciation goes to the Transformation Lab workshop series participants who presented a broad and deep understanding of the Pay-As-You-Go (PAYG) Solar Home System (SHS) space and contributed to a series of recommendations to improve the sustainability and transformative footprint of the problem space, which can be organised broadly into three categories: academic, technical and policy- related. We also acknowledge our colleagues at ACTS who took time to review, comment and give suggestions to this chapter, and those who supported the Transformative Knowledge Network in one way or another.

8 We would like to express our sincere gratitude to the participants in the two T-Labs conducted in 2016 and 2018 in Hebei Province, for sitting together to explore a more multi-dimensional perspective on green transformation in China. We are extremely grateful to Mr Wang Jiankun, our gatekeeper for field research. His sincerity and trust had directly led to the successful implementation of the research. We are deeply appreciative to Prof. Robert Walker for his enthusiasm and immense knowledge throughout his participation.

9 We are deeply appreciative of our collaborators in the Xochimilco T-Lab; we have attempted to reflect their knowledge and perspectives faithfully in this chapter, while acknowledging that what we present here is filtered through our lens as project conveners. We would like to thank the work of Beatriz Ruizpalacios and the technical support of Rodrigo García Herrera and Patricia Pérez-Belmont. We also acknowledge the complementary funding from the National Science Foundation Grant No. 1414052, CNH: The Dynamics of Multi-Scalar Adaptation in Megacities (PI H. Eakin).

10 We acknowledge the collaborative inputs of all those involved in the TRCSS, SASH-KN, and the T-Lab associated with this project, including the network of organisations that appear in Figure 10.8 (The Gurgaon Water Forum: A Transdisciplinary Network).

11 We would like to acknowledge the inputs of those already mentioned with regard to Chapters 5, 6 and 9.

12 While great efforts have been made to include those whose work has contributed to the ideas and substance of this chapter and the insights emerging from this book, there are a host of individuals and organisations without whom this chapter would not have been possible, including the many hundreds of stakeholders who have engaged with the project in each of the hubs. We offer them our thanks.

ABBREVIATIONS AND ACRONYMS

AIDWA	All India Democratic Women's Association
AITUC	All India Trade Union Congress
ACTS	African Centre for Technology Studies (Kenya)
ASH	Africa Sustainability Hub, hosted by ACTS (Kenya)
ASU	Arizona State University (USA)
ATPS	Africa Technology Policy Studies Network
BHFP	Brighton and Hove Food Partnership (UK)
BNU-SSSDPP	Beijing Normal University School of Social Development and Public Policy
BSUFN	Brighton and Sussex Universities Food Network (UK)
CCDAR	Centre for Ecology, Development and Research
CENIT	Centre de Investigaciones para la Transformación (Argentina)
CGWB	Central Ground Water Board (India)
CITU	Centre of Indian Trade Unions
CPA	Collective Practical Approach
CPU	Collective Practical Understanding
CTD	Centre for Technology and Development
DLF	Delhi Land and Finance Ltd (real estate developer) and associated DLF Foundation (philanthropic arm)
ESRC	Economic and Social Research Council (UK)
FG	field development group
FGD	focus group discussion
FORHEAD	Forum on Health, Environment and Development
GMUC	Gurgaon-Manesar Urban Complex (India)

GRP	Gurgaon Rejuvenation Project
GWF	Gurgaon Water Forum
HVM	Haryana Vigyan Manch
ICIPE	International Centre for Insect Physiology and Ecology
ICSU	International Council of Scientific Unions
IDS	Institute of Development Studies (UK)
INTA	Instituto Nacional de Tecnología Agropecuaria)
IP(R)	intellectual property (rights)
ISC	International Science Council
ISSC	International Social Science Council
JNU	Jawaharlal Nehru University (India)
KEPSA	Kenya Private Sector Alliance
KG	knowledge generation group
KOSAP	Kenya Off-Grid Solar Access Project
LANCIS-IE	Laboratorio Nacional de Ciencias de la Sostenbilidad, Instituto de Ecología, Mexico
MDG	Millennium Development Goal
MECS	Modern Energy Cooking Services programme
MNC	Multinational Corporation
MSP	Multi-stakeholder platform
NCR	National Capital Region (India)
NEMA	National Environment Management Authority
NGO	Non-Governmental Organization
NSSI	Network System of Solution Implementation
PAYG	Pay-As-You-Go
PIPA	Participatory Impact Pathways Analysis
RSPL	Ltd Rohit Surfactants Private, Ltd
RWAs	Resident welfare associations
SASH&KN	South Asia Sustainability Hub & Knowledge Network
SCIT	Social Carriers of Innovation for Transformations
SDG	Sustainable Development Goal
SEI	Stockholm Environment Institute
SES	social–ecological system
SG	system design group
SGSD	Society for Geo-Informatics and Sustainable Development
SHS	Solar Home Systems
SME	small and medium-sized enterprise
SRC	Stockholm Resilience Centre (Sweden)
SSRP	Sussex Sustainability Research Programme (University of Sussex, UK)
STEPS	Centre Social, Technological and Environmental Pathways to Sustainability Centre (UK)

SUWM	Sustainable Urban Water Management
TKN	transformative knowledge network
ToC	theory of change
TRCSS	Transdisciplinary Research Cluster on Sustainability Studies
UK	United Kingdom of Great Britain and Northern Ireland
UNAM	National Autonomous University of Mexico
USA	United States of America

CONTRIBUTORS

Dinesh Abrol, TRCSS, JNU – Transdisciplinary Research Cluster on Sustainability Studies, Jawaharlal Nehru University, New Delhi

Marina Apgar, Institute of Development Studies/STEPS Centre, University of Sussex, UK

Joanes Atela, African Centre for Technology Studies (ACTS) ICIPE, Duduville Campus, Kasarani, Nairobi,

Rob Byrne, SPRU – Science Policy Research Unit/STEPS Centre, University of Sussex, UK

Lakshmi Charli-Joseph, Laboratorio Nacional de Ciencias de la Sostenibilidad (LANCIS), Instituto de Ecología, Universidad Nacional Autónoma de México, Ciudad de México, México

Victoria Chengo, African Centre for Technology Studies (ACTS) ICIPE, Duduvile Campus, Kasarani, Nairobi, Kenya

Almendra Cremaschi, Centro de Investigaciones para la Transformación, Universidad Nacional de San Martín, Argentina

Rachael Durrant, SPRU – Science Policy Research Unit/STEPS Centre, University of Sussex, UK

Hallie Eakin, School of Sustainability, Arizona State University, Tempe AZ, USA

Adrian Ely, SPRU – Science Policy Research Unit/STEPS Centre, University of Sussex, UK

Edward Hackett, Heller School for Social Policy and Management, Brandeis University, Waltham MA, USA

Chulin Jiang, School of Social Development and Public Policy, Beijing Normal University, China

Pravin Kushwaha, TRCSS, JNU – Transdisciplinary Research Cluster on Sustainability Studies, Jawaharlal Nehru University, New Delhi

David Manuel-Navarrete, School of Sustainability, Arizona State University, Tempe AZ, USA

Anabel Marin, Institute of Development Studies/ STEPS Centre, University of Sussex, UK (formerly Centro de Investigaciones para la Transformación, Universidad Nacional de San Martín, Argentina)

Fiona Marshall, SPRU – Science Policy Research Unit/STEPS Centre, University of Sussex, UK

Kennedy Mbeva, African Centre for Technology Studies (ACTS), Kenya

David Ockwell, School of Global Studies/STEPS Centre, University of Sussex, UK

Per Olsson, Stockholm Resilience Centre, Sweden

Joel Onyango, African Centre for Technology Studies (ACTS), Kenya

Nathan Oxley, Institute of Development Studies/STEPS Centre, University of Sussex, UK

Laura Pereira, Stockholm Resilience Centre, Stockholm University; Centre for Complex systems in Transition, Stellenbosch University

Ritu Priya Mehrotra, TRCSS, JNU – Transdisciplinary Research Cluster on Sustainability Studies, Jawaharlal Nehru University, New Delhi

Beatriz Ruizpalacios, Laboratorio Nacional de Ciencias de la Sostenibilidad (LANCIS), Instituto de Ecología, Universidad Nacional Autónoma de México, Ciudad de México, México

Ruth Segal, SPRU – Science Policy Research Unit/STEPS Centre, University of Sussex, UK

Rebecca Shelton, School of Sustainability, Arizona State University, Tempe AZ, USA

J. Mario Siqueiros-García, Instituto de Investigaciones en Matemáticas Aplicadas y en Sistemas (IIMAS), Universidad Nacional Autónoma de México

Rachael Taylor, Independent researcher, London, UK

Aschalew Tigabu, African Centre for Technology Studies (ACTS)

Patrick Van Zwanenberg, Centro de Investigaciones para la Transformación, Universidad Nacional de San Martín, Argentina

Elise Wach, Institute of Development Studies/STEPS Centre, University of Sussex, UK

Lichao Yang, School of Social Development and Public Policy, Beijing Normal University, China

Olive Zgambo, Centre for Complex systems in Transition, Stellenbosch University

FIGURES

TABLES

PREFACE

This book has a long history. The organisations and individuals involved have links that in some cases stretch back decades. These have been strengthened as a result of sustained support for the STEPS Centre from the UK Economic and Social Research Council from 2006 to 2021 and funding for the Pathways network provided by the Transformations to Sustainability programme from 2014 to 2019. These types of long-term initiatives are important for building trusted relationships across countries, especially among early career researchers (who make up half of the authors). The resulting book represents the combined efforts of researchers, activists, public servants, representatives of the private sector and other collaborators across five continents – many more people than appear in the author list. It embodies an attempt to learn across disciplines, cultures and contexts, and to collaborate across local, national and international scales towards shared objectives.

The work reported in Chapters 5–10 took place between 2014 and 2019, however writing up processes differed and, in most cases, concluded at various points in 2020. In every hub represented in the book, the arrival of the SARS-CoV-2 virus/Covid-19 presented significant challenges and, as editor, I struggled to keep to my own schedule for finalising the manuscript. The limitations on in-person interactions made the task of integration and conclusion especially challenging and I am truly grateful to all those involved for their patience and unwavering support in finalising the work. The responsibility for any imperfections resulting from the constrained conditions under which the book was completed falls primarily to me.

During the production period, we tragically lost one of our colleagues to the virus. Dr Pravin Kushwaha, aged just 43 at the time of his passing in May 2021, was committed to social justice and to helping others through his research and practice. He had previously joined with other colleagues from the Gurgaon

Water Forum and associated networks to deliver thousands of food packets to migrant workers following the first Indian lockdown in March 2020. In many ways Pravin exemplified the dedication to research, activism and international collaboration that has underpinned the 'Pathways' network and enabled the completion of the book. We dedicate this publication to his memory.

Adrian Ely, June 2021

SECTION 1
Introduction

1

INTRODUCTION

Adrian Ely

Sustainable development: universal goals across a divided world

The Sustainable Development Goals (SDGs), which grew out of the Rio+20 UN Summit in Rio da Janeiro in 2012 and were agreed at the UN General Assembly in 2015, represent potentially the most ambitious, comprehensive and internationally recognised development agenda that the world has ever seen. In comparison to their forerunners the Millennium Development Goals (MDGs), the 2030 Agenda and the SDGs are 'universal' and are envisaged to be implemented by "all countries and all stakeholders" through to 2030 (United Nations 2015). They are also transformative in their ambition, requiring systemic changes that go beyond incremental shifts in policy, behaviour or the use of technology – changes that empower the most vulnerable and genuinely "leave no-one behind".

Five years later, unity around the goals has been unsettled by the shock of Covid-19, an infectious agent responsible for numerous medical crises, economic recessions and socio-political upheavals across the world. At the time of writing this chapter (September 2020) the ability of national governments to adopt a collaborative rather than a competitive approach to addressing Covid-19 hangs in the balance, and in many ways the world looks more divided than ever. International networks of scientists and researchers are struggling to overcome this division.

As with Covid-19 and, earlier, the MDGs, the current international development agenda poses questions for the global research community. What does this idea of "Transforming our World" (the title of the 2030 Agenda) actually mean when it is translated to the very different contexts in which we find ourselves? How can we understand and help to bring about the kinds of transformative change that the SDGs necessitate? What is the role of research – in particular

DOI: 10.4324/9780429331930-2

research that is rooted within the social sciences but extends to incorporate other disciplinary and practice-based inputs – in these transformations?

This book tries to address these questions. The research detailed in this volume (which took place pre-Covid-19) engages with the specificities of different contexts around the world, while seeking general lessons that can be drawn about transformations to sustainability and the role of research within them. It thus documents a new approach (or approaches) that contribute to the enterprise of "transdisciplinary" research, in which collaborations between academic and non-academic partners attempt not only to understand the world and diagnose systemic challenges of sustainability, but also to contribute to overcoming them.

The next section of this chapter firstly outlines the rationale and emergence of the 'Pathways' Transformative Knowledge Network, from which the co-authors are drawn, and highlights the sustainable development challenges with which it engaged between 2014 and 2020. In the following section, we point to some of the theoretical concepts and transdisciplinary approaches that the network applied across and beyond traditional schools of social and natural science. These provided a basis for significant cross-learning between the network hubs – a key objective of the network. We next explore the role that research and researchers can play in contributing to transformations to sustainability, posing questions that will be answered in the next nine chapters of this volume. Each of these sections directs the reader to the most relevant chapters, in which the issues are discussed in much greater detail. Acknowledging the multiple potential audiences to the volume (open access online), we lastly summarise the organisation of this book and provide a roadmap to its use.

Introducing the 'Pathways' network

This book draws upon a five-year period of transdisciplinary research that has involved over a hundred researchers across five continents in the 'Pathways' transformative knowledge network (TKN). The background and configuration of the TKN and the approaches to organising its work over the five years in question are detailed in Chapter 2. Emerging out of a set of collaborations involving the following organisations and the STEPS Centre (a collaboration between SPRU – the Science Policy Research Unit and the Institute of Development Studies at the University of Sussex), the network was established to undertake cutting edge, independent, critical, engaged research, to offer a common facility for communication, impact and engagement with action and policy and to create a joint platform for learning and exchange between members, including faculty, students. Through the generous support of the 'Transformations to Sustainability' programme, the network was able to experiment with these and other activities in a network that spanned various regions across the globe (see Figure 1.1).

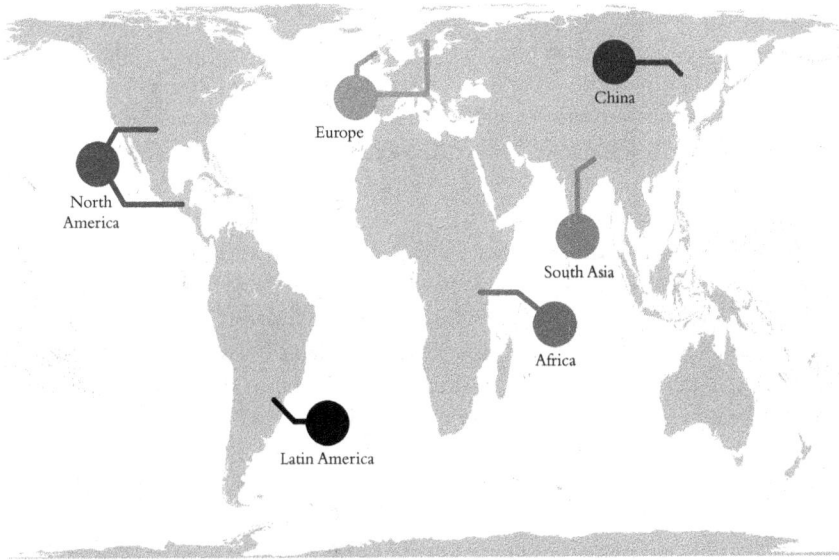

FIGURE 1.1 The organisations that are members of the 'Pathways' Transformative Knowledge Network and their geographical distribution.

The nodes in the network above are represented by the following hubs and organisations:

Latin America hub
• Centre for Research on Transformation (CENIT), Buenos Aires, Argentina

Europe hub
• STEPS Centre, University of Sussex, UK
• Stockholm Resilience Centre, Sweden

Africa hub
• African Centre for Technology Studies, Nairobi, Kenya
• African Technology Policy Studies Network, Nairobi, Kenya
• Stockholm Environment Institute Africa Centre, Nairobi, Kenya

China hub
• Beijing Normal University School of Social Development and Public Policy, China

South Asia hub
• Transdisciplinary Research Cluster on Sustainability Studies, Jawaharlal Nehru University, New Delhi, India

North America hub
• Arizona State University, USA
• National Autonomous University of Mexico, Mexico

The STEPS Centre's 'pathways' approach (Leach et al. 2010), discussed further in Chapter 3, provided some of the conceptual grounding for the work by highlighting the importance of (indeed the necessity for) multiple 'pathways' of social-technological-environmental change, combining to serve the interlinked challenges of environmental sustainability, poverty alleviation and social justice. This plurality was also reflected in the TKN's activities, and the diversity of contexts in which we worked.

The early phases of the 'Pathways' TKN adopted a distributed and bottom-up approach to identifying the sustainability challenges that would be the focus of each hub. These foci were organised around three broad themes that cut across many of the Sustainable Development Goals detailed in Table 1.1. In the individual hubs, the research involved transdisciplinary networks selected by teams from each of the six hub organisations listed in Figure 1.1 and below:

Theme 1 – Sustainable agricultural and food systems for healthy livelihoods (SDGs 1, 2, 3, 9, 11, 12, 15)
- Transformations to sustainable food systems in Brighton and Hove/ Europe hub – STEPS Centre, University of Sussex, UK with inputs from Stockholm Resilience Centre, Sweden
- The future of seeds (and agriculture) in Argentina/South America hub – Centre for Research on Transformation (CENIT), Buenos Aires, Argentina

Theme 2 – Low carbon energy and industrial transformations (SDGs 1, 3, 5, 7, 8, 9, 10, 13)
- Low carbon energy transitions that meet the needs of the poor/Africa Sustainability Hub – African Centre for Technology Studies, Nairobi, Kenya
- China's green transformations/ China Hub – Beijing Normal University School of Social Development and Public Policy, China

Theme 3 – Water and waste for sustainable cities (SDGs 1, 2, 3, 6, 8, 9, 10, 11, 12, 14, 15)
- Water governance challenges, Mexico City/ North America hub – Arizona State University, USA and National Autonomous University of Mexico, Mexico
- The urban system of water and waste management in Gurgaon, India / South Asia hub – Transdisciplinary Research Cluster on Sustainability Studies, Jawaharlal Nehru University, New Delhi India

Between 2015 and 2019, the TKN experimented with diverse approaches to researching and intervening in the sustainability challenges above – bringing together different kinds of networks and applying a range of social science methods. Working together, the TKN also had the ambition of experimenting, documenting and comparing across the hubs in the network with the objective of "learning across disciplines, cultures and contexts" (Ely and Marin 2016).

This book thus represents an effort to bridge this internationally shared normative agenda for sustainable development with concrete action research initiatives in a set of specific contexts across the world. It generates fresh insights into the role that social science can play in these initiatives, and provides lessons for future transdisciplinary research that aims to connect the global and the local. While these pages provide only a condensed and partial account of the experiences that have emerged, they offer an important resource for future efforts that strive towards a collective and shared understanding of ways in which humanity can respond to the multiple challenges of sustainable development.

In search of transformations to sustainability

Representing universal goals in a divided world, the 2030 Agenda identifies a series of 17 aspirational goals (see Table 1.1) and 169 targets, all agreed in New

TABLE 1.1 The Sustainable Development Goals (United Nations 2015)

Goal 1	End poverty in all its forms everywhere
Goal 2	End hunger, achieve food security and improved nutrition and promote sustainable agriculture
Goal 3	Ensure healthy lives and promote well-being for all at all ages
Goal 4	Ensure inclusive and equitable quality education and promote lifelong learning opportunities for all
Goal 5	Achieve gender equality and empower all women and girls
Goal 6	Ensure availability and sustainable management of water and sanitation for all
Goal 7	Ensure access to affordable, reliable, sustainable and modern energy for all
Goal 8	Promote sustained, inclusive and sustainable economic growth, full and productive employment and decent work for all
Goal 9	Build resilient infrastructure, promote inclusive and sustainable industrialisation and foster innovation
Goal 10	Reduce inequality within and among countries
Goal 11	Make cities and human settlements inclusive, safe, resilient and sustainable
Goal 12	Ensure sustainable consumption and production patterns
Goal 13	Take urgent action to combat climate change and its impacts*
Goal 14	Conserve and sustainably use the oceans, seas and marine resources for sustainable development
Goal 15	Protect, restore and promote sustainable use of terrestrial ecosystems, sustainably manage forests, combat desertification, and halt and reverse land degradation and halt biodiversity loss
Goal 16	Promote peaceful and inclusive societies for sustainable development, provide access to justice for all and build effective, accountable and inclusive institutions at all levels
Goal 17	Strengthen the means of implementation and revitalise the Global Partnership for Sustainable Development

* Acknowledging that the United Nations Framework Convention on Climate Change is the primary international, intergovernmental forum for negotiating the global response to climate change.

York in 2015. But behind these lie the radically different contexts – at national and subnational levels – in which these ambitions are to be realised. Citizens and communities across the planet are searching for transformations to sustainability that cater to their own needs and worldviews.

Theories around social transformations have a long pedigree and have recently come to the fore in social science research related to transformations to sustainability (Hackmann and St Clair 2012). Chapter 3 provides a detailed overview of this area of research as a background to some of the conceptual approaches that have been applied in the different hubs of the 'Pathways' network. It draws upon multiple disciplines including classical sociology and political economy and more recent notions of socio-technical system transitions and social ecological resilience. Drawing together these bodies of literature and the analytical and normative commitments of the 'pathways approach' for grassroots empowerment, the book provides a new synthesis of knowledge around 'social transformations to sustainability', rooted in theory and action. Through deploying a range of theories and flexible methodological approaches defined as 'transformation laboratories' (T-Lab, see Chapter 4), the TKN has generated a set of hub-based experiences that engage with locally defined transformations. These are recounted in detail in Chapters 5–10. Together, they form the basis of a new approach to conceptualising 'transformative pathways to sustainability' and a reference for future praxis. While not making any claims about transformations emerging as a result of our work (or even being steered by the contributions of our time-limited project), these chapters document the processes through which the six hub teams endeavoured to conduct transdisciplinary research that goes beyond analysis to action.

Learning across disciplines, cultures and contexts

An important contribution of the 'Pathways' TKN and of this book is how this search for transformative pathways to sustainability has emerged differently in each of the hubs. The project was designed in such a way as to enable this process of cross-learning (Marin et al. 2016; Ely et al. 2020), in particular by encouraging interactions between early career researchers across the network and sharing leadership between the global North and global South (the network was co-led from the UK and Argentina hubs).

The hub organisations, teams and transdisciplinary networks (with whom they worked in T-Labs) differ greatly across disciplinary and institutional dimensions. The individual hub activities are clarified in Chapters 5–10, each of which provides a chronological and reflective account of the various stages that the hub team went through in their transdisciplinary research and the insights that emerged. Unsurprisingly, these insights are grounded in diverse theoretical literatures (briefly explored earlier in Chapter 3) and based on different methodological approaches (covered in Chapter 4). Through providing a flexible approach (using what we describe as theoretical and methodological 'anchors') we were able to draw some conclusions from learning that has taken place across selected hubs (Chapter 11) and the whole network (Chapter 12).

This book is the output of a project that has been fortunate to benefit from significant resources. At the same time, it takes place within a context of a much broader field of 'transformations to sustainability' work. Indeed, the field is expanding so rapidly and in so many directions that it is impossible to keep up with the various contributions that are emerging. It has therefore not been possible to do justice to the many parallel insights that are emerging from the different corners of the world. Nevertheless, we hope that the work presented here can combine with the efforts of wider international networks in a way that furthers both our theoretical and practical understanding of sustainability challenges and how social transformations can overcome them.

In the following pages, the book engages with the following emerging questions, drawing on experiences from the six hubs of the 'Pathways' Transformative Knowledge Network:

• How are transformations to sustainability conceptualised across different theoretical and scholarly traditions, and how does this influence the organisation of transdisciplinary research?
• How can we, as researchers, understand and help to bring about the kinds of transformative change that the 2030 Agenda calls for?
• What broader lessons does this point to regarding the role of research – in particular research that is rooted within the social sciences but extends to incorporate other disciplinary and practice-based inputs – in these transformations?

The organisation of this book and a roadmap to its use

This volume appeals to multiple different types of readers, from academic researchers in the social and natural sciences to transdisciplinary scholars with a history of engaged, problem- and solution-oriented research. It will be of use to policy-makers or research funders with an interest in how knowledge can contribute to sustainable development initiatives. It will also appeal to practitioners – whether they find themselves within the private sector, in non-government organisations or indeed in communities around the world, striving to solve their own sustainability challenges. Here we provide a 'roadmap' explaining how this book can best be used, and the resources that each of the chapters provide to their various potential readerships. As an open access online publication, this book can be read either in its entirety or as individual chapters.

The first section of the book (including this chapter) provides an introduction to the book and the project that it draws upon. The next chapter describes the 'Pathways' Transformative Knowledge Network, its genesis, hub partners and their distinctive disciplinary and contextual backgrounds. It explains some of the differences between the cases that each team has focussed upon, including the themes that have been addressed (sectoral or cross-sectoral), the histories of engagement with non-academic actors in each locality and the disciplinary backgrounds of the team members.

The second section of the book explores some of the tools and approaches that were applied throughout the project, as well as some of the conceptual insights that have emerged as the work has progressed.

Chapter 3 extends the description in this chapter by beginning to analyse the different approaches to theory adopted in the project as a whole and in each of the hubs. In view of the book's focus on transformative change – a search for profound and long-term reconfiguration of systems and structures – the chapter reviews some of the theoretical literature in this area and how it has been applied in the 'Pathways' Transformative Knowledge Network.

Chapter 4 describes the TKN's approach to Transformation Labs, positioning it alongside earlier work on social innovation labs (Westley and Laban 2015) and exploring some of the insights that have emerged from applying this approach in very diverse contexts.

Section 3 focusses upon the six international cases. The chapters outline the experiences of each hub in the Transformative Knowledge Network and draw from process documentation and reflection by the teams who were responsible. These relate back to some of the concepts outlined in Chapters 2–4 and explore how they "played out" in different contexts, each characterised by varying disciplinary traditions and socio-political cultures. The six chapters can be read individually by anyone with a particular interest in the geographical region or the sustainability challenge in question. They are arranged as follows and 'paired' to reflect the thematic focus of the work and the architecture of the project:

Agri-food transformations

    5 UK – Towards a More Sustainable Food System in Brighton and Hove
    6 Argentina – Bioleft: a collaborative, open-source seed breeding initiative for sustainable agriculture

Transformations in Energy and Industry

    7 Kenya – Making Mobile Solar Energy Inclusive
    8 China – The Economic Shock of a Green Transition in Hebei

Transformations in Urban and Peri-Urban Spaces

    9 Mexico – Wetlands Under Pressure: The Experience of the Xochimilco T-Lab
    10 India – Enabling Transformations to Sustainability: Rethinking Urban Water Management in Gurgaon, India

Section 4 offers a conclusion to the book and is made up of two chapters.

Chapter 11 focusses on one particular area of application of the 'pathways' approach – that associated with the notion of framing and the contribution that 're-framing sustainability challenges' can make to transformative change. The chapter draws upon the work in the Mexico, UK and Argentina cases but is of wider analytical relevance.

Chapter 12 draws on the work in all six of the hubs and identifies further conceptual contributions and comparative insights. Building on the theoretical foundations in Chapter 3 and the intervening chapters, it pulls together the lessons from the transdisciplinary research in each hub, and develops a synthesis on 'transformative pathways to sustainability'. Finally, it lays out a future agenda for internationally networked, engaged social science research on sustainability transformations.

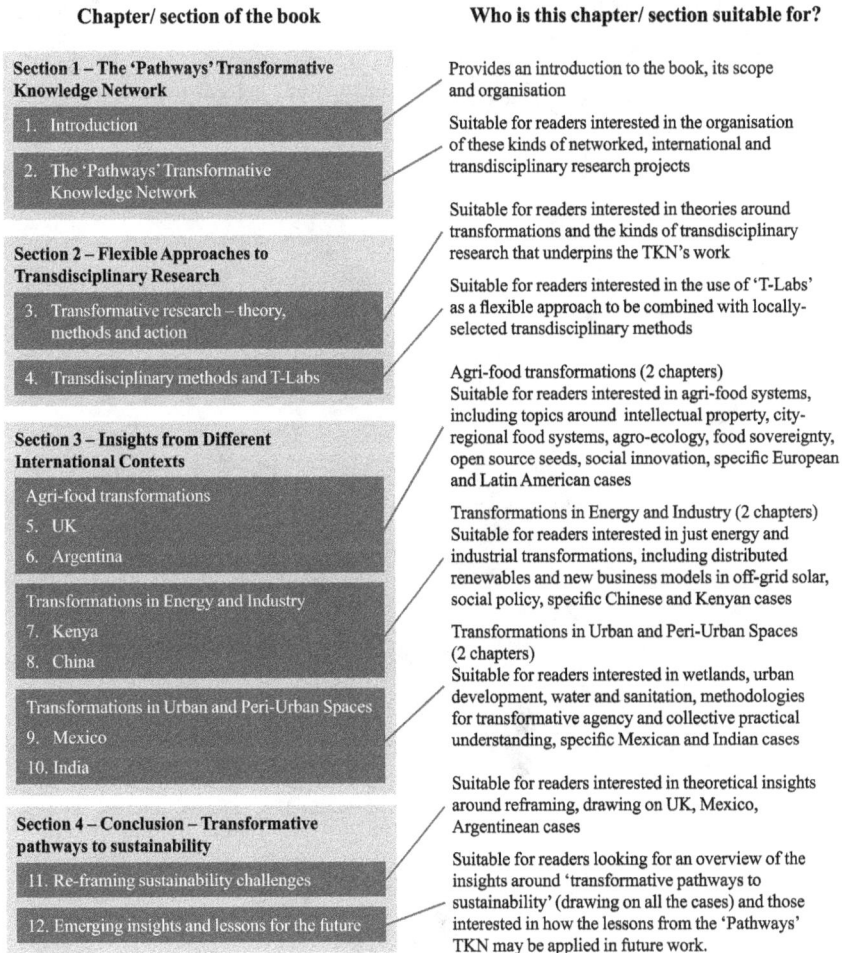

Chapter/ section of the book	Who is this chapter/ section suitable for?
Section 1 – The 'Pathways' Transformative Knowledge Network	Provides an introduction to the book, its scope and organisation
1. Introduction	Suitable for readers interested in the organisation of these kinds of networked, international and transdisciplinary research projects
2. The 'Pathways' Transformative Knowledge Network	Suitable for readers interested in theories around transformations and the kinds of transdisciplinary research that underpins the TKN's work
Section 2 – Flexible Approaches to Transdisciplinary Research	Suitable for readers interested in the use of 'T-Labs' as a flexible approach to be combined with locally-selected transdisciplinary methods
3. Transformative research – theory, methods and action	
4. Transdisciplinary methods and T-Labs	Agri-food transformations (2 chapters) Suitable for readers interested in agri-food systems, including topics around intellectual property, city-regional food systems, agro-ecology, food sovereignty, open source seeds, social innovation, specific European and Latin American cases
Section 3 – Insights from Different International Contexts	Transformations in Energy and Industry (2 chapters) Suitable for readers interested in just energy and industrial transformations, including distributed renewables and new business models in off-grid solar, social policy, specific Chinese and Kenyan cases
Agri-food transformations	
5. UK	
6. Argentina	
Transformations in Energy and Industry	
7. Kenya	Transformations in Urban and Peri-Urban Spaces (2 chapters) Suitable for readers interested in wetlands, urban development, water and sanitation, methodologies for transformative agency and collective practical understanding, specific Mexican and Indian cases
8. China	
Transformations in Urban and Peri-Urban Spaces	
9. Mexico	Suitable for readers interested in theoretical insights around reframing, drawing on UK, Mexico, Argentinean cases
10. India	
Section 4 – Conclusion – Transformative pathways to sustainability	Suitable for readers looking for an overview of the insights around 'transformative pathways to sustainability' (drawing on all the cases) and those interested in how the lessons from the 'Pathways' TKN may be applied in future work.
11. Re-framing sustainability challenges	
12. Emerging insights and lessons for the future	

FIGURE 1.2   A roadmap suggesting how different parts of this book may be most effectively used by readers with different interests.

References

Ely, A. and Marin, A. (2016) Learning about 'Engaged Excellence' across a Transformative Knowledge Network, *IDS Bulletin* 47(6). doi: 10.19088/1968–2016.200

Ely, A., Marin, A., Charli-Joseph, L., Abrol, D., Apgar, M., Atela, J., Ayre, B., Byrne, R., Choudhary, B. K., Chengo, V., Cremaschi, A., Davis, R., Desai, P., Eakin, H., Kushwaha, P., Marshall, F., Mbeva, K., Ndege, N., Ochieng, C., Ockwell, D., Olsson, P., Oxley, N., Pereira, L,. Priya, R., Tigabu, A., Van Zwanenberg, P. and Yang, L. (2020) Structured Collaboration across a Transformative Knowledge Network: Learning across Disciplines, Cultures and Contexts? *Sustainability*. doi: 10.3390/su12062499

Hackmann, H. and St Clair, A.L. (2012) Transformative Cornerstones of Social Science Research for Global Change. Paris: International Social Science Council

Leach, M., Scoones, I. and Stirling, A. (2010) *Dynamic Sustainabilities: Technology, Environment, Social Justice*. London: Earthscan.

Marin, A., Ely, A. and van Zwanenberg, P. (2016) Co-Design with Aligned and Non-Aligned Knowledge Partners: Implications for Research and Coproduction of Sustainable Food Systems, *Current Opinion in Environmental Sustainability* 20: 93–98.

United Nations. (2015) Transforming Our World: The 2030 Agenda for Sustainable Development, Resolution adopted by the General Assembly on 25 September 2015.

Westley, F. and Laban, S. (eds) (2015) *Social Innovation Lab Guide*. Waterloo, ON: Waterloo Institute for Social Innovation and Resilience.

2

THE 'PATHWAYS' TRANSFORMATIVE KNOWLEDGE NETWORK

Adrian Ely and Anabel Marin

Introduction and background

The 'Pathways' transformative knowledge network (TKN) is an international partnership of research hubs, collaborating to explore processes of social transformation and to share insights across disciplines, cultures and contexts. This chapter describes the network, one of three funded under the Future Earth 'Transformations to Sustainability' programme, and provides some background to the various hubs, their disciplinary backgrounds and histories of engaged research. It describes the design of the network and the elements that enabled cross-learning between the experiences of each of the hubs. The chapter also provides a brief introduction to the theoretical and methodological anchors of the project, which are discussed further in Chapters 3 and 4 respectively.

The Pathways TKN represents the primary activity of the 'Pathways to Sustainability' global consortium. This grew out of an academic centre funded by the UK Economic and Social Research Council (ESRC) – the STEPS (Social, Technological and Environmental Pathways to Sustainability) Centre – and a network of partners around the world. Since the inception of the STEPS Centre in 2006, project-based collaborations between the Centre and each of the hubs helped to shape the interpersonal relationships and enhanced understanding of intellectual and political synergies that enabled a closer partnership.

In 2013, a proposal was developed, describing a consortium "bound together by common values rooted in a commitment to independent, challenging, normatively-formed, engaged research, a joint vision for understanding and supporting pathways to sustainability, and a common interest in transformative research and action". The regional partners came together with a focus on the three activities of "research", "impact and engagement" and "learning and exchange", and various hubs in the consortium hosted launch events to showcase

DOI: 10.4324/9780429331930-3

and share research being conducted in China (April 2015), Africa (June 2015), Latin America (November 2015) and South Asia (January 2016), engaging with networks across their countries and regions, drawing on financial support the STEPS Centre's Phase 2 grant from the ESRC. Table 2.2 provides more information on the institutional host arrangements at the time of the launch of each hub. The original proposal in 2013 suggested that some of the consortium's activities would move towards rotation between hubs either annually (in the case of annual symposia) or every three years (in the case of co-ordination of the consortium), and extension and rotation between the various hubs (in the case of summer schools).

Working together across the consortium provided great opportunities for cross-learning, motivated by the search for mutual understanding of how humanity can respond to the shared challenge of sustainable development and overcome the differences that act as a barrier to its realisation (as outlined in the previous chapter). Among several attempts to secure support for these types of activities, the consortium was fortunate to be funded in two rounds (seed-funding and network grant – described in Table 2.1) of the Transformations to Sustainability Programme (T2S). The T2S programme was coordinated by the International Social Science Council (ISSC – now the ISC), funded by the Swedish International Development Cooperation Agency (SIDA) and implemented in partnership with the National Research Foundation of South Africa. In the seed-funding round, additional support came from the UK ESRC Newton Fund.

Towards a Transformative Knowledge Network

The work of the 'Pathways' Transformative Knowledge Network would have been impossible without the support (financial and otherwise) of the Transformations to Sustainability Programme. To some extent, the activities of the 'Pathways' TKN (including its conceptualisation as a 'Transformative Knowledge Network') reflect the ambitions of the T2S programme – to support an innovative, solution-oriented approach to sustainability research that:

- Is framed and led by social scientists
- Involves all relevant knowledge holders – from social, natural and engineering sciences, the humanities, civil society, media and policy domains – at all stages of the research process
- Involves researchers in all regions of the world, including low- and middle-income countries

(T2S 2019)

As a contribution to Future Earth,[1] the programme showed remarkable vision, recognising the role of transdisciplinary social science and a desire to build this as an international research field. Emerging from an alliance of international environmental, biosphere, biodiversity and earth system sciences programmes, including the International Human Dimensions Programme on Global Environmental Change (IHDP, initiated in 1990 by ISSC), Future Earth foreshadowed a broader 'coming together' of natural and social sciences (including the merger of ISSC and ICSU – the International Council for Scientific Unions – to become the International Science Council in 2018). Unlike many of the various Future Earth initiatives at the time, the programme built primarily on thinking within the ISSC (Hackmann and St Clair 2012) and the 2013 World Social Science Report (UNESCO/ISSC 2013), and was rare in being social science-led.

A condition of funding was that the Transformative Knowledge Networks were led or co-led from the global South. The UK and Argentina teams (the authors of this chapter) had contacted each other in parallel with the idea of applying to the call, and it was decided that Adrian Ely and Anabel Marin would co-lead the proposal. Beyond 'Pathways', the other two Transformative Knowledge Networks supported by the programme were:

- Acknowl-EJ (Academic-Activist Co-Produced Knowledge for Environmental Justice)[2]
- T-learning (Transgressive Social Learning for Social-Ecological Sustainability in Times of Climate Change)[3]

The programme convened annual Transformative Knowledge Workshops in 2014 (Potsdam, Germany, hosted by the Institute for Advanced Sustainability Studies), 2015 (Durban, South Africa, alongside the World Social Science Forum), 2016 (New Delhi, India, hosted by the 'Pathways' India hub), 2017 (Buenos Aires, Argentina, hosted by the 'Pathways' Argentina hub) and 2018 (Fukuoka, Japan, alongside the World Social Science Forum). These contributed to creating and maintaining an international community of scholars and practitioners involved in T2S research, fostering inter- and transdisciplinary dialogue across regions and networks. The 2014 event involved a broad range of experts and also heard from the 38 projects that had been awarded seed-funding. The 2015 workshop included representatives of 8 short-listed proposed TKNs, including the three that were eventually funded. The 2016 and 2017 events were hosted and co-organised by two of the hubs of the 'Pathways' TKN, and primarily involved members of the three TKNs. In 2018 several members of the 'Pathways' network joined a workshop that brought together the three TKNs and a new cohort of grantees from the T2S programme, for which financial support had been provided by the NORFACE-Belmont Forum group of donors. Activities in the three TKNs outlived their periods of funded research, and various representatives (especially those from Latin America) gathered at the Transformations 2019 conference in Santiago, Chile, to once again share insights.

TABLE 2.1 Key moments in the creation, organisation and co-ordination of the Transformative Knowledge Network, building on Ely et al. (2020)

Month	Event	Venue(s) where relevant	Collaborative developments
2010 onwards	Development of networks and establishment of the 'Pathways to Sustainability' global consortium	International, with notable launches of individual hubs in Nairobi, Beijing, New Delhi, Argentina.	Initial connections made, with growing appreciation of different disciplinary backgrounds and institutional histories.
March 2014	ISSC launches call for 'Transformations to Sustainability' programme seed grants	International	Collaborative proposal development
September 2014	30,000 Euros seed grant awarded		
September 2014–March 2015	Co-design workshops in each hub produce **case-specific concept notes**, feeding into TKN proposal	Argentina, China, India, Kenya, Mexico, UK	Sharing of contextual background, "problem space" and proposed transdisciplinary research projects
December 2014	ISSC launches call for 'Transformations to Sustainability' programme TKN grants	International	Collaborative proposal development, incorporating insights from seed-funding stage
October 2015	850,000 Euros TKN grant awarded		
April 2016	Inception workshop including **adapted PIPA processes**, T-Lab discussions and strategic planning	Buenos Aires, Argentina	Further sharing of ideas around Transformation Labs, 'Pathways' methods and hub case studies
June 2016	*Baseline survey circulated for completion by all hub teams*	*All hubs*	*Sharing insights and experiences across hubs*
May 2016–August 2017	First round of T-Lab workshops, including **collaborative planning process (T-Lab format)** and **internal** & external **reporting**	Argentina, China, India, Kenya, Mexico, UK	Sharing of initial research data, T-Lab design, implementation and learning, as well as future plans in each hub

Date	Process / document	Location / hubs	Purpose
July 2017	*Mid-point survey circulated for completion by all hub teams*	*All hubs*	*Sharing insights and experiences across hubs*
September 2017	T-Lab training and reflection workshop, including identification of thematic insights and **theory of change discussions**	Dundee, Scotland (alongside Transformations 2017 conference)	Identification of key themes for exploration: T-Labs, theories of change, framing, innovation
October 2017–October 2018	Second round of T-Lab workshops, including **internal & external reporting**	Argentina, China, India, Kenya, Mexico, UK	Sharing of further data, T-Lab experiences (positive and negative) and future plans in each hub
October 2018	Final workshop, including further **discussions around theory, research and action**	Nairobi, Kenya	Time-constrained discussions of theoretical and methodological differences, as well as emerging insights. Reflective project evaluation.
November 2018	*Final survey circulated for completion by all hub teams*	*All hubs*	*Sharing insights and experiences across hubs*
October 2019	Follow-up workshop, including reflection on lessons, planning for publications and future work	Santiago, Chile (alongside Transformations 2019 conference)	Time-constrained discussion of insights around theoretical and methodological anchors, reframing, innovations, etc.
June 2019–May 2021	Collaborative book writing, exchange of drafts, online discussions	International	Deeper appreciation of cross-learning, differences between various hubs, difficulties faced and emerging insights.

Processes and documents that directly underpin some of the hub chapters (5–10) in this book are in bold.

Co-design of the 'Pathways' TKN project

Transdisciplinary engagement with diverse partners in each of the hubs started with the seed-funding, which was awarded in 2014 and supported a process of co-design (Marin et al. 2016), defined by Moser (2016) as "first phase of the knowledge co-production process, in which researchers and non-academic partners jointly develop a research project and define research questions that meet their collective interests and needs". This took the form of multi-stakeholder workshops in each of the six hubs of the Pathways network that identified local research foci through engaging knowledge partners/ stakeholders, identifying locally defined sustainability challenges and agreeing on tentative project activities in concept notes (which fed into the proposal for the TKN). In many cases this process of co-design built on longer relationships between the research teams and knowledge partners in their locality (explored in Table 2.1).

The locally identified sustainability challenges, organised around three broad domains, were researched in transdisciplinary projects led by the teams from each of the six hub organisations listed below:

Theme 1 – Sustainable agricultural and food systems for healthy livelihoods
- Transformations to sustainable food systems in Brighton and Hove/Europe hub – STEPS Centre, University of Sussex, UK and Stockholm Resilience Centre, Sweden (discussed further in Chapter 5)
- The future of seeds (and agriculture) in Argentina/Latin America hub – Centre for Research on Transformation (CENIT), Buenos Aires, Argentina (discussed further in Chapter 6)

Theme 2 – Low carbon energy transitions
- Low carbon energy transitions that meet the needs of the poor/Africa Sustainability Hub – African Centre for Technology Studies, Africa Technology Policy Studies Network, Stockholm Environment Centre – Africa, Nairobi, Kenya (discussed further in Chapter 7)
- China's green transformations/China Hub – Beijing Normal University School of Social Development and Public Policy, China (discussed further in Chapter 8)

Theme 3 – Water and waste for sustainable cities
- Water governance challenges, Mexico City/North America hub – Arizona State University, USA and National Autonomous University of Mexico, Mexico (discussed further in Chapter 9)
- The urban system of water and waste management in Gurgaon, India/South Asia hub – Transdisciplinary Research Cluster on Sustainability Studies, Jawaharlal Nehru University, New Delhi India (discussed further in Chapter 10)

The co-design and emergence of the transdisciplinary work differed in each case. Hubs were paired as described above in order to help foster collaboration

TABLE 2.2 Description of consortium hubs that make up the TKN, and disciplinary and transdisciplinary research history in each hub at the outset of the project

Consortium Hub	Institutional host arrangement at launch	System and problem space	Primary disciplines represented	History of engagement with this problem
Europe	STEPS Centre, including SPRU – Science Policy Research Unit and Department of Geography (University of Sussex) and Institute of Development Studies, UK Stockholm Resilience Centre, Sweden	System: food system in the city of Brighton and Hove, and in particular the production in the South Downs National Park and Brighton-Lewes Downs Biosphere Region. Problem space: the food system in Brighton and Hove is unsustainable because of limitations to local food supply and environmentally damaging production and consumption practices	Science and technology policy Development Studies Ecology Biotechnology Tropical agricultural ecology Environmental sciences Science and technology studies	Some non-academic engagement, but limited prior research on this specific topic. Existing relationships with local and national research community and (in some cases) civil society and local growers.
Latin America	CENIT (Centro de Investigación para la Transformación) – Centre for Research on Transformation, Buenos Aires, Argentina	System: the seed and agricultural sector in Argentina, and the functions that seeds play in maintaining agricultural biodiversity and economic and social diversity of agriculture Problem space: the risk of further loss of social, ecological and economic diversity in agriculture as a result of the increasing mercantilisation of seeds and the consequent market concentration in world and regional seed markets	Economics Agronomy Science and technology policy Intellectual property law	Over 5 years of experience in sustainability and development issues in the seed and agriculture. Sectors. Existing professional relationships with many key actors in the seed sector, especially in civil society groups, the national seed industry, agricultural extension, and government.

(Continued)

Consortium Hub	Institutional host arrangement at launch	System and problem space	Primary disciplines represented	History of engagement with this problem
Africa	The Africa Sustainability Hub, involving the African Centre for Technology Studies, the African Technology Policy Studies Network and the Stockholm Environment Institute Africa Centre	System: enabling sustainable and equitable access to Solar Home Systems (SHS) for all via mobile-based payment systems in Kenya. Problem space: access to and payment of SHSs especially for the low-income cohort	Environment and Development Studies Environmental Sciences Economics Environmental Studies	The Africa Sustainability Hub (ASH) has been in existence for only a year, with low carbon energy a focus of work. The hub already enjoyed professional relationships with the research, civil society, government, and development partners
China	Small team School of Social Development and Public Policy, Beijing Normal University	System: S City, Hebei Province. Problem space: social impacts are not taken into account in the process of green transformation in China	Anthropology Public policy Participatory research Management	The hub has been working on this problem since August 2015
North America	School of Sustainability, Arizona State University, USA National Laboratory for Sustainability Sciences (LANCIS – Laboratorio Nacional de Ciencias de la Sostenibilidad), Institute of Ecology, National Autonomous University of Mexico	System: we focus on the process of informal/irregular urbanisation of the Xochimilco wetland system, Mexico City, and the associated cultural & ecological services. Problem space: a lack of an effective strategy to slow/halt/manage the urbanisation of Xochimilco wetland socio-ecosystem	Sustainability Science Ecology Applied Mathematics and Systems Research	Previous 2 years work in the area, with members of the broader team working in Xochimilco for much longer

| South Asia | The South Asia Sustainability Hub & Knowledge Network (SASH&KN) under the Transdisciplinary Research Cluster on Sustainability Studies – involving the following Centres at Jawaharlal Nehru University, New Delhi, India:
 • Centre for Studies in Science Policy
 • Centre of Social Medicine and Community Health
 • Centre for the Study of Regional Development
 • Centre for Informal Sector & Labour Studies | System: Gurgaon-Manesar urban Complex in the vicinity of National Capital Territory of New Delhi, India.
 Problem space: systemic problems of overexploitation of sources of surface and ground water, growing inequity in distribution of water, rising non-priority use of water, decreasing reliability of supply are making the water supply system of the region highly vulnerable and dependent on underground and distant sources of surface water supplies | Science and technology policy
 Public health
 Regional development
 Labour studies | Current site-specific work has started only during the last three months – civil society, researchers, government and media are being engaged |

Details of the system, problem space, primary disciplines and history of engagement are drawn from baseline surveys in each hub. These evolved as the project progressed (see Chapters 5–11).

and cross-learning between countries in the global North and global South. This pairing was used at various points through the project to foster cross-learning, e.g. by encouraging participants to share their rationales for particular decisions around research and engagement (e.g. exchanging T-Lab designs in a specific format prior to the first T-Lab workshop), or to share their experiences (e.g. of positive and negative aspects of T-Labs) and lessons (e.g. relating to the specific domains in which they were working). Nevertheless, the process of co-design, and the inevitable consequences of problem reframing that often occurs in co-design processes, made the initial domain-based structure of the paired hubs less salient than other, less visible points of comparison such as approaches used in engagement or the scale or goals of implementation.

The approach to domain-specific pairing represents just one element of the design of the network that aimed strategically to foster co-learning and exchange. The next section describes various other elements of this design in more detail.

Structured design to allow for co-learning and exchange

The TKN project was designed to provide flexibility for location-specific decisions about transdisciplinary research and engagement (including methods, discussed in Chapter 4), thus allowing reflection within each individual hub around how to improve transdisciplinary practice. Beyond the independently coherent hub-based work, the project allowed for the collection of standardised (as well as hub-specific) data at symmetrical points across all hubs, in an attempt to compare and learn across contexts. In this way, the transdisciplinary research processes in each hub were integrated into the design of the wider project. Table 2.1 illustrates how the hub research was organised in T-Labs (discussed in detail in Chapter 4) and punctuated by moments for data collection, sharing and co-learning and collaborative reflection across the network.

At the inception workshop in April 2016, the representatives of each hub team undertook an adapted and simplified 'participatory impact pathways analysis' (PIPA) (Douthwaite et al. 2007; Ely and Oxley 2014) to map out the stakeholders that would be engaged during the course of their transdisciplinary research. This method adopted the funder's pre-determined categories of stakeholders (defined at the outset of the project in formal reporting requirements): academia, research body, think tank, NGO, public administration, civil society and others. Some hubs found that these were insufficient in their specificity, so in those cases hubs added sub-categories that catered to their own situation. Beyond identifying the category of each stakeholder, hubs were asked to make subjective assessments of their degree of power (power over the transformation) and their degree of alignment with the research team's own framing of the sustainability challenge. Results of each of these hub-specific processes were included in the inception workshop report, which proposed surveys (collecting qualitative data) and structured reporting on T-Labs (including qualitative data on process and quantitative data on stakeholder participation) to provide an empirical basis for comparison and cross-learning. Bi-monthly teleconferences via Skype, Zoom or GoToMeeting were set as the primary means for TKN-wide interaction.

Structured reporting by hubs took place after each of the two T-Lab workshops (specific events in each hub that were used for data collection). Hubs were invited to produce internal reports for circulation around the network, which were similarly structured to include questions on decisions taken, methods used, changes observed, findings made and lessons learnt. At each of the two events, hubs also reported on the participation of different stakeholders across academic and non-academic groups in each hub (again drawing on the same categories as had been used in the PIPA and similar subjective measures of power and alignment). This comparative method offered a way to begin to understand the hubs' different approaches to transdisciplinary research, and to consider how these related to the disciplines, cultures and contexts that were prevalent in each of the hubs (represented, e.g. in Figures 5.3 and 8.1).

The project also conducted three internal surveys (baseline, mid-point and final, indicated in italics in Table 2.1) in which members of each of the hub teams were asked similar questions regarding their research process. These sources (reports and surveys) have been drawn on significantly in the accounts in Chapters 5–10. During the project they were uploaded to a SharePoint, which provided a document repository for these outputs and other literature (academic or otherwise) that could support analysis and comparison of the processes occurring in each hub. The SharePoint also provided a site for peer review (e.g. of T-Lab designs, on the basis of templates shared in advance) and discussion fora, offering opportunities for continuous exchange of ideas and experiences between the different hubs.

While bi-monthly teleconferences (involving individuals across up to 16 time zones) were valuable enough to be continued over a year after the project funding had ceased, the use of Microsoft SharePoint, selected largely because of problems using Google in China, diminished as the project progressed due to preferences for different platforms across geographies and generations (e.g. Slack/Zoom/Skype). This was particularly notable for the 'real-time collaborative drafting' function.

Beyond virtual interactions, a series of exchange visits were also built into the design of the network (and the budgets of each hub). These were used to aid project planning, collaborative writing (see 'cross-learning blogs' below) and planning future work and funding proposals. They were particularly targeted at early career researchers and took the form of:

- Adrian Ely (UK hub) spending over four months with the Argentina hub (April–August 2016) at the outset of the project to aid with planning and early writing
- Joanes Atela visiting China in October 2016 to exchange insights with the China team and plan future work

- Lichao Yang visiting Kenya in April 2017[4]
- Representatives from the USA/Mexico teams attending the T2S programme workshop in India in 2017
- Anabel Marin visiting the UK hub (January 2019) to report on the work of Bioleft and prepare for the culmination of the project[5]

Co-learning blogs were incorporated into the design of the project as a prompt to paired hubs to think together and produce collaborative work. These offered the opportunity for collaborative writing without the constraints that more formal demands (e.g. co-authored journal articles) necessarily involve, e.g. the identification of a shared theoretical framework, presentation of full data, methods. All in all, seven blogs were published during the formal timeframe of the project (see below, with urls all accessed 30/9/2020.).

UK-Argentina hubs

Seeding Ideas: knowledge brokering and recombination for agricultural transformations, by Adrian Ely, Paddy Van Zwanenberg, Elise Wach, Martin Obaya and Almendra Cremaschi – https://steps-centre.org/blog/seeding-ideas-knowledge-brokering-recombination-agricultural-transformations/

China-Africa hubs

Transformations from Beijing to Nairobi and back: what can we learn from each other? by Yang Lichao, Kennedy Liti Mbeva and Jiang Chulin – https://steps-centre.org/blog/transformations-beijing-nairobi-back-can-learn/

North America hub

What 'agency' do researchers have in transformative research projects? by Hallie Eakin, Lakshmi Charli-Joseph and J. Mario Siqueiros-García – https://steps-centre.org/blog/agency-researchers-transformative-research-projects/

India hub

The Power of a T-Lab: sharing lessons on water and justice in Gurgaon, India by Dinesh Abrol, Pravin Kushwaha and Bikramaditya K. Choudhary–https://steps-centre.org/blog/the-power-of-a-t-lab-sharing-lessons-on-water-and-justice-in-gurgaon-india/

Beyond these co-learning blogs between paired hubs (that were incorporated into the project design), representatives of other hubs and even other TKNs collaborated on a number of blogs:

UK and Argentina hubs and other TKNs

Research, Convening and Bridging: sharing insights from the ISSC's Transformative Knowledge Networks, by Adrian Ely (with contributions from Joanes

Atela, Mirna Inturias, Dylan McGarry, Iokiñe Rodríguez and Patrick Van Zwanenberg) – https://steps-centre.org/blog/research-convening-bridging-sharing-insights-isscs-transformative-knowledge-networks/

North America and Argentina hubs

Living Aulas: what connects 'undisciplinary' research on sustainability? by Almendra Cremaschi and Rebecca Shelton – https://steps-centre.org/blog/living-aulas-create-space-for-undisciplinary-researchers

UK, Argentina and North American hubs and other TKNs

What does transformative research for sustainability look like? by Patrick van Zwanenberg, Hallie Eakin, Ethemcan Turhan, Mutizwa Mukute and Fiona Marshall – https://steps-centre.org/blog/transformative-research-sustainability-look-like/

Taken together, the approach to the design of the project and the various processes for data collection and sharing described above provided the basis for a uniquely international exploration of the role of transdisciplinary social science in transformations to sustainability. From an organisational learning perspective (Argyris and Schön 1996), these approaches provided opportunities for single-loop learning (instrumental learning through theoretically informed action) and double-loop learning (questioning the underlying theories

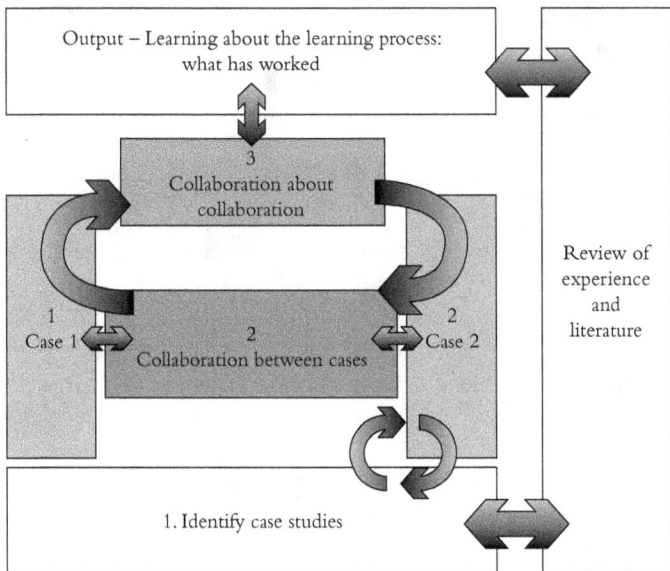

FIGURE 2.1 Schematic Representation of the collaboration process (adapted from Hackett and Eakin 2015).

in order to improve them). For example, in each hub, there was a process of learning about what activities or approaches were effective or not as the projects unfolded in each locale (single-loop learning) and, as described by Hackett and Eakin (2015) in work during the seed-funding stage, learning from and across collaborative contexts. The project was also designed to foster triple-loop learning, particularly through reflection on the processes of cross-hub interaction (learning about the learning and collaboration process), so that these insights could inform future networked transdisciplinary research projects.

While the network architecture and some symmetry of research design across hubs were beneficial in enabling comparison, significant flexibility was required. There was a degree of shared understanding around the notion of social transformations across the consortium (based on the years of previous collaborative work); however, the ways in which these applied to the selected sustainability challenges was open to interpretation. Further, it was difficult to anticipate what would be the appropriate approaches or methods for each context, what local collaborators would be involved, and what opportunities for action and change would materialise once the projects were initiated.

The challenge for the network then was to allow as much flexibility as possible, while adopting a process through which the decisions on theory, method or approach made within each hub could be documented and compared, if not in real-time, at a moment when the hub teams could pause for reflection. This challenge is common to projects taking a complexity-aware approach, recognising emergence, while working within institutional and funding parameters that push towards pre-defined and linear planning.

A compromise involved the adoption of 'anchors' that provided a common language and approach, without constraining the creativity and freedom of hubs to carry out the work that they saw as worthwhile and potentially impactful, within their chosen theoretical and epistemological traditions.

Theoretical anchors

Hubs in the 'Pathways' TKN favoured a diversity of epistemological approaches, differing in their theorisation of transformations, change processes and the role of researchers therein. These differences link to the different disciplines that were prominent in each hub (Table 2.2) but also the regionally specific academic and socio-political lineages on which they drew (discussed further in Chapter 3).

Individuals from all hubs had – at different points and to varying extents – collaborated with members of the STEPS Centre, whether around topics such as resilience (Leach 2008), technology regulation (Van Zwanenberg et al. 2011), grassroots innovation (Fressoli et al. 2014) and the politics of sustainable development (STEPS Centre 2010; Leach et al. 2012; Ely et al. 2013), and the wider pathways approach articulated in Leach et al. (2010). This history provided us with a number of theoretical "anchors" that offered a basis for further collaboration:

- **Systems** – "particular configurations of dynamic interacting social, technological and environmental elements" (Leach et al. 2010).

As described in Chapter 1, the focus on *systemic* transformation was shared across hubs. This included a definition of the system (including explicit attention to how the system was framed) in the original co-design phase (see Table 2.1). Lessons that emerged from the project (discussed in Chapters 3 and 12) contributed to the delineation of "systemic" approaches to transformations research, alongside "structural" and "enabling" approaches that were also reflected in some of the examples outlined in this book (Scoones et al. 2018).

- **Framings** – "the different ways of understanding or representing a social, technological or natural system and its relevant environment. Among other aspects, this includes the ways system elements are bounded, characterized and prioritized, and meanings and normative values attached to each" (Leach et al. 2010).

Building on Goffman's (1974) seminal work, the notion of framing has a long history in policy studies (Schön & Rein 1994; Levidow and Murphy 2003; Ely et al. 2009) and was familiar to many across the consortium. The co-design workshops and concept notes that emerged from them identified different framings and the project offered significant opportunities to explore processes of re-framing (see Chapter 11).

- **Pathways** – "the particular directions in which interacting social, technological and environmental systems co-evolve over time" (Leach et al. 2010).

Concept notes identified dominant and alternative pathways, but adopted different lenses through which these were characterised in each context. At the same time, the pathways approach (and the notion of pathways) played a different role in each case. In some cases (see Chapter 9 – Mexico) they were combined with ideas around transformative agency (Westley et al. 2013) while in others (see Chapter 10 – India) class was a more central organising concept. In some cases (see Chapter 8 – China) gender played a more central role in the work, while others (Chapter 7 – Kenya) engaged more with issues of poverty as a focus for transformational change. Taken together, these different approaches offer insights into the notion of *transformative pathways* to sustainability (Chapter 12).

As anchors, these concepts represented heuristic starting points rather than a rigid theoretical framework. The rationale was that there was at least some familiarity with them across each of the hubs, and thus they could act as a *lingua franca* through which more abstract theoretical notions could be explored (see Chapter 3). The role of the project was not to test these concepts (derived from work led from the global North) for their applicability in different contexts but to explore their limitations and put forward alternatives grounded in the contexts in which the research was conducted. Indeed, a key ambition of the project was to foster transdisciplinary approaches that prioritised historical and contemporary characteristics of the hubs rather than being driven by those in the Northern-dominated literature (Van Zwanenberg et al. 2016).

Methodological anchors

In each hub locality, transformations (processes of deep systemic change) were already ongoing – understood as centred on technologies, market incentives, state-led support or citizen mobilisation (Scoones et al. 2015). The project aimed to further elucidate these processes and – through strategic use of transdisciplinary social science research and evidence – help to steer them in more environmentally sustainable and socially just directions. A previous review of transdisciplinary research in sustainability science (Brandt et al. 2013) supported the view taken within the TKN that research methods needed to be selected on the basis of local preferences, rather than standardised across the network. At the same time, some commonalities were desirable in order to support comparison and cross-learning. Based on key contributions from Stockholm Resilience Centre (Per Olsson and Laura Pereira), we adopted the overall approach of 'T-Labs' – processes involving research and transdisciplinary engagement to address a complex sustainability problem or challenge – around which different hubs could experiment with different methods for research and engagement. T-Labs (shorthand for Transformations laboratories) were first experimented with in the run-up to the Transformations 2015 conference hosted by Stockholm Resilience Centre, and add to the panoply of strategic approaches to enable or unleash systemic change through experimentation in 'labs', including living labs (Bergvall-Kåreborn & Ståhlbröst 2009; Keyson et al. 2017), transition labs (Nevens et al. 2013), social labs (Hassan 2014), social innovation labs (Westley and Laban 2015) or real-world labs (Wagner, et al. 2016; Schäpke et al. 2018). They are differentiated on the basis of their focus on transformations in social-ecological systems/ human-nature interactions and their open-endedness (being strategically facilitated to allow for emergence, as discussed in more detail in Chapter 4).

Like the theoretical concepts above, the notion of T-Labs acted as an anchor to be negotiated and experimented with, rather than a methodological tool or protocol to be implemented in a standard manner across the TKN. Chapters 4 and 5–10 provide further information on how the T-Lab concept was operationalised in different contexts.

The structured approach to collaboration outlined above (and discussed further in Ely et al. 2020) balanced the need for a coherent international project design with the need for deep context-specificity. The use of theoretical and methodological anchors that provided the flexibility for transdisciplinary work in each hub to be locally co-designed and implemented was valued by the network team, based on a reflective self-evaluation of the project conducted at the final workshop in October 2018. T-Labs provided an opportunity for local independence in a way similar to what has been described as "framed creativity" in studies of adaptive co-management (Olsson et al. 2004).

As the following chapters describe in more detail, this approach provided insights both in terms of single-loop (learning through theoretically informed action, in this case enabling individual hubs to adopt more effective research and engagement methods in the future) and double-loop learning (questioning the underlying theories in order to improve them, in this case via shared reflection alongside teams from other hubs in the network). The experience provided a wealth of insights and mainly tacit knowledge about international collaboration in transdisciplinary social science for sustainability transformations. Only a tiny proportion of the lessons learnt from the 'Pathways' TKN are codifiable in a volume such as this. However, as the next chapter explains, the overriding motivation behind the project was – from the outset – much more than the production of formal research outputs such as academic publications.

Notes

1 Launched in 2015, Future Earth is a ten-year initiative to advance Global Sustainability Science, build capacity in this rapidly expanding area of research and provide an international research agenda to guide natural and social scientists working around the world.
2 http://acknowlej.org, accessed 30/9/2020.
3 http://transgressivelearning.org/, accessed 30/9/2020.
4 Reported in the following blog – https://steps-centre.org/blog/learning-across-continents-sustainable-transformations-visit-china-africa/, accessed 30/9/2020.
5 Reported in the following blog – http://bioleft.org/en/2019/01/28/bioleft-en-el-reino-unido-seminarios-academicos-y-agricultura-urbana/, accessed 30/9/2020.

References

Argyris, C. & Schön, D.A. (1996) *Organizational Learning II: Theory, Method and Practice.* Redwood City, CA: Addison-Wesley.
Bergvall-Kåreborn, B. & Ståhlbröst, A.(2009) Living lab: An open and citizen centric approach for innovation. *International Journal of Innovation and Regional Development* 1(4): 356–370.
Brandt, P., Ernst, A., Gralla, F., Luederitz, C., Lang, D.J., Newig, J., Reinert, F., Abson, D.J., von & Wehrden, H.A. (2013) Review of transdisciplinary research in sustainability science. *Ecological Economics* 92: 1–15.
Douthwaite, B., Alvarez, S., Cook, S., Davies, R., George, P., Howell, J., MacKay, R. & Rubiano, J. (2007) Participatory impact pathways analysis: a practical application of program theory in research for development. *Canadian Journal of Program Evaluation* 22(2): 127–159.

Ely, A. & Marin, A. (2017) Learning about 'Engaged Excellence' across a transformative knowledge network. *IDS Bulletin* 47(6): 73–86.

Ely, A., Marin, A., Charli-Joseph, L., Abrol, D., Apgar, M., Atela, J., Ayre, B., Byrne, R., Choudhary, B. K., Chengo, V., Cremaschi, A., Davis, R., Desai, P., Eakin, H., Kushwaha, P., Marshall, F., Mbeva, K., Ndege, N., Ochieng, C., Ockwell, D., Olsson, P., Oxley, N., Pereira, L,. Priya, R., Tigabu, A., Van Zwanenberg, P. & Yang, L. (2020) Structured collaboration across a Transformative Knowledge Network: Learning across disciplines, cultures and contexts? *Sustainability* 12(6): 2499.

Ely, A. & Oxley, N. (2014) *STEPS Centre Research: Our Approach to Impact*, STEPS Working Paper 60. Brighton: STEPS Centre.

Ely, A., Smith, A., Leach, M., Stirling, A. & Scoones, I. (2013) Innovation politics Post-Rio+20: hybrid pathways to sustainability? *Environment and Planning C* 31(6): 1063–1081.

Ely, A. Stirling, A, Wendler, F. & Vos, E. (2009) The process of framing, in Dreyer, M. & O. Renn (Eds.) *Food Safety Governance: Integrating Science, Precaution and Public Involvement*. Berlin Heidelberg: Springer Verlag, pp. 47–56.

Fressoli, M., Arond, E., Dinesh Abrol, D., Smith, A., Ely, A. & Dias, R. (2014) When grassroots innovation movements encounter mainstream institutions: implications for models of inclusive innovation. *Innovation and Development* 4(2): 277–292.

Goffman, E. (1974) *Frame Analysis: An Essay on the Organization of Experience*. Boston: Northeastern University Press.

Hackett, E. & Eakin, H. (2015) ISSC 'Transformations to Sustainability' Programme Concept Note- Water Governance Challenges, Mexico City and Phoenix Research Note from the ASU Water Workshop, 12 December 2014, STEPS Centre and Arizona State University, https://steps-centre.org/wp-content/uploads/ISSC-Concept-note_ASU.pdf, accessed 29/9/2020.

Hackmann, H. & St Clair, A.L. (2012) *Transformative Cornerstones of Social Science Research for Global Change*. Paris: International Social Science Council.

Hassan, Z. (2014) *The Social Labs Revolution*. Oakland, CA: Berrett–Koehler Publisher, Inc.

Keyson, D.V., Guerra-Santin, O. & Lockton, D. (Eds.) (2017) *Living Labs: Design and Assessment of Sustainable Living*. New York: Springer International Publishing.

Leach, M. (Ed.) (2008) *Re-framing Resilience: A Symposium Report*, STEPS Working Paper 13. Brighton: STEPS Centre.

Leach, M., Rockström, J., Raskin, P., Scoones, I., Stirling, A.C., Smith, A., Thompson, J., Millstone, E., Ely, A., Arond, E., Folke, C. & Olsson, P. (2012) Transforming innovation for sustainability. *Ecology and Society* 17(2): 11.

Leach, M., Scoones, I. & Stirling, A.C. (2010) *Dynamic Sustainabilities: Technology, Environment and Social Justice*. Abingdon: Routledge/Earthscan.

Levidow, L. & Murphy, J. (2003) Reframing regulatory science: trans-Atlantic conflicts over GM crops. *Cahiers D'économie et Sociologie Rurales* 68–69: 48–74.

Marin, A., Ely, A. & van Zwanenberg, P. (2016) Co-design with aligned and non-aligned knowledge partners: implications for research and coproduction of sustainable food systems. *Current Opinion in Environmental Sustainability* 20: 93–98. www.sciencedirect.com/science/article/pii/S1877343516300562 (accessed 30 November 2016).

Moser, S. (2016) Can science on transformation transform science? Lessons from co-design. *Current Opinion in Environmental Sustainability* 20: 106–115.

Nevens, F., Frantzeskaki, N., Gorissen, L. & Loorbach, D. (2013) Urban transition labs: co-creating transformative action for sustainable cities. *Journal of Cleaner Production* 50: 111–122.

Schäpke, N., Stelzer, F., Caniglia, G., Bergmann, M., Wanner, M., Singer-Brodowski, M., Loorbach, D., Olsson, P., Baedeker, C. & Lang, D.J. (2018) Jointly experimenting for transformation? Shaping real-world laboratories by comparing them. *GAIA* 27(1): 85–96.

Olsson, P., Folke, C. & Berkes, F. (2004) Adaptive co-management for building resilience in social–ecological systems. *Environmental Management* 34(1): 75–90.

Pathways Network. (2018) *T-Labs: a Practical Guide – Using Transformation Labs (T-Labs) for Innovation in Social-ecological Systems*. Brighton, UK: STEPS Centre.

Schön, D. & Rein, M. (1994) *Frame Reflection: Towards the Resolution of Intractable Policy Issues*. New York: Basic Books.

Scoones, I., Leach, M. & Newell, P. (Eds.) (2015) *The Politics of Green Transformations*. Abingdon: Routledge/Earthscan.

Scoones, I., Stirling, A., Abrol, D., Atela, J., Charli-Joseph, L., Eakin, H., Ely, A., Olsson, P., Pereira, L., Priya, R., van Zwanenberg, P. & Yang, L. (2018) *Transformations to Sustainability*, STEPS Working Paper 104. Brighton: STEPS Centre.

STEPS Centre. (2010) *Innovation, Sustainability, Development: A New Manifesto*. Brighton: STEPS Centre.

T2S. (2019) *Transformations to Sustainability: About the Programme*, https://transformations tosustainability.org/about-the-programme/, accessed 16/8/2019.

UNESCO/ISSC. (2013) *World Social Science Report 2013: Changing Global Environments*. Paris: United Nations Educational, Scientific and Cultural Organisation & International Social Science Council.

Van Zwanenberg, P., Ely, A. & Smith, A. (2011) *Regulating Technology: International Harmonization and Local Realities*. Abingdon: Routledge.

Van Zwanenberg, P., Marin, A. & Ely, A. (2016) *How Do We End the Dominance of Rich Countries Over Sustainability Science?* https://steps-centre.org/blog/how-do-we-end-the-dominance-of-rich-countries-over-sustainability-science/, accessed 9/9/2019.

Wagner, F., Schäpke, N., Stelzer, F., Bergmann, M. & Lang, D. J. (2016) BaWü-labs on their way: Progress of real-world laboratories in Baden-Württemberg. *GAIA* 25(3): 220–221.

Westley, F. & Laban, S. (Eds.) (2015) *Social Innovation Lab Guide*. Waterloo, ON: Waterloo Institute for Social Innovation and Resilience.

Westley, F.R., Tjornbo, O., Schultz, L., Olsson, P., Folke, C., Crona, B. & Bodin, Ö. (2013) A theory of transformative agency in linked social-ecological systems. *Ecology and Society* 18(3): 27.

SECTION 2

Emerging themes across the transformative knowledge network

3

TRANSFORMATIONS

Theory, research and action

Adrian Ely

Introduction: a reflexive approach

The previous two chapters have provided a background to the 'Pathways' transformative knowledge network (TKN), its genesis, ambitions and overall transdisciplinary approach. This chapter draws attention to earlier work that has engaged with concepts of transformation and describes the long history of action/activist research that has emerged in response to various sustainability problems. This raises questions about the positionality of researchers in this process, and the implications of epistemological frameworks and normative commitments for transdisciplinary science. In considering these implications, the chapter tries to adopt a reflexive approach (in line with wider pathways thinking) that recognises how structures and circumstances condition our work.

In adopting such an approach, it is apt to ask "why write a book?" The years of person-time and the other resources that went in to the production of this output could be seen as being in tension with the project's transformational ambitions. Even if the original proposal outputs included "possibly an edited volume incorporating experiences and insights at the local and global level", this was not a firm commitment. Indeed, as our final report provided to the funder made clear, some of our most important achievements were not academic in nature at all, but rather embodied in the actions and networks that had emerged from our work. The fact that we are writing a book, and the nature of the publication itself (and its constituent chapters) is in part driven by our different institutional settings. In various ways these shape the expectations placed upon us, and to some extent cast us in our roles as researchers, scientists or activists. Production of an edited volume can be seen as a response to universities' demands for "knowledge products" (Russell et al. 2008). But this is only part of the answer. Despite the differences in publishing cultures across the TKN, the documentation of our collective efforts

DOI: 10.4324/9780429331930-5

in this format (alongside many other media, in different formats and languages) was seen as worthwhile. Further, the interactions necessary for the production of this shared output, years after the formal end of the project, helped us to realise our ambitions to learn across disciplines, cultures and contexts. Attempting to distil some of this learning into book form has been an important part of the research process.

This learning highlighted the different emphases on theory, research and action possessed by the various hubs, and the researchers within them. There are transdisciplinary action research histories in each of the different regions from which the TKN membership is drawn, of which many of us are aware. However, their imbalanced representation in formal academic literature (especially that confined to the English language) means that most analyses are deeply situated in the Western tradition. Despite the shared insights and cross-learning that we have achieved, the format of this document to some extent continues in that tradition. Nevertheless, the project offered the opportunity of a considered reflection of transformations research and how science itself may need to be transformed with a focus on coproduction and learning rather than codification of knowledge products. As such, this document should be read as a partial and particular reflection on the TKN's work, rather than seen as the culmination of its activities.

The chapter begins by outlining some of the existing theory around transformations, and then considers the role of research in transformations and the need to reflect on framings. We then move beyond research to action, and point to relevant literatures from around the world that have bridged this divide. Coming back to the project, we consider how we attempted to adopt a reflexive approach that did not prioritise knowledge (theory/research) or action but saw them as tightly interwoven. The learning that emerged was to some extent codifiable but the transformative pathways we sought are much more about the changes in individuals, and in the actions and networks that resulted from the project than whatever is contained within the pages of this book.

Sustainability, change and transformation

For decades, researchers of sustainable development have recognised that the urgency and scale of sustainability challenges require systemic changes rather than changes at the level of individuals, populations, technologies or behaviours (Meadows et al. 1972; Schot et al. 1997; Berkes et al. 2003). The challenges are particularly complex, when we recognise that sustainability itself is viewed from very different perspectives (Leach et al. 2010a) and from global to local levels (Steffen et al. 2015). Hackmann and St Clair (2012) provide an academic perspective on systemic responses to "ever-expanding environmental problems and disaster risks on the one hand, and converging crises of climate, inequality, food, water, finance and social discontent on the other", highlighting the role of social science. A contemporary political recognition of the need for systemic change is underlined by the title of the 2030 Agenda for sustainable development and the SDGs 'Transforming our World' (United Nations 2015). But multiple transformations can be conceived, each with their own underlying rationales and politics (Scoones et al. 2015), As Feola (2015) argues, "high conceptual elasticity and lack of empirical grounding of the concept of transformation generate the risk of voiding the term of meaning". Prior to embarking on a study of transformative pathways to sustainability, therefore, it is worth reviewing some of the contours of the conceptual debates around term.

Approaches to understanding such processes of transformation in social systems date back at least as far as Marx's (1859; 1867) recognition of shifts in relations between "base" and "superstructure", or more recently Polanyi's (1944) work "The Great Transformation". Such approaches have been characterised by Scoones et al. (2018) as "structural", in that they focus on deep changes in the structural relations of politics, economy and society. While notions of social sustainability (although expressed in different terms) are fundamental to these analyses, the environment sustainability element is minor. Writers such as Fraser (2014) have taken some of Polanyi's ideas forward to analyse contemporary ecological, social and financial crises. Individual scholars have adopted structural approaches as a largely analytical lens on transformations, pointing towards the relationships between carbon-based economies and power (Mitchell 2011) and considering the structural implications of decarbonisation (Newell and Paterson 2012) or degrowth (D'Alisa et al. 2014).

More recent work, by growing communities of scholars, has looked at change in socio-technical (Grin et al. 2010), ecological and socio-ecological (Olsson et al. 2014) systems. Scoones et al. (2018) label these approaches 'systemic' and characterise them as focussing on particular features such as species, actors or technologies (and the relations between them). Those literatures focussing on socio-technical system *transitions*, especially those adopting a *transition management* perspective (Grin et al. 2010), see government as a central actor introducing incentives, investments and policy initiatives can help to bring about changes in a way that fosters instrumental objectives including social and environmental sustainability (see, e.g. Kemp and Rotmans 2005; Kern and Howlett 2009). Scholarship is seen as being able to inform such policy initiatives, suggesting that knowledge underpins action.

In contrast to such controlled *transitions*, Stirling (2015) points to transformations as "more plural, emergent and unruly political re-alignments, involving social and technological innovations driven by diversely incommensurable knowledges, challenging incumbent structures and pursuing contending (even unknown) ends" (Stirling 2015: 1). Under this perspective, the role of government is less central, and greater agency (sometimes in adversarial relations with government) is attributed to civil society. This might take the form of coalitions and alliances are formed (Schmitz 2015), advocacy 'from below' through social movements (Scoones et al. 2015) or action through grassroots innovation networks (Smith and Ely 2015). While this distinction between transition and transformation is not evidenced by bibliometric analysis of the literatures (at least in the energy field – Chappin and Ligtvoet 2014), it is adopted to varying extents in the chapters of this book and shared by other scholars highlighting resistance movements (Temper et al. 2018) who argue that "while transitions literature tends to focus on artifacts and technologies, we suggest that a resistance-centred perspective focuses on the creation of new subjectivities, power relations, values and institutions".

Socio-ecological systems scholars draw upon studies of resilience that have emerged from ecology (Holling 1973), applying and extending the concepts to analyse interactions with human (social) systems (Folke et al. 2002). In translating these studies to the policy field, they have largely moved beyond the expert-led decision-making and governmental management approaches to an appreciation of complex socio-ecological systems undergoing adaptive cycles at multiple, hierarchically structured scales (Gunderson and Holling 2002; Olsson et al. 2006). While these approaches have their critics, social-ecological systems play an important conceptual role in informing the notion of T-Labs (Chapter 4) and specific hub work (e.g. Mexico).

Patterson et al. (2015, 2017) and Blythe et al. (2018) also point to these "systemic" approaches in their account of four approaches to transformations, namely, "socio-technical transitions and transition management" and "socio-ecological transformations", to which they add transformative adaptation (e.g. Pelling 2011) and "sustainability pathways" (e.g. Leach et al. 2010a). There is significant scope for interaction between these approaches (see, e.g. West et al. 2014 on synergies between the socio-ecological and pathways approaches). In a broad review, Foela (2015) offers a sophisticated framework for comparing different systemic approaches, based on "system model", "form and temporal range", "seat of causality and social consciousness" and "outcome" to distinguish between different approaches, and makes a plea for the testing of "different concepts and theories of transformation in empirical research" – a plea to which this book responds.

A third category of 'transformations' studies described by Scoones et al. (2018) highlight the agency and uncertainties inherent in choosing the aims and direction of transformation, and focus on revealing the different values, knowledge and relationships (including power relations) involved in change. These "enabling" approaches emphasise human agency, collective action, political mobilisation and emancipation, and aim to challenge incumbent interests and control, thus representing a move from analysis or policy advocacy to engaged scholarship and research as activism. Examples include community-led environmental action, hacker/maker spaces for grassroots innovation or commoning approaches to sustainable local economies (Scoones et al. 2020). While often attending to localised challenges, enabling approaches often reflect a desire to contribute to structural or systemic transformation at higher levels.

These various concepts can help us not only to understand transformative social-technological-environmental change as it has unfolded in the past, but can also inform work of transdisciplinary scholars working in different contexts towards the 2030 Agenda. In such a complex sphere, moving from analysis to action means not only identifying (and supporting) alternative pathways, but also challenging incumbency (and the structures with which it is entangled) in contexts where power relations are often highly skewed in favour of unsustainable production and consumption. It raises difficult and fundamental questions for networks embedded primarily within academic research organisations that are not geared towards transformation. It requires attention to political rigour as well as academic rigour (Temper et al. 2018, 2019) and an alertness to the risks through which scholarship in this area may become implicated in unsustainable practices, social inequality and injustice (elsewhere referred to as the "dark side of transformation"; Blythe et al. 2018).

The work described in this book draws insights from structural and systemic approaches, and to varying extents adopts enabling approaches that involve transdisciplinary collaboration, a recognition of different perspectives and framings and a normative commitment to contributing to directions of progressive social change.

The role of research in transformative pathways to sustainability

Brand (2016) writes that the term "transformation" can be used either analytically (to analyse past and present changes in order to assess and explain them).or strategically (to denote the kinds of changes required to overcome environmental and social challenges). Likewise, "transformative pathways to sustainability" can be an analytical tool or a strategic tool. This book explores a move from the use of the pathways approach to understand the direction in which interacting social, technological and ecological systems co-evolve to one that attempts to contribute to the emergence of those directions, supporting plural alternative pathways with a commitment to environmental sustainability, poverty alleviation and social justice. As such, it exemplifies what Feola (2015) describes as the solution-oriented or "transformational social science" (Hackmann and St Clair 2012) perspective as a direct call for the social sciences "to take a more strategic and operational approach to issues of change", while retaining a commitment to plurality.

Given the different political contexts evidence in the Pathways Network hubs, significant flexibility was required in order to operationalise the notion of 'transformational social science', acknowledging the institutional and external pressures imposed on researchers and other members of the teams in each case.

Flexibility was also required due to the different *disciplinary cultures* that were prominent in each hub (see Chapter 2). While the theoretical anchors discussed in the previous chapter (systems, framings, pathways) to some extent provided a common language across each hub, theoretical conceptions of transformation differed. This sometimes translated into divergences in epistemological views, which combined with different objectives and strategies around the appropriate role of researchers in studying or intervening in systems. These different objectives, and the underlying theories of transformation that were applied in each case, are compared in Table 3.1.

TABLE 3.1 Objectives and underlying theories of transformation from TKN hubs

Hub	General objective of project/case study	Underlying theories of transformation that inform the choice of method
UK	To design and implement research and "transformation laboratories" with the aim of enhancing the supply of local, sustainably produced food into Brighton and Hove (and drawing wider lessons for the UK's agricultural transformations).	Transformation is influenced by changing cognitive, affective and political economic drivers that work across individuals, groups and systems. Pathways, politics of green transformations, governance of sustainable socio-technical transitions, transformative pathways.
Argentina	To design and implement "transformation laboratories" (T-Labs) with the aim of creating an experimental space in which coalitions of heterogeneous actors can agree on a sustainability problem in the agricultural seed sector and develop and prototype possible solutions.	Transformation involves experimentation with novel, more sustainable socio-technical practices and the development of alternative 'path breaking' socio-technical configurations.
Africa Hub (Kenya)	To use the T-Lab approach to explore how Kenya can enable sustainable and equitable access to solar home systems for all via mobile-based payment systems, especially those who can't participate in micro-financing schemes.	The T-Lab involved different stakeholders (government, NGOs, civil society, private sector development partners, research and academia) who provided rich and diverse insights into what needs to be done or changed to enable equitable, sustainable access for all, to solar PV systems via mobile-based payment systems.
China Hub	This study engages in the social dimensions of green transformation in order to provide a more holistic picture of the transformations to sustainability.	Transformations in China are driven by a number of actors. The change agents are different stakeholders in transformation, including laid-off workers, former plant owners, local government officials, scholars, NGOs, etc.
Mexico	To design and implement a process known as "transformation laboratories" with the aim of identifying, mobilising and activating individual and collective agency of actors involved in the social-ecological dynamics of the Xochimilco urban wetland.	Transformation is about bottom-up building of collective agency through reframing systems dynamics – transformations to sustainability; transformative agency; pathways.
South Asia Hub (India)	To design and implement transformation labs as a process with the aim of promoting a collective strategy for intervention to bring together the mobilised publics specifically representing poor and marginalised along with middle classes to develop the collective practical understanding and build alliances for enabling their participation in planning and decision-making processes of water and waste water management.	Transformation is conceptualised as enabling the people as a whole specifically poor and marginalised to enhance their access to resources and capabilities for mobilisation of power to innovate and foster regime change that helps to create conditions for the realisation of ecologically and socially just development.

Adapted from Ely et al. 2020.

Researchers' framings of sustainability

Researchers play an important role in framing sustainability transformations, and this calls for reflexivity, given the power they hold as actors within them. Working across and beyond different disciplines alerts us to the fact that sustainability is subject to very different and conflicting understandings. One of the tools deployed by the STEPS Centre's "pathways" approach to transdisciplinarity is a conscious appreciation of framings, which are defined as "the different ways of understanding or representing a social, technological or natural system and its relevant environment" (Leach et al. 2010a). The notion of framings is represented in Figure 3.1 and accompanying Table 3.2, both originally drawn from Leach et al. (2010a).

This explicit attention to different framings, adopted within a transdisciplinary approach, aims to recognise the role of power in shaping knowledge and action. Contending *analytical* framings from the various natural and social sciences – let alone contending *actor* framings – differ in "the ways system elements are bounded, characterized and prioritized, and meanings and normative values attached to each" (Leach et al. 2010a: 4). This aspect of the pathways approach has been applied previously in domains such as energy (Byrne et al. 2011), agriculture (Van Zwanenberg et al. 2011), bioenergy (Cavicchi and Ely 2016), health (Leach et al. 2010b) and urban waste management (Randhawa et al. 2020) to understand how the framings of more powerful actors come to dominate in policy discourse over those of more marginalised groups. This can lead to a locking in of policy to the specific pathways favoured by those powerful actors, and the occlusion and crowding out of alternative perspectives and "subaltern" pathways (Stirling 2012). In these cases, framings have been identified empirically in

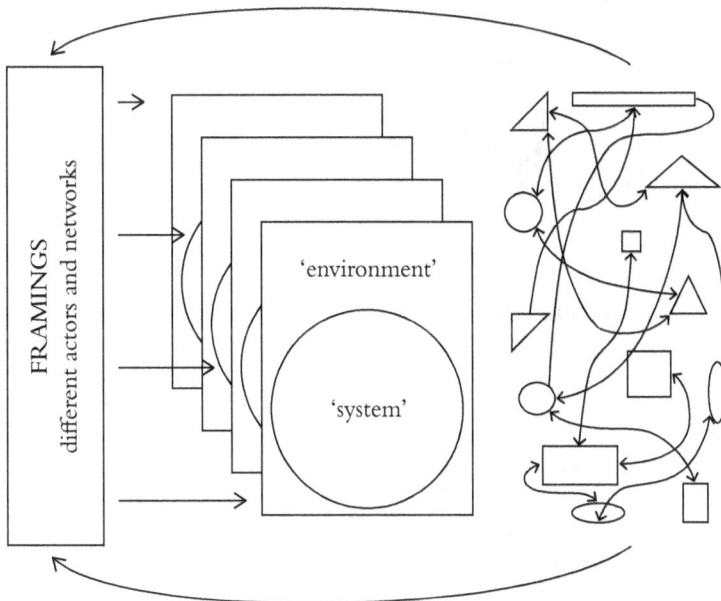

FIGURE 3.1 Multiple framings (adapted from Figure 3.1 from Leach et al. 2010a, p. 44).

TABLE 3.2 Dimensions of framing

Choice of elements	Subjective judgements
• Scale	• Perspectives
• Boundaries	• Interests
• Key elements and relationships	• Values
• Dynamics in play	• Notions of relevant experience
• Outputs	• Goals

Box 3.1 from Leach et al. (2010a, p. 45).

the narratives that are adopted and repeated (or neglected and ignored) on the basis of documentary evidence.

The 'Pathways' TKN's action-orientation required a different approach. In each of the cases described in this book, attention has been given to how systems and their potential transformations to sustainability have been framed, by both actors and analysts. Each locally defined sustainability challenge (see Chapter 4) reflected a particular framing, emerging from the co-design of each local project. Maintaining a self-reflective and critical approach that recognises the power that researchers (and their disciplinary and theoretical assumptions) have to frame sustainability challenges in particular ways has been important as the research has progressed (Marshall et al. 2018).

The chronological histories presented in Chapters 5–10 illustrate how researcher framings influenced the work carried out in each hub. However, they also show how transdisciplinary interaction led plural framings to guide the work from the outset. Engagement with non-academic partners in each of the cases in this book started at the co-design phase (see Chapter 2 for a discussion of the phases of the project), launching "from the assumption that scientific knowledge combined with others' knowledge is itself a powerful agent of change" (Moser 2016). Through the T-Labs, these framings evolved as the projects progressed, leading to reframing processes discussed further in Chapter 11. This reflected the project's shift from research to action, and a focus on transdisciplinary learning.

From research to action: transdisciplinary research and its intellectual heritages

Working across more than one scientific discipline in parallel (multidisciplinarity) and in combination (interdisciplinarity) has long been recognised as a feature of problem-oriented, action research. There is increasing interest in transdisciplinary research from the sustainability transformations community (Hackmann and St. Clair 2012; Mauser et al. 2013) alongside significant conceptual efforts from European groups like TD-Net (Hirsch Hadorn and Pohl 2007; Hirsch Hadorn et al. 2008) and a recognition of the diversity of approaches used in different countries (Von Wehrden et al. 2019). Earlier appeals to transdisciplinarity (although other terms were used) were made by Western researchers in international development (Chambers 1983; Hall 1992 to "participatory research") or in science and technology policy studies (Gibbons et al. 1994 to "mode 2" knowledge production). However, many of these ideas developed alongside and were pre-dated by a multitude of different intellectual heritages from across the globe.

Influenced by Paolo Freire's notion of *conscientization* and Nyerere's policies in Tanzania (among other phenomena), the original 'Participatory Research Project' at the International Centre for Adult Education in Toronto in 1976 had interacted with and learnt from other colleagues in India, Venezuela, Tanzania and the Netherlands (Rahman 2008). Latin American scholars in the 1970s and 1980s called for new forms of research combining theory, action and participation (Fals-Borda 1979), as other sought new trajectories of socio-technical change that better responded to local priorities, problems and circumstances (Herrera 1979; Sunkel and Gligo 1981).

Reflecting a long history of participatory action research in South Asia (Rahman 1985) and debates around the role of science and society dating back to Gandhian-based Sarvodaya movement (e.g. Krishna 2001), components of the Indian research system have attempted to foster collaboration with non-academic (especially rural) sectors of society since shortly after independence. In China, non-expert ("peasant scientist") participation in research was encouraged during Mao's time (Oldham 1964); however, has more recently been less well-established outside specialist groups, e.g. in the agricultural domain (e.g. Li et al. 2009; Song and Vernooy 2010).

African scholars and practitioners have also pointed towards ideas that resonate with the notion of transdisciplinarity, highlighting the importance of knowledge being rooted in particular socio-cultural and historical contexts (Urama et al. 2010). Much of the work from the continent – theoretical and experimental – has roots that go back to post-colonial periods and reflect both nationalist ideologies and pan-Africanist politics (Mangu 2006; Nabudere 2006).

In contemporary Europe, transdisciplinary research thrives around networks associated with the Wuppertal Institute (https://wupperinst.org/en/), ETH Zurich and TD-NET (www.transdisciplinarity.ch/en/td-net/Ueber-td-net.html) and DRIFT (https://drift.eur.nl/) among others. Considering transdisciplinary research as a component of sustainability science Brandt et al. (2013) investigate the process phases, knowledge types and the intensity of involvement of practitioners displayed by 236 peer-reviewed transdisciplinary papers. Their findings are presented in relation to five pre-identified challenges, represented in Table 3.2.

As transdisciplinary research has been formalised to become a focus of study and excellence in itself, terminologies have become entrenched within particular networks and to some extent more fragmented (as noted by Brandt et al. 2013). Klein (2020) provides a wide-ranging review of sustainability and

TABLE 3.3 Challenges for undertaking transdisciplinary approaches in sustainability science

Challenge	Finding of review (Brandt et al. 2013)
Coherent Framing.	Transdisciplinary Research in Sustainability Science is Increasing, but Under Diverse Term
Integration of Methods	Method Sets Used are Independent of Process Phases and Knowledge Types
Research Process and Knowledge Production	There is a Gap Between 'Best Practice' Transdisciplinary Research as Advocated and Transdisciplinary Research as Published in Scientific Journals
Practitioners' Engagement	Knowledge is Interchanged, Yet Empowerment is Rare
Generating Impact	Generating Transdisciplinary Research with High-Scientific Impact Remains Challenging

Derived from Brandt et al. (2013).

transdisciplinarity by focussing in on specific keywords to elucidate shifts from interdisciplinarity and different forms of learning and knowledge.

In other work, transdisciplinary interactions between researchers and other societal groups throughout the process have been referred to "co-production". Differing from both interactional constitutive co-production (as defined by Jasanoff 2004) this term has assumed an important role in recent research in transformations to sustainability. Miller and Wyborn (2018) review the history and theory around co-production from a much broader set of disciplines and fields (including public and business administration, science and technology studies and sustainability science), arguing that some convergence is visible across traditions. They argue that co-production practices should recognise and value both process and outcomes, summarising as follows:

1 Be inclusive in the diversity of participants, the power accorded to them, and the processes and objectives of co-production. Ensure that the institutions that enable co-production attend carefully to the credibility, legitimacy, and accountability this entails.

2 Acknowledge that co-production is a process of reconfiguring science and its social authority. Such processes require participants to be reflexive about the inherently political nature of producing knowledge in the service of changing social order at local to global scales.

3 Recognise that public engagement, deliberation, and debate will shape the content and relevance of knowledge and its ability to help construct and empower institutions to facilitate sustainability.

Norström et al. (2020) put forward their own principles for knowledge co-production, which they describe as "part of a loosely linked and evolving cluster of participatory and transdisciplinary research approaches that have emerged in recent decades"; their perspective urges that coproduction processes be "context-based", "pluralistic", "goal-oriented" and "interactive". They suggest that "many researchers still face incentive structures that primarily reward disciplinary science that does not engage with society" while "many practitioners work within organisations that do not incentivise critical reflection, ongoing learning and revision of actions". But coproduction challenges the distinction between research and practice (pointing towards a praxis mode), and indeed between knowledge and action. If "co-production is a process of reconfiguring science and its social authority" as Miller and Wyborn suggest, then it implies questioning the modernist assumption that (research-based) knowledge should inform action in the first place. Instead, action research by individuals, teams and networks proceeds through a constant negotiation of unfolding pathways, which is conditioned by the various knowledge systems, power relations and institutional structures within which the various actors are embedded. Whether or not this implies a necessity for modernist practices themselves to be transformed (Arora 2019), it at least calls for attention to positionality and an engagement with power in transformative action research. Within the wider context of this book, it leads us to question whether "transformative pathways" may involve shifts in authority away from science, and incorporate processes both of learning and unlearning.

Transformation, positionality and learning

As discussed in Chapter 2, the hubs in the TKN shared a normative commitment to understanding *and supporting* pathways to sustainability, and ambitions during the project to evaluate change and understand "what has worked". The diversity of contexts presented particular challenges with respect to the double loop learning approach, which is more reflexive than linear models of evaluation and learning that often adopt predefined theories and indicators of change.

Just as they had adopted different conceptual understandings of transformation, the TKN hubs defined different theories of change (representing their understandings of how their own interventions would contribute to transformation.) We had started to do this at the inception workshop in Buenos Aires using an adapted participatory impact pathways analysis approach (PIPA – see Ely and Oxley 2014) and at the T-Labs training and reflection workshop in Dundee in 2017, where hub teams drew diagrams describing the strategies adopted. The discussions in Dundee also provided us with an opportunity to reflect on our positionality as researchers. Brief notes from the discussion – a snapshot capturing the thinking at the time – are represented in Table 3.4. The positionality of researchers as "elites" in many contexts, and the power imbalances between hub teams and others in the T-Labs (also discussed in Chapter 4) had already been recognised at earlier stages of the project (see Ely and Marin 2017) but the Dundee meeting allowed them to be revisited in the light of project work to date (resonating with insights from another of the TKNs on 'political rigour' as a necessary complement to academic rigour in transformations research – see Temper et al. 2019).

TABLE 3.4 Summarised notes around theories of change and positionality identified by Pathways TKN hubs at the T-Lab training and reflection workshop Dundee, 2017

	Argentina	UK	Mexico	India	China	Kenya
Theory of Change	Looking at alternative forms of agriculture, working towards empowering farmers directly and indirectly. Open-source seed system in place.	Goal to change the land use around the city. Small and marginal farmers.	Strategy oriented towards informally organised groups. Aim to reframe the problem.	Assertive, agenda-setting, mobilisation towards building new imagination about the problem.	Green policies that are already in place, so not looking for concrete intervention. By creating knowledge and awareness they are fostering change beyond the project.	Role of knowledge production.
Positionality	Collaboration with different agencies and working to ensure access to seed availability to farmers.	Generating new knowledge as well as synthesising existing knowledge.	Facilitators developing action towards creating agency. Risk: will agency be maintained?	Researchers cannot be drivers without being transformed themselves, so main role is trying to link the objectives of the groups, identify opportunities and try to mobilise the groups.	Knowledge facilitators by empowering actors, e.g. existing knowledge. Agent of empowerment.	Also knowledge facilitators and synthesisers of knowledge – by putting actors together they understand how the technology impacts. Acting as agents of understanding.

Note that these should be viewed as a partial "snapshot", and continued to evolve as the project progressed (see Chapter 12).

The T-Lab training and reflection workshop (Dundee) 2017 provided 21 members of the TKN (meeting in person) the opportunity to identify emerging themes that were most deserving of discussion and reflection. These included framing and reframing, theories of transformation and theories of change, research methods, innovation and alternatives, and networks and collective agency. These were discussed (as far as time allowed) at the workshop, and elements of these themes were drawn upon to devise a common format for the hub-specific chapters that follow (Chapters 5–10).

The workshop also raised the issue of how we might monitor and evaluate our interventions, leading to discussions of the kinds of 'impacts' we were seeking in each hub. These differed greatly, which made it difficult to identify or characterise any general 'baseline' against which transformative change could be measured. While some hubs monitored specific changes that could be seen as an element of transformation (e.g. the area planted to open-source seed that was used as a measure in Argentina, or the network methods applied in Mexico in Chapter 9), most hubs struggled to identify ways to measure transformation, let alone to evaluate the role that research had played within it.

Monitoring and evaluation has in recent years been moving towards approaches that employ participatory and reflexive use of theory of change both as a process and as a product (e.g. Britt and Patsalides 2013; Douthwaite et al. 2017; Moore et al. 2018). In contrast to naïve linear views that see research leading to outputs, leading to outcomes and thus impact (which is subject to measurement), these recent approaches focus instead on reflecting on underlying assumptions about how change happens in line with the ambitions of double loop learning described in Chapter 2. Through regular reflection, the aim is to build middle range theory of how change happens, as it happens.

The use of adapted PIPA approaches, followed by reflection and learning both within hub teams (individual T-Labs) and across hub teams (in Dundee and Nairobi), served this aim. While we struggled to build any overarching theory, the TKN's move from the linear view towards a more complexity-aware approach helped us to understand better how – in different contexts – transdisciplinarity can contribute to transformational outcomes.

This led to a deeper appreciation of the role of transdisciplinary research and engagement in transformative change that (re-)emphasised the importance of emergence. In most hubs (as is clear from Chapters 5–10), exogenous factors such as policies, parallel movements or specific events contributed at least as much to outcomes as the work of the research teams. The structural and systemic perspectives on transformation described above helped us to understand these contributions and in many cases to work with them to enable transformative pathways.

The process of reflection thus saw research and action proceeding in parallel rather than either one being seen as prior. Knowledge about transformation was being built as the hub processes developed; however, in many cases, commitments to action were made in advance of any codification or theorisation of what needed to be done. These processes of coproduction are difficult to record in real-time and even afterwards, but they delivered "less conventional outcomes" (Norström et al. 2020) such as internationally embedded networks including Bioleft (Chapter 6), methodological innovations (see Chapter 9), collective practical understanding (see Chapter 10), new institutions, trusted relationships and a shared sense of understanding and commitment that long-outlasted the funded project (see Chapter 12).

As such, the formal research paradigm (and resulting knowledge products such as this book) captures only a subset of the experimentation and learning that took place within the emergent T-Lab processes. The remaining chapters of this book try to capture some that learning in a way that is accessible to researchers and others. But a far greater proportion of the learning (and unlearning) remains uncodified, residing in the individuals and (international, intergenerational) networks that have emerged since the early stages of the project. The essence of the transformative pathways to sustainability sought in the project is embodied in these individuals and networks as much as in any of the resultant publications, even if it is the publications that receive the academic attention.

References

Arora, S. (2019) 'Admitting uncertainty, transforming engagement: towards caring practices for sustainability beyond climate change', *Regional Environmental Change* 19(6): 1571–1584.

Brand, U. (2016) '"Transformation" as a New Critical Orthodoxy', *Gaia* 25(1): 23–27. doi:10.14512/gaia.25.1.7

Brandt, P., Ernst, A., Gralla, F., Luederitz, C., Lang, D. J., Newig, J., Reinert, F., Abson, D. J. & von Wehrden, H. (2013) 'A Review of Transdisciplinary Research in Sustainability Science', *Ecological Economics* 92: 1–15.

Berkes, F., Colding, J., Folke, C. (Eds.) (2003) *Social-ecological Systems: Building Resilience For Complexity and Change*, Cambridge University Press, Cambridge.

Blythe, J., et al. (2018) 'The Dark Side of Transformation: Latent Risks in Contemporary Sustainability Discourse', *Antipode* 50(5): 1206–1223.

Britt, H. & Patsalides, M. (2013) *Complexity-Aware Monitoring*. Discussion Note, Monitoring and Evaluation Series; Washington, DC, USA: USAID.

Cavicchi, B. & Ely, A. (2016) *Framing and Reframing Sustainable Bioenergy Pathways: The Case of Emilia Romagna*, STEPS Working Paper 88, Brighton: STEPS Centre.

Chambers, R. (1983) *Rural Development: Putting the Last First*, Harlow: Prentice Hall.

Chappin, J.L. & Ligtvoet, A. (2014) 'Transition and Transformation: A Bibliometric Analysis of Two Scientific Networks Researching Socio-technical Change', *Renewable and Sustainable Energy Reviews* 30: 715–723.

D'Alisa, G., Federico D. & Kallis, G. (Eds.) (2014) *Degrowth: A Vocabulary for a New Era*, Abingdon: Routledge.

Douthwaite, B., Apgar, J.M., Schwarz, A.-M., Attwood, S., Sellamuttu, S.S. & Clayton, T.A (2017) 'New Professionalism for Agricultural Research for Development', *International Journal of Agricultural Sustainability*, 15: 1–15. doi:10.1080/14735903.2017.1314754.

Ely, A. & Oxley, N. (2014) *STEPS Centre Research: Our Approach to Impact*, STEPS Working Paper 60, Brighton: STEPS Centre.

Ely, A. & Marin, A. (2017) 'Learning about 'Engaged Excellence' across a transformative knowledge network', *IDS Bulletin* 47(6): 73–86.

Ely, A., Marin, A., Charli-Joseph, L., Abrol, D., Apgar, M., Atela, J., Ayre, B., Byrne, R., Choudhary, B. K., Chengo, V., Cremaschi, A., Davis, R., Desai, P., Eakin, H., Kushwaha, P., Marshall, F., Mbeva, K., Ndege, N., Ochieng, C., Ockwell, D., Olsson, P., Oxley, N., Pereira, L,. Priya, R., Tigabu, A., Van Zwanenberg, P. & Yang, L. (2020) Structured collaboration across a Transformative Knowledge Network: Learning across disciplines, cultures and contexts? *Sustainability* 12(6): 2499.

Fals-Borda, O. (1979) 'The Application of Participatory Action-Research in Latin America', *International Sociology* 2(4): 329–347.

Feola, G. (2015) 'Societal Transformation in Response to Global Environmental Change: A Review of Emerging Concepts', *Ambio* 44(5): 376–390.

Folke, C., Carpenter, S., Elmqvist, T., Gunderson, L., Holling C.S. & Walker, B. (2002) 'Resilience and Sustainable Development: Building Adaptive Capacity in a World of Transformations', *Ambio* 31(5): 437–440.

Grin, J., Rotmans, J. & Schot, J. (Eds.) (2010) *Transitions to Sustainable Development: New Directions in the Study of Long-Term Transformative Change*, Abingdon: Routledge.

Gunderson, L. & Holling, C.S. (2002) *Panarchy: Understanding Transformations in Human and Natural Systems*, Washington: Island Press.

Hackmann, H. & St Clair, A.L. (2012) *Transformative Cornerstones of Social Science Research for Global Change*, Paris: International Social Science Council.

Hall, B.L. (1992) 'From Margins to Center? The Development and Purpose of Participatory Research', *The American Sociologist* 23(4): 15–28.

Herrera, A.O. (1979) *Desarrollo, medio ambiente y generación de tecnologías apropiadas*, Lima: ECLAC.

Hirsch Hadorn, G.H. & Pohl, C. (2007) *Principles for Designing Transdisciplinary Research*, Munich: Oekom verlag.

Hirsch Hadorn, G., Hoffmann-Riem, H., Biber-Klemm, S., Grossenbacher-Mansuy, W., Joye, D., Pohl, C., Wiesmann, U. & Zemp, E. (Eds.) (2008) *Handbook of Transdisciplinary Research*. Proposed by the Swiss Academies of Arts and Sciences, Heidelberg: Springer.

Holling, C.S. (1973) 'Resilience and Stability of Ecological Systems', *Annual Review of Ecology and Systematics* 4: 1–23.

Jasanoff, S. (Ed.) (2004) *States of Knowledge: The Co-production of Science and Social Order*, London: Routledge.

Kemp, R. & Rotmans, J. (2005) 'The Management of the Co-Evolution of Technical, Environmental and Social Systems', in K.M. Weber & J. Hemmelskamp (Eds.), *Towards Environmental Innovation Systems*, Berlin and Heidelberg: Springer-Verlag. pp. 33–55.

Kern, F. & Howlett, M. (2009) 'Implementing Transition Management as Policy Reforms: A Case Study of the Dutch Energy Sector', *Policy Sciences* 42(4): 391–408.

Klein, J. T. (2020) 'Sustainability and Collaboration: Crossdisciplinary and Cross-Sector Horizons', *Sustainability* 12(4): 1515

Krishna, V.V. (2001) 'Changing S&T Policy Cultures, Phases and Trends in Science and Technology in Indian "Science and Technology Policy"', *Science and Public Policy* 28(3): 179–194.

Leach, M., Scoones, I. & Stirling, A. (2010a) *Dynamic Sustainabilities: Technology, Environment, Social Justice*, London: Earthscan.

Leach, M., Scoones, I. & Stirling, A (2010b) 'Governing Epidemics in an Age of Complexity: Narratives, Politics and Pathways to Sustainability', *Global Environmental Change* 20(3): 369–377.

Li, X., Qi, G. & X. Xu (2009) 'Emergence of Farmer-Centered Agricultural Science and Technology Policy in China', in I. Scoones and J. Thompson (Eds.), *Farmer First Revisited: Innovation for Agricultural Research and Development*, Rugby: Practical Action Publishing.

Mangu, A.M. B. (2006) 'Democracy, African intellectuals and African Renaissance', *International Journal of African Renaissance Studies*, 1(1): 147–163.

Marshall, F., Dolley, J. & Priya, R. (2018) 'Transdisciplinary Research as Transformative Space Making for Sustainability: Enhancing Propoor Transformative Agency in Periurban Contexts', *Ecology and Society* 23(3): 8.

Marx, K. (1859) *A Contribution to the Critique of Political Economy*, Moscow: Progress Publishers.

Marx, K. (1867) *Capital: A Critique of Political Economy – Volume 1*, London: Penguin.

Mauser, W. Klepper, G., Rice, M., Schmalzbauer, B.S., Hackmann, H., Leemans, R. & Moore, H. (2013) 'Transdisciplinary Global Change Research: The Co-creation of Knowledge for Sustainability', *Current Opinion in Environmental Sustainability* 5: 420–431.

Meadows, D.H., et al. (1972) *The Limits to Growth: A Report for the Club of Rome's Project on the Predicament of Mankind*, New York: Universe Books.

Miller, C.A. & Wyborn, C. (2018) 'Co-production in Global Sustainability: Histories and Theories', *Environmental Science and Policy*. doi: 10.1016/j.envsci.2018.01.016

Mitchell, T. (2011) *Carbon Democracy: Political Power in the Age of Oil*, London: Verso.

Moore, M.L., Olsson, P., Nilsson, W., Rose, L. & Westley, F.R. (2018) 'Navigating Emergence and System Reflexivity as Key Transformative Capacities', *Ecology and Society* 23: 38.

Moser, S. (2016) 'Can Science on Transformation Transform Science? Lessons from Co-design', *Current Opinion in Environmental Sustainability* 20: 106–115.

Nabudere, D.W. (2006) 'Towards an Afrokology of Knowledge Production and African Regeneration', *International Journal of African Renaissance Studies* 1(1): 7–32.

Oldham, G. H. G. (1964) 'Science in Mainland China: A Tourist's Impressions', *Science* 147: 706–714.

Olsson, P., Galaz, V. & Boonstra, W.J. (2014) 'Sustainability Transformations: A Resilience Perspective', *Ecology and Society* 19(4): 1.

Olsson, P., Gunderson, L.H., Carpenter, S.R., Ryan, P., Lebel, L., Folke, C. & Holling, C.S. (2006) 'Shooting the Rapids: Navigating Transitions to Adaptive Governance of Social-Ecological Systems', *Ecology and Society* 11(1): 18.

Newell, P. & Paterson, M. (2010) *Climate Capitalism: Global Warming and the Transformation of the Global Economy*, Cambridge: Cambridge University Press

Norström, A.V., Cvitanovic, C., Löf, M.F., West, S., Wyborn, C., Balvanera, P., Bednarek, A. T., Bennett, E. M., Biggs, R., de Bremond, A., Campbell, B. M., Canadell, J. G., Carpenter, S. R., Folke, C., Fulton, E. A., Gaffney, O., Gelcich, S., Jouffray, J., Leach, M., Le Tissier, M., Martín-López, B., Louder, E., Loutre, M., Meadow, A. M., Nagendra, H., Payne, D., Peterson, G. D., Reyers, B., Scholes, R., Speranza, C. I., Spierenburg, M., Stafford-Smith, M., Tengö, M., van der Hel, S., van Putten, I. and Österblom, H. (2020) 'Principles for knowledge co-production in sustainability research', *Nature Sustainability* 3, 182–190.

Patterson, J., Schulz, K., Vervoort, J., Adler, C., Hurlbert, M., van der Hel, S., Schmidt, A., Barau, A. Obani, P., Sethi, M., Hissen, N., Tebboth, M., Anderton, K., Börner, S. & Widerberg, O. (2015) *Transformations Towards Sustainability': Emerging Approaches, Critical Reflections, and a Research Agenda*. Earth System Governance Working Paper No. 33. Lund and Amsterdam: Earth System Governance Project.

Patterson, J., Schulz, K., Vervoort, J., van der Held, S., Widerberg, O., Adler, C., Hurl-bert, M., Anderton, K., Sethi, M. & Barau, A. (2017) 'Exploring the Governance and Politics of Transformations Towards Sustainability', *Environmental Innovation and Societal Transitions* 24: 1–16.

Pelling, M. (2011) *Adaptation to Climate Change. From Resilience to Transformation*, Oxford: Routledge.

Polanyi, K. (1944) *The Great Transformation: The Political and Economic Origins of our Time*, Boston: Beacon Press.

Rahman, M.A. (1985) 'The Theory and Practice of Participatory Action Research', in O. Fals-Borda (Ed.), *The Challenge of Social Change*, London: Sage Publications. pp. 107–132.

Rahman, M.A. (2008) 'Some Trends in the Praxis of Participatory Action Research', Chapter 3 in Reason and Bradbury (Eds.) *The SAGE Handbook of Action Research*, Sage, London, pp. 49–62.

Randhawa, P., Marshall, F., Kushwaha, P.K. & Desai, P. (2020) 'Pathways for Sustainable Urban Waste Management and Reduced Environmental Health Risks in India: Winners, Losers, and Alternatives to Waste to Energy in Delhi', *Frontiers in Sustainable Cities* 2(14).

Russell, A.W., Wickson, F. & Carew, A.L. (2008) 'Transdisciplinarity: Context, Contradictions and Capacity', *Futures* 40: 460–472.

Schmitz, H. (2015) 'Green Transformation – Is There a Fast Track?', in I. Scoones, M. Leach and P. Newell (Eds.), *The Politics of Green Transformations*, Abingdon: Routledge/Earthscan. pp. 170–184.

Schot, J.W., Brand, E. & Fischer, K. (1997) 'The Greening of Industry for a Sustainable Future: Building an International Research Agenda', *Business Strategy and the Environment* 6: 153–162.

Scoones, I., Leach, M. & Newell, P. (Eds.) (2015) *The Politics of Green Transformations*, Abingdon: Routledge/Earthscan.

Scoones, I., Stirling, A., Abrol, D., Atela, J., Charli-Joseph, L., Eakin, H., Ely, A., Olsson, P., Pereira, L., Priya, R., van Zwanenberg, P. & Yang, L. (2018) *Transformations to Sustainability*, STEPS Working Paper 104, Brighton: STEPS Centre.

Scoones, I., Stirling, A., Abrol, D., Atela, J., Charli-Joseph, L., Eakin, H., Ely, A., Olsson, P., Pereira, L., Priya, R., van Zwanenberg, P. & Yang, L. (2020) 'Transformations to Sustainability: Combining Structural, Systemic and Enabling Approaches', *Current Opinion in Environmental Sustainability* 42: 65–75.

Smith, A. & Ely, A. (2015) 'Green Transformations from Below? The Politics of Grassroots Innovation', in I. Scoones, M. Leach & P. Newell (Eds.), *The Politics of Green Transformations*, Abingdon: Routledge/Earthscan. pp. 102–118.

Song, Y. & Vernooy, R. (2010) 'Seeds of Empowerment: Action Research in the Context of the Feminization of Agriculture in Southwest China', Gender, *Technology and Development* 14(1): 25–44.

Steffen, W., Richardson, K., Rockström, J., Cornell, S.E., Fetzer, I., Bennett, E.M., et al. (2015) 'Planetary Boundaries: Guiding Human Development on a Changing Planet', *Science* 347(6223): 1259855.

Stirling, A.C. (2014) 'From Sustainability, through Diversity to Transformation: Towards More Reflexive Governance of Vulnerability', Chapter 16 in A. Hommels, J. Mesman & W. Bijker (Eds.) *Vulnerability in Technological Cultures: New Directions in Research and Governance*, Cambridge,: MIT Press. pp. 305–332.

Stirling, A. (2015) 'Emancipation Transformations: From Controlling "The Transition" to Culturing Plural Radical Progress', in I. Scoones, M. Leach & P. Newell (Eds.), *The Politics of Green Transformations*, London: Routledge, pp. 54–67.

Sunkel, O. & Gligo, N. (Eds.) (1981) *Estilos de desarrollo y medio ambiente en la America Latina*, Mexico DF: Fondo de Cultura Economica.

Temper, L., McGarry, D. & Weber, L. (2019) 'From Academic to Political Rigour: Insights from the "Tarot" of Transgressive Research', *Ecological Economics* 164: 106379.

Temper, L., Walter, M., Rodriguez, I., Kothari, A. & Turhan, E. (2018) 'A Perspective on Radical Transformations to Sustainability: Resistances, Movements and Alternatives', *Sustainability Science* 13(3): 747–764.

United Nations. (2015) 'Transforming our World: The 2030 Agenda for Sustainable Development'. https://sdgs.un.org/2030agenda

Urama, K., Ogbu, O., Bijker, W., Alfonsi, A., Gomez, N. & Ozor, N. (2010) *The African Manifesto for Science, Technology and Innovation*, Nairobi: African Technology Policy Studies Network.

Van Zwanenberg, P., Ely, A. & Smith, A. (2011) *Regulating Technology: International Harmonisation and Local Realities*, Abingdon: Earthscan.

von Wehrden, H., Guimarães, M.H., Bina, O., Varanda, M., Lang, D. J, John, B., Gralla, F., Alexander. D., Raines, D., White, A. & Lawrence, R. J. (2019) 'Interdisciplinary and Transdisciplinary Research: Finding the Common Ground of Multi-faceted Concepts', *Sustainability Science* 14: 875–888.

West, S., Haider, J., Sinare, H. & Karpouzoglou, T. (2014) *Beyond Divides: Prospects for Synergy between Resilience and Pathways Approaches to Sustainability*, STEPS Working Paper 65, Brighton: STEPS Centre.

4

TRANSDISCIPLINARY METHODS AND T-LABS AS TRANSFORMATIVE SPACES FOR INNOVATION IN SOCIAL-ECOLOGICAL SYSTEMS

Laura Pereira, Per Olsson, Lakshmi Charli-Joseph, Olive Zgambo, Nathan Oxley, Patrick Van Zwanenberg, J Mario Siqueiros-García and Adrian Ely

Introduction

This chapter outlines the theoretical and methodological aspects of the Transformation Laboratories ('T-Labs') approach used throughout the project to bring together multiple researchers, stakeholders and knowledge partners in a coproduction/ transdisciplinary research mode. This includes a discussion of the origins and negotiation of the term, and the development of the 'T-Labs' concept throughout the course of the project. It discusses the ways in which different hubs applied the T-Lab approach alongside (or through incorporating) other transdisciplinary social science methods. The chapter draws significantly on "T-Labs: A Practical Guide" – a publication produced by the 'Pathways' Network on the basis of the experiences of experimenting with T-Labs across the different hubs (Pathways Network 2018).

Origins and meaning of the T-Lab concept

The T-Labs approach had previously been coined and used in the run-up to the Transformations 2015 conference, hosted by the Stockholm Resilience Centre and piloted in three experiments focussing on fisheries, algorithms and urban development. The insights and experiences from these T-Labs were fed back into the conference and helped to set the scene for the scientific discussions that it hosted (Transformations Conference 2015). The 'Pathways' transformative knowledge network (TKN) was seen as an opportunity to explore and further develop the idea of T-Labs. This involved experimenting with the approach in different initiatives and in more diverse settings around the world.

The concept was first discussed across the network at the inception workshop in April 2016. There, T-Labs were recognised as a process involving research and transdisciplinary engagement to address a complex sustainability problem or challenge. They are specifically designed to guide transformations

DOI: 10.4324/9780429331930-6

in *social-ecological systems* (SES) towards sustainability, by supporting changes in the conditions that made these systems unsustainable in the first instance. They include a set of stakeholders who may have different roles and perspectives, but who have an interest in solving the problem and some ability to provoke change.

T-Labs build upon the concept of social innovation labs (Westley and Laban 2012). They are designed and facilitated processes aimed at supporting multi-stakeholder groups to address complex social-ecological system problems by creating "safe" spaces to discuss and launch innovations. They further develop the concept of social innovation labs to incorporate social-ecological dynamics (Ely and Marin 2016; Charli-Joseph et al. 2018; van Zwanenberg et al. 2018). T-Labs aim to produce social-ecological innovations which help to create a more just and sustainable outcome for people and other parts of nature (see also Schäpke et al. 2018). The T-Lab is designed to afford diverse groups the opportunity for deeper reflexivity and engagement (Pereira et al. 2020). These transformative spaces seek to foster transformation and not just innovation within social-ecological systems.

A T-Lab aims to:

- frame the challenge, find change-makers and strengthen their individual and joint capacities to more effectively address the challenge;
- develop change strategies that test multiple solutions, which could help to solve the challenge;
- create early prototypes of interventions and build momentum for action.

Prototypes could be new business models, services or kinds of governance that fundamentally change human-environment interactions and contribute to changes for a better future.

The Social Innovation Lab Guide emphasises imagining high potential interventions, gaining system sight, redefining problems and identifying opportunities in the broader context with the potential to tip systems in positive directions (Westley and Laban 2012). The contributions of these 'real-world labs' to transformation include experimental methods, a transdisciplinary mode of research, scalability and transferability of results, as well as scientific and societal learning and reflexivity (Schäpke et al. 2018). Other similar examples include living labs (Bergvall-Kåreborn and Stahlbrost 2009; Bergvall-Kåreborn et al. 2009; von Wirth et al. 2019), real-world labs (Schäpke et al. 2015; 2018), urban living labs (Bulkeley et al. 2016; Voytenko et al. 2016; Naumann et al. 2018) and urban transition labs (Nevens et al. 2013). The growing interest in 'labs' responds to a demand for places which allow creative, cross-sector and cross-disciplinary decision-making and innovation. Expertise in psychology and group dynamics, complex adaptive systems theory, design thinking, computer modelling and visualisation tools has fed into ideas of lab approaches.

More broadly, these approaches rely on conditions such as broad-based research (across disciplines and methods), co-creation of solutions (across sectors and including citizens) a specialised physical environment (a 'safe enough space' where participants are more likely to be creative), clear process design and facilitation (including explaining how any particular workshop links to wider changes), rapid prototyping (of the social innovation, e.g. testable model, software, plan or intervention to be designed) (see pp. 47–53 in the Social Innovation Lab Guide, Westley et al. 2015), multi-disciplinary support staff (and facilitators) and continual learning (supporting the roll-out of the lab's outputs). The main focus of these labs has been on achieving social change, and more specifically changes in relationships between people and between people and their social environment. However, they tend to miss human-environment relationships and connectedness between nature and human society, which is particularly important for achieving sustainability transformations. The 'Pathways' Network attempted to use T-Labs to attend to these relationships through a focus on social-ecological systems.

T-Labs offer a methodological approach for working with the emergence of bottom-up and collaborative planning initiatives specifically targeting sustainability transformations in social-ecological systems. Based on Zgambo (2018), a T-Lab is a space for:

- facilitated, collective learning about the nature of a problem or challenge;
- learning about different kinds of possible solutions, or pathways of possible change;
- helping to create a collective sense of the need for change – within and beyond the stakeholders directly involved;
- developing strategies for affecting change;
- identifying which actors have transformative potential.

When is a T-Lab appropriate?

T-Labs are still a "new and experimental concept" across much of the world, and to the best of our knowledge, the food system T-Lab held in South Africa was the first to be undertaken in the Global South (Pereira et al. 2020) and there was a sharing and learning experience from that process that fed directly into the 'Pathways' Network T-Labs. Previously, T-Labs had only been used in Western contexts (Transformations Conference 2015), and so there is a need for interrogating when they are appropriate and when alternative processes of convening are better suited to other situations (Pereira et al. 2018).

T-Labs are intervention processes that require thorough planning, but are still flexible enough to allow emergence and the unexpected to occur. Ideally, the form a T-Lab takes is dependent on the local context and the people involved. Key elements of a successful T-Lab include having a complex problem to address, the participation of a motivated and diverse group of stakeholders who are willing to take a leading role, a window of opportunity to address the problem, a shared goal of an action plan as an outcome and skilful facilitation. The following are some of the conditions under which a T-Lab may be an effective intervention (Zgambo 2018):

1   There is a complex SES challenge to address
2   There is a diverse group of participants with transformative capacity or agency
3   Identifiable action-oriented outcome(s) can be the end goal of process

TABLE 4.1 When to use/not use a T-Lab

When to use T-Labs	When not to use T-Labs
A transition or transformation is taking place in a social-ecological system	There is no interest in, or sense of ownership of, the problem
There is a complex problem related to this transformation	There is limited capacity or interest to invest significant time to the process
There are people with significant ownership over the problem and strong motivation to change it	There is no flexibility to explore or change the focal question/challenge
There is confusion and disagreement about what is going on and why	
There is a collective sense of urgency	

4   There is a strongly motivated convenor
5   There has been little to no niche impact on the regime (i.e. no successful implementation of the alternative innovations in the dominant regime)
6   There is tension in the regime, or noticeable shifts in the culture or economic or political scene that can serve as potential windows of opportunity for T-Lab innovations to take effect.

It is also important to recognise when a T-Lab may not be the most appropriate approach (see Table 4.1).

As researchers are finding themselves at the intersection of action and analysis, where they navigate the fine line between actively intervening in processes to enable change, while also being able to provide a critical analysis of what types of changes are occurring, some researchers are finding themselves as 'transformative space-makers' (Marshall, Dolley and Priya 2018). T-Labs are an example where research has opened up a space for productive collaboration and interaction between diverse stakeholders with the intention that there may be actionable outcomes with which policy and other decision-making actors can engage.

What does a T-Lab involve?

Once it has been determined that a T-Lab is appropriate for the given problem, it is necessary to design the process. This means thinking in more depth about the system and the associated sustainability problem, what further research is needed, and who can be involved.

Defining the system and the problem

The team convening the T-Lab should make sure they agree on the basic problem framing (noting that this can change as the T-Lab proceeds). This can then be explored in more detail through research and workshops.

An important aim in T-Labs is to create networks of change-makers and support distributed **agency**. Agency refers to the capacity of a person or group to act according to its motivations, values and goals. In a social-ecological system, agency is shaped by a number of important elements, which relate to their power relative to other actors (Westley et al. 2013). They include:

- how people see or frame the system
- the capacities and skills that they have to act
- their social networks
- their values and beliefs
- constraints such as poverty or inequality.

Defining the system therefore can include mapping the capacities and constraints, social networks and values and beliefs. This, in turn, can help to reflect on these elements and how they can be strengthened or changed, individually or collectively. This can also help to identify the relationships between people, and between people and ecosystems and technology.

Using research

To design a T-Lab, careful research is needed to understand the problem and the system components and interactions. This may involve reviewing the existing literature, and undertaking new research to fill in gaps where necessary. It also involves scoping and interviewing participants who will be included in the T-Lab about the challenge. Methods might include:

- visits to sites affected by the problem (businesses, farms, nature reserves, villages or urban areas)
- group discussions
- semi-structured interviews with individuals
- Q-Method
- Agency Network Analysis.

These methods can help to identify and understand who should be involved, how they perceive the problem and actions taken to address it.

Designing workshops

T-Lab workshops are highly facilitated events, typically taking place over 1–3 days, and usually reconvened 2–3 times. They provide an opportunity to bring together those identified as core actors that represent key components of the system in focus. At these events different ways to 'see' the system can be explored together as well as identifying the roots of the problem. This goes beyond a technical understanding of the system to appreciate different framings, perspectives and values. In the 'Pathways' Network, most of our cases used two main workshops to structure the T-Lab process. These were interspersed with a number of other engagements.

The T-Labs methodology aims to help broaden the set of actors who are involved and bring together contrasting views to reveal dilemmas and generate creative, collaborative responses. This often results in bringing together actors that usually do not meet together and are more or less aligned with each other.

Bringing together powerful actors with marginalised ones for the first time can be a powerful enabler of innovation. However, there are many challenges involved in bringing such diverse actors together. Innovation is not a neutral process. Ideas are shaped by politics and power relations in any group of people, including in 'Labs'. The content of a T-Lab – dealing with social and ecological issues – means that these dynamics are even more important. Sustainability problems often have disproportionate effects on people who are marginalised – by power, poverty, age/ generation, language, gender, sexuality, race, ethnicity, class, culture and so on. If done well, tensions can be turned into constructive ways forward and can help generate novel re-combinations of existing ideas. However, the ethics of bringing a diverse set of actors with different power dynamics together needs to be explicitly addressed in the design phase of the T-Lab (see Pereira et al. 2019).

Review and reflection

The T-Lab process includes time to review and reflect on what has been learnt at each stage. This includes:

- Feedback to the participants of workshops on what was discussed and what happens next;
- Reflections among the project team about what has been learnt at each stage.

While a T-Lab process is a deliberate attempt to support on-going transformations, because we are dealing with complex adaptive social-ecological problems, it is unpredictable and emergent. This requires methods to keep track of what is happening and that can give real-time feedback to the learning process.

Participatory methods

The methods used across the hubs had the objectives of both a) enhancing our understanding of whatever phenomena we were interested in, and b) a means of trying to support or nurture interventions, including forming alliances, supporting struggle, reframing debates, challenging power, etc. That is, they all attempted to bridge research and action, in ways that involve engagement with communities of practice.

Based on experiences and insights from the Pathways TKN, we illustrate (Table 4.2) the variety of the different methods that the six hubs used in their T-Lab processes. However, these are by no means an exhaustive list of methods that can be used in T-Labs (or even the full list of those used in the TKN).

TABLE 4.2 Participatory methods in Pathways TKN T-Labs

Hub	Method and purpose/general description	Techniques
UK Hub	**Open space** [Qualitative method] Engaging actors, appreciating different actors' perspectives, histories and positioning relative to the transformations at play; allow stakeholders to openly share perspectives on different questions and bridge between otherwise unrelated areas.	Participatory workshop
	Continuum methods, specifically Evaluation H [Qualitative method] Identify different actors' positions and perspectives (especially at the extremes), foster discussion across them, identify challenges and opportunities and work towards solutions. Gather participants together to position themselves in relation to each other and to open up debate. It can be effective if participants represent different sectors, backgrounds, or types of involvement in the issue being explored, particularly if these different stakeholders do not interact often. A significant question is written at the top of a wall, table, or large sheet of paper (the work surface). Participants place their responses along a horizontal line halfway down, which offers a continuum, e.g. good to bad, easy to difficult, important to not important. Participants are also asked to write the factors which influence why their response was placed where it was on the line. The factors identified can be positive or negative, and are usually attached to vertical lines at either end of the continuum (hence the 'H' or rugby post name). The factors are then clustered. Discussion explores how to overcome negative factors or support positive ones.	Facilitated, participatory workshop
Latin America (Argentina) Hub	**Q-Method** [Mixed method] Identify competing discourses about the nature of sustainability challenges, their drivers, and their possible solutions in the seed sector, and map areas of consensus and disagreement between different groups of stakeholders; Identify different actors' perspectives, foster discussion across them, identify where alliances between different actors are possible, and work towards solutions.	World Café; Open Space Technology

(Continued)

Hub	Method and purpose/general description	Techniques
Africa (Kenya) Hub	**Participatory Impact Pathways Analysis (PIPA)** [*Qualitative method*] Identify impact pathways to detect key stakeholders with interest and influence in policy, business and technology; to elicit the various pathways for transformation; target what pathways (i.e. engagements, networks) could be engaged in the process so as to enhance uptake of the research outputs.	Participatory workshop
China Hub	**Multi-stakeholders' process engagement** [*Qualitative method*] Identify change agents (e.g. laid-off workers, former plant owners, local government officials, scholars, NGOs) on local environmental transformation; navigate the power dynamics inherent in local transformation, and foster reflection to provide guidance for new ways of engaging with environmental policy at the larger context of transformation. Uncover how gender relations affect a development problem by showing that gender relations may affect the solution and what could be done, and to identify the different roles and gender divisions of labour in the household (pre– and post– green transformation), as an important approach to ensure gender equality and women's empowerment.	In-depth semi-structured interviews & focus group; Gender analytical tools (Triple Roles Approach)
	Role play simulation [*Qualitative method*] All participants play different roles in response to a situation introduced by a facilitator. The situation can either be the one under discussion, or another (fictional or real) situation where a similar problem is faced. The volunteers all stand on a starting line, and the facilitator announces hypothetical policies or projects which will be implemented. Based on their roles, the volunteers take either a step forward (if they are to benefit from the policy), backward (if it will have negative impact on them) or stay still (if it will have no impact). At the end, participants discuss the differences between the winners and losers, and how this exercise compares to their own experience. This method allows participants to imagine how different actors might respond to the problem, or to see the varied effects of policies and interventions on different stakeholders in a given setting. A fictional or similar setting can be used when the situation under discussion is sensitive, and participants may not feel completely free to express their opinions.	Role-play

Hub	Method description	Methods
		[Ego net; action] nets; Cognitive maps
North America (Mexico) Hub	**Agency Network Analysis (ANA)** *[Mixed method]* Describe the actor's agency profile by identifying individual agency through collecting information about actors' social network, the practices they share with the members of their social network, their representation of the SES, and the position they occupy in it.	
	Avatars – Agents of Change *[Qualitative method]* Drawing a character or an archetype that represents us in specific situations can make our participation in that group/situation more open and effective. Each participant draws their character on a large sheet of paper and lists five 'powers' that it has (e.g. the ability to listen well, ability to guide others, communication, and so on). Participants are invited to imagine their personages taking responsibility for different things, embodying different roles, and cooperating with others in new ways. The characters (or Avatars) show the variety and strength of capacities among the participants.	Graphic self-representation
	Mapping significant and valued elements *[Qualitative method]* Participants identify the elements of the system that are most significant and valued by them. They start as individuals by listing 2 elements, then find symbols to represent these elements with materials. They then discuss as a small group why they value these elements, what they provide and any associated emotions. Participants then construct a map of the system using physical objects (e.g. dough, colours, small modelling objects, pebbles, pictures, small branches) in their small group, then share the maps with the wider group. This method encourages participants to focus on specific parts of the system and think about how they are valued. By discussing them, differences in value and importance are revealed. The method allows discussion of the deeper significance and cultural meaning of different parts of the system.	Participatory mapping
South Asia (India) Hub	**Multi-stakeholder processes for the mobilised publics through the development of their Collective Practical Understanding (CPU) and actions** *[Mixed method]* Coproduction of knowledge, knowledge sharing, dialogues and engagement with institutions of planning and governance for demonstrating the possibilities of alternative pathways. Development of multi-stakeholder-knowledge-enhancing platform enabling social mobilisation and awareness, including direct actions, participation and real-world experiments. Mapping of knowledge, values and institutions of mobilised publics and organising them for the creation of a multi-stakeholder platform for individual and collective actions.	Citizens science; Citizens watch and citizens journalism approaches & tools; Real-world experiments

Adapted from Ely et al. (2020). More detailed discussion of the methods used in each hub appears in Chapters 5–10.

For more ideas on methods, see the Social Innovation Lab Guide (Westley and Laban 2012), which gives detailed guidance on workshop design and the principles behind social innovation labs.[1]

Key insights

Depending on the nature of their defined problem space and the groups they convened, different hub teams in the 'Pathways' Network adopted some of the following approaches in their first T-Labs:

- create a collective sense of the need for change
- make visible alternative views about the problem and the possible solutions
- help to negotiate and create some kind of consensus across different views
- help to develop, or aim to develop some more specific social-ecological innovations.

Experiences in the 'Pathways' Network pointed to two types of innovations that might emerge from T-Labs:

- new innovations that can 'bridge' different (and to some extent conflicting) framings, offering the possibility of a route through an unsustainable impasse. We have previously referred to these as 'bridging innovations' (van Zwanenberg et al. 2018)
- innovations that draw on the resources of different actors who have been brought together through the T-Lab process. These may be novel recombination between 'bottom-up' (or grassroots) efforts and top-down (government-led or high-tech-based) initiatives. We have previously described these as 'hybrid innovations' (Ely et al. 2013).

In the 'Pathways' Network, there were important differences in the extent to which T-Labs were convened (or spontaneously emerged) that will be explored in the subsequent chapters.

- What were the key insights that came out of the project?

  - T-Labs are a process, not a method, event or set of events. Their adaptability was illustrated by the varying ways in which they were implemented (see Chapters 5–10).
  - There was considerable negotiation over the terminology of T-Labs, and T-Labs (even the word) was sometimes rejected (e.g. in India) for being too scientistic.
  - There were instances where T-Labs contributed to change; however, causality was difficult to attribute (explored further in Chapter 12).

- Failure to identify change (in terms of short-term impact) does not necessarily mean failure. In some cases unexpected events contributed to change alongside the work of the hubs (e.g. transformative agency was mobilised following the earthquake response in Mexico, and fundraising in India led to further work in Gurgaon).
- Insights from wider work on 'transformative spaces' in the global South may help strengthen the T-Lab approach going forward. Some of these were explored further in the special issue of Ecology and Society (Pereira et al. 2018) and a synthesis paper (Pereira et al. 2020).

Note

1 Another useful resource is the STEPS Centre's "Methods and Methodologies" site https://steps-centre.org/methods/ (accessed 20/5/2020).

References

Bergvall-Kåreborn, B. and Stahlbrost, A. (2009) 'Living Lab: an open and citizen-centric approach for innovation', *International Journal of Innovation and Regional Development*, 1(4): 356. doi: 10.1504/IJIRD.2009.022727.

Bergvall-Kåreborn, B. et al. (2009) 'A milieu for innovation: defining living labs', in Huizingh, K. R. E. et al. (eds) *Proceedings of the 2nd ISPIM Innovation Symposium: Simulating Recovery – the Role of Innovation Management*. ISPIM, New York, pp. 1–12.

Bulkeley, H., et al. (2016) 'Urban living labs: governing urban sustainability transitions', *Current Opinion in Environmental Sustainability*. Elsevier, 22, pp. 13–17. doi: 10.1016/J.COSUST.2017.02.003.

Charli-Joseph, L. et al. (2018) 'Promoting agency for social-ecological transformation: a transformation-lab in the Xochimilco social-ecological system', *Ecology and Society*, 23(2). doi: 10.5751/ES-10214–230246.

Ely, A. and Marin, A. (2016) 'Learning about "Engaged Excellence" across a Transformative Knowledge network', *IDS Bulletin*, 47(6). doi: 10.19088/1968–2016.200.

Ely, A., Smith, A., Leach, M., Stirling, A. and Scoones, I. (2013) 'Innovation Politics Post-Rio+20: Hybrid Pathways to Sustainability?', *Environment and Planning C* 31(6): 1063–1081.

Marshall, F., Dolley, J. and Priya, R. (2018) 'Transdisciplinary research as transformative space making for sustainability: enhancing propoor transformative agency in periurban contexts', *Ecology and Society*. The Resilience Alliance, 23(3). doi: 10.5751/ES-10249–230308.

Naumann, S., Davis, M., Moore, M. L. and McCormick, K. (2018) 'Utilizing Urban living laboratories for social innovation', in Elmqvist, T, Bai, X, Frantzeskaki, N., et al. (eds) *Urban Planet*. Cambridge, UK: Cambridge University Press, pp. 197–217.

Nevens, F., Frantzeskaki, N., Gorissen, L. and Loorbach, D. (2013) 'Urban transition labs: co-creating transformative action for sustainable cities', *Journal of Cleaner Production* 50, pp. 111–122. doi: 10.1016/j.jclepro.2012.12.001.

Olsson, P., Galaz, V. and Boonstra, W. J. (2014) 'Sustainability transformations: a resilience perspective', *Ecology and Society*, 19(4), p. 1. doi: 10.5751/ES-06799-190401.

Pathways Network. (2018) *T-Labs: A Practical Guide–Using Transformation Labs (T-labs) for Innovation in Social-Ecological Systems*. Brighton, UK: STEPS Centre.

Pereira, L., Drimie, S., Zgambo, O. and Biggs, R. O. (2020) 'Planning for change: transformation labs for an alternative food system in the Western Cape', *Urban Transformations*. doi: 10.1186/s42854-020-00016-8.

Pereira, L., Frantzeskaki, N., Hebinck, A., Charli, L., Scott, J., Dyer, M., Eakin, H., Galafassi, D., Karpouzoglou T., Marshall, F., Moore, M. L., Olsson, P., Mario Siqueiros-García, J., van Zwanenberg, P. and Vervoort, J. M. (2020) 'Transformative spaces in the making: key lessons from nine cases in the global South', *Sustainability Science*, 15, pp. 161–178.

Pereira, L. M., et al. (2018) 'Designing transformative spaces for sustainability in social-ecological systems', 23(4). doi: 10.5751/ES-10607–230432.

Schäpke, N., Singer-Brodowski, M., Stelzer, F., et al. (2015) 'Creating space for change: real-world laboratories for sustainability transformations. The case of Baden-Württemberg', *GAIA* 24, pp. 281–283. doi: 10.14512/gaia.24.4.17.

Schäpke, N., et al. (2018) 'Jointly experimenting for transformation? Shaping real-world laboratories by comparing them', *GAIA – Ecological Perspectives for Science and Society*, 27(1), pp. 85–96. doi: 10.14512/gaia.27.S1.16.

Smith, A. and Raven, R. (2012) 'What is protective space? Reconsidering niches in transitions to sustainability', *Research Policy*, 41(6), pp. 1025–1036. doi: 10.1016/j.respol.2011.12.012.

Transformations Conference. (2015) Transformations 2015 conference website. http://transformations2015.org/, accessed 27/9/2019.

van Zwanenberg, P., et al. (2018) 'Seeking unconventional alliances and bridging innovations in spaces for transformative change: the seed sector and agricultural sustainability in Argentina', *Ecology and Society*. The Resilience Alliance, 23(3). doi: 10.5751/ES-10033–230311.

von Wirth, T., et al. (2019) 'Impacts of urban living labs on sustainability transitions: mechanisms and strategies for systemic change through experimentation', *European Planning Studies*, 27(2), pp. 229–257. doi: 10.1080/09654313.2018.1504895.

Voytenko, Y., Evans, J. and Schliwa, G. (2016) 'Urban living labs for sustainability and low carbon cities in Europe: towards a research agenda', *Journal of Cleaner Production*, 123, pp. 45–54. doi: 10.1016/J.JCLEPRO.2015.08.053.

Westley, F. R. and Laban, S. (2012) *Social Innovation Lab Guide*. Waterloo, Canada. doi: 10.1002/yd.20002.

Zgambo, O. (2018) *Exploring Food System Transformation in the Greater Cape Town Area*. MPhil Thesis, Stellenbosch: Stellenbosch University.

SECTION 3

Insights from different international contexts

5

TOWARDS A MORE SUSTAINABLE FOOD SYSTEM IN BRIGHTON AND HOVE, UK

Adrian Ely, Elise Wach, Rachael Taylor, Ruth Segal and Rachael Durrant

Introduction

Brighton and Hove is a city on the South coast of the United Kingdom (UK) with a population of approximately 273,369 (United Kingdom Census, 2011). The city is surrounded by a highly biodiverse and productive chalk reef system to the South and endangered chalk downland habitats to the North. Two recent events have increased attention towards biodiversity conservation and wider sustainability issues in the area (including agricultural land). First, in April 2011 the South Downs National Park became operational (South Downs National Park Authority 2012), bringing a shift in responsibility for planning to the wider area. About 40% of the city sits within the boundaries of the national park. Second, in June 2014 Brighton and Lewes Downs (including the city of Brighton and Hove and the county town of Lewes) became the first completely new World Biosphere site established in the UK for almost 40 years. The University of Sussex is a member of the Brighton and Lewes Downs Biosphere Partnership, and research undertaken as part of these initiatives informed the proposed study.

Beyond this, the hub drew significantly upon the work of the Brighton and Hove Food Partnership (BHFP), a local multi-stakeholder platform that aims to create a sustainable, healthy and fair food system for the city. BHFP's 2012 strategy "Spade to Spoon: Digging Deeper" (BHFP 2012) stated:

- "26% of the city's ecological footprint (the amount of land and resources we use) relates to food (also known as the city's 'foodprint')".
- "To produce enough food to feed the population of Brighton & Hove we need approximately 70,000 hectares of productive agricultural land".

DOI: 10.4324/9780429331930-8

- "Each year the food produced on that land requires approximately 750,000 barrels of oil and almost 625 million tonnes of fresh water. In all, this generates an estimated half-a million tonnes of greenhouse gases".
- "We have about half the number of recommended allotment plots. The total number of plots at the beginning of 2011 was 2,795, which is 10.9 per 1,000 people. There are 1,612 residents on the waiting list".
- "The infrastructure supporting the local food supply chain is not as advanced as in some regions, which have developed local distribution centres, established cooperative wholesalers and invested in local processing (e.g. mills or abattoirs)".
- "Over recent years, the number of Brighton & Hove residents employed in agriculture has fallen by 40% (the average UK drop is closer to 20%)".

The UK hub's work grew out a well-documented and well-researched understanding of the dominant agri-food pathway in the UK – one characterised by market-driven consolidation of both production and supply chains leading to ever larger-scale (more mechanised, input-intensive and less local) production and serving national and international supermarket chains. It also built upon several years of research, conducted by colleagues within the University of Sussex, which engaged with alternative agri-food pathways in Brighton and Hove and the surrounding area. This included research on:

- Studies of the history of organic farming in the UK (Smith 2006) looking at the influence of the niche on the incumbent regime (the dominant pathway).
- 'Grassroots innovation niches' such as community growing (White and Stirling 2013), which studied the role of community-organised, not-for-profit urban agriculture (within the city itself).
- The role of civil society organisations in food system transitions (Durrant 2014) – a doctoral project that had examined civil society networks beyond the city, including larger community-supported agriculture initiatives such as Tablehurst and Plaw Hatch Farms.
- A study of Seedy Sunday – the UK's largest and longest-running seed swap, which takes place in Brighton every February (Balázs et al. 2016).
- 'ARTS' (Accelerating and Rescaling Transitions to Sustainability) – an EU project in which the role of civil society and policy action in Brighton and Hove had been examined alongside similar phenomena across other European cities (Durrant et al. 2018).

As such, several of the research team had engaged with these issues in the preceding years.

Findings and relationships from this work fed into a co-design workshop in January 2015, at which researchers gathered together with local and national civil society organisations and commercial and non-commercial growers. While encouraging, the contribution of the urban agriculture pathway (White and

Stirling 2013) to serving the city's food needs was seen by participants at the workshop as limited in a context of insufficient access to land and a range of other constraints. Therefore, participants decided that the study should build upon the current understanding of how these pathways – i.e. the urban agriculture pathway and the dominant agri-food pathway – interacted, focussing on what was termed the "missing middle". This was the current and potential contribution of commercial scale farms that are slightly larger than the community gardens and allotments in the city (which receive government support) but smaller than farms which receive significant amounts of government subsidies. As they do not qualify for community or grant support, they were perceived as being at risk of economic collapse in the current economic context, particularly given high rates of attrition among these types of farms at a UK level (Willis 2017, Winter et al. 2016). On the other hand, their size and positionality could also enable them to engage in experimentation and innovation towards sustainable food systems (not only in production techniques but also in supply chain experimentation).

While it was clear that 65% of holdings in the South Downs National Park are less than 100Ha in size (South Downs National Park Authority 2012), the extent to which these and other farms local to Brighton and Hove served the city, and the sustainability of their operations, was unclear. Using interviews and desk research, the study proposed to collect examples of good practice, integrating sustainable production methods with local medium-sized supply chains (e.g. serving small, specialist wholefood supermarkets in Brighton and Hove) in the hope of pointing to lessons for other parts of the country. At the same time, the research proposed to investigate the constraints facing medium-sized farmers in serving the city. Reflecting the interest of the Argentinean team's focus (see Chapter 8) and the local interest in seed saving and exchange (exemplified by Seedy Sunday), seed was of particular interest to the research team.

The boundaries adopted at the outset of the project, therefore, were the food system in the city of Brighton and Hove, and in particular the production of food in the South Downs National Park and Brighton and Lewes Downs Biosphere Region (see map below). The "problem space" was defined as: "The food system in Brighton and Hove is unsustainable because of limitations to local food supply and environmentally damaging production and consumption practices". The transformation required to overcome it was seen as "increased localisation of supply and encouraging innovation for sustainable food production and consumption".

The baseline survey helped to map the situation (according to the research team) at the outset of the project. The existence of various box schemes and supermarkets that offered local produce to a minority of consumers suggested some recognition of the problem space among the general public. In comparison, the problem was recognised as important by civil society and academic groups. In particular, the problem was widely recognised among those studying environmental sustainability and food policy across the UK as well as locally (e.g. across Brighton-Sussex University Food Network – a locally run knowledge centre on the theme of food). In terms of mobilisation, there was seen to be a powerful civil society movement at national and international levels, focussing on local, sustainable food production. In Brighton and Hove there was already some mobilisation, but not necessarily co-ordinated across the city region (beyond the work of BHFP, which primarily focussed within the city). The private sector was seen to have responded in a limited way, with a limited number of restaurants and retailers in the city that prioritised locally produced (or environmentally sustainably produced) food. Some farmers had innovated to develop novel retail approaches to serve this niche (e.g. farmers' markets, box schemes). In terms of governance, at the national level, the UK government offered very limited, if any, support for localised food networks prioritising environmental and social sustainability, although some support came from national charities (and the national lottery). At the local level, Brighton and Hove City Council recognised the need to localise food production and were strong partners within BHFP. Through the City Food Strategy (BHFP 2012) they aimed to work with local communities on food projects for health, rehabilitation and other social goals, though their focus has been more on the consumption side than on production, with the exception of community gardens and allotments.

Although there were no major conflicts associated with the problem space, the baseline survey highlighted some general political issues about inequality and access to land. A more specific tension emerged from the observation that consumers usually demanded cheap, diverse (but often unsustainable) food supplies, which can often be supplied more efficiently by vertically integrated supermarket chains than by local suppliers and retailers.

Theory, research and action

The hub adopted a theoretically informed approach combining empirical research and stakeholder engagement. The pathways approach (Leach et al 2010) provided the primary theoretical underpinning of the work, with policy actors as the key audience and a strategic approach to communications envisaged as a way to raise awareness and bring about changes in knowledge, attitudes and skills.

Theories of change developed as the project evolved. The co-design workshop – which was undertaken in January 2015, at a time when funding for the research was yet to be secured – was supplemented by a Participatory Impact Pathways Analysis (PIPA) exercise involving Adrian Ely and Nathan Oxley (STEPS Centre Communications Manager) at the inception workshop in April 2016. As a route to developing an instrumental theory of change for the project, the PIPA exercise produced a network map identifying research organisations, local and national NGOs, government organisations, private sector enterprises (including farmers, digital sales platforms, retailers and restaurants) and local media as key strategic partners. Brighton and Hove Food Partnership was recognised as a powerful convenor, and consumers were identified as the most powerful group in terms of enabling transformation. All actors other than large farmers, consumers and national media were seen as normatively aligned with the research team (i.e. likely to be welcoming of the transformation being envisaged). A continuous process of research, iterative communication and reflection with these stakeholders was proposed as a way of understanding how policy did, and could, support transformative pathways involving sustainable agriculture in the "missing middle".

Our more general conceptual theory of transformation was only codified later, at the T-Lab training and reflection workshop in Dundee in August 2017, in the following terms: "Transformation is influenced by changing cognitive, affective and political economic drivers that work across individuals, groups and systems". Concepts of particular relevance to this theory of transformation were identified, including the 'pathways' approach (Leach et al. 2010), 'politics of green transformations' (Scoones et al. 2015), 'governance of sustainable socio-technical transitions' (Smith, Stirling and Berkhout 2005), and 'transformative pathways' in particular (Ely and Marin 2016).

The research involved two stages. Prior to the first T-Lab workshop we conducted interviews with small- to medium-sized farms and gardens, policymakers and retailers, and surveyed attendees of Seedy Sunday 2017. Whereas the interviews were envisaged as a core part of the study design, the survey was an additional research activity commissioned by the organisers of Seedy Sunday. Following the first T-Lab workshop we conducted desk research, supplemented by further interviews. During this stage we focussed less on researching the context in Brighton and Hove, and more on drawing lessons from other localities. Our instrumental theory of change thus moved towards one of 'seeding ideas' and knowledge brokering.

Our ambitions for action rested on engagement of different groups of stakeholders through T-Lab workshops. The engagement methods selected for use during the T-Lab 1 workshop were intended to bring together diverse stakeholders who may not have engaged with one another on a regular basis. The specific methods planned for the T-Lab were a roundtable session taking feedback from stakeholders on the research findings; an adapted Evaluation H exercise to elicit a broad range of divergent perspectives on the ease of supplying sustainably produced food to Brighton and Hove (see below on Evaluation H); and an exercise mapping positive and negative factors, building on discussions from the Evaluation H (and moving towards the identification of positive actions and social innovations). The methods used took an 'open space' approach to allow themes, priorities and ideas to emerge from discussions, thus accommodating a pathways perspective of plurality and diversity. After the T-Lab 1 workshop we hoped to catalyse further action by maintaining contact and networking through additional workshops and events, and by publishing a briefing at the end of the project that pointed to specific opportunities for policy innovations (related to a revision of the Whole Estate Plan (WEP) for the Downland Estate – see Box 5.1). Overlapping with and informing this second stage were two further projects associated with the Sussex Sustainability Research Programme (see below).

BOX 5.1 THE DOWNLAND ESTATE

The Downland Estate, which now includes over 4,000 hectares of farmland, has been owned and commercially managed by Brighton and Hove City Council since 1913. The land was initially acquired to protect the city's drinking water supply and control development; however, a range of more diverse aims and objectives were first formalised in 2005 (codified in the Downland Initiative Feasibility Study – see Smiths Gore and University of Reading 2006). These include income and capital provision as well as the facilitation of conservation, education, public access and agriculture. During 2018–2019, the Council began to revise the Whole Estate Plan (WEP) for the Downland Estate, in order to provide a coherent strategy for managing this portion of the South Downs National Park.

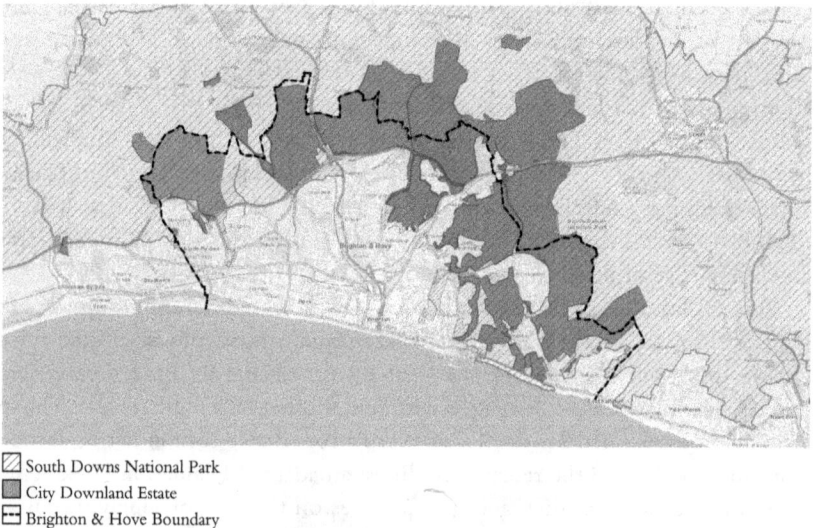

South Downs National Park
City Downland Estate
Brighton & Hove Boundary

FIGURE 5.1 Map showing the City Downland Estate in relation to Brighton and Hove and the South Downs National Park.

Unlike other hubs (e.g. Argentina) the UK hub moved from engaging with a more aligned to a less aligned group of stakeholders as it progressed. We also found that we engaged successively with increasingly powerful groups. This is illustrated pseudo-quantitatively in Table 5.1, which draws upon the highly subjective assessments of power and alignment produced at each convening event.

As a stakeholder without a direct economic stake in the way that land is managed (both within the city limits and across the South Downs National Park and Brighton and Lewes Downs Biosphere Region including the Downland Estate),

TABLE 5.1 Average alignment and power of actors/individuals as estimated from PIPA exercise and first and second T-Lab workshop reports

Event	Average "power"	Average "alignment"
Co-design workshop	Not recorded	Not recorded
Initial network mapping (PIPA) at inception workshop, April 2016	1.39	0.96
T-Lab workshop 1, December 2016	1.12	1.0
T-Lab workshop 2, July 2018	1.69	0.73

Average "power" estimated on a scale of 0–5 (0 = envisaged to have no influence, 5 = the most powerful actors). Average "alignment" estimated on a scale of −1 to +1 (−1 = expected to be negative or resistant, 0 = expected to be uninterested; awareness/persuasion needed, +1 = expected to be positive or welcoming with regard to transformation).

or any specific political ties, we were able to convene multi-stakeholder groups over numerous occasions during the life of the project. This is significant and is partly a result of the reputation of the University, which had been built up over several decades, as well as (more recently) the Brighton and Sussex Universities Food Network (BSUFN). This apparent legitimacy of researchers both as convenors (of aligned and non-aligned groups) and as a source of authoritative knowledge called for a careful approach. We therefore entered the T-Lab events without our own predefined goals, attempting to foster a process through which goals would emerge on the basis of the shared discussions (resulting in more shared ownership of the outcomes). We also needed to be cognisant of our limitations as mediators (Ely and Marin 2017), and to be constantly aware of the limitations on our resources. The UK hub had comparatively fewer resources than the other hubs, and – recognising this – we were not able to position ourselves as key agents of transformation. It was therefore challenging to convene events with a transformative agenda without inappropriately raising expectations among other stakeholders.

Although they did not lead to any concrete initiatives, the T-Lab events provided a forum where new ideas could be discussed and new connections were made (as evidenced by emails received after the events), which potentially forms the basis for policy advocacy going forward. The events also played a role in establishing and strengthening links between researchers (across disciplines at the Universities of Sussex and Brighton) and other groups (Council, civil society, private sector), some of which continue to grow in areas that are related to, but not directly the focus of, our project. At the same time, they built on earlier research and relationships, just as the project has done since its outset in 2015.

In addition to the T-Lab events, impact-oriented evidence, taking the form of provocative discussion papers and talks, was presented to increasingly powerful (and non-aligned) audiences. This may not have led to a direction-change in knowledge, attitudes or skills, but provided an impetus for alliance-building, debate and challenge.

Taken overall, this way of working is strongly aligned with Ely and Marin's 'transformative pathways' approach, developed during the early stages of this project, which envisages the role of transdisciplinary research as follows:

> In seeking transformative pathways, in which directions are potentially unknown (or at least uncertain) but normative commitments are shared, the role of transdisciplinary research becomes one of fostering, supporting or reconfiguring such coalitions and alliances, and working with them to co-construct and mobilise impact-oriented evidence.
>
> *(Ely and Marin 2017)*

This remained the approach through both of the T-Lab workshops described below.

Key moments in the T-Lab process

The research and T-Labs proceeded through various stages. The two T-Lab workshops described here were punctuation marks in a longer, ongoing process of research and engagement, advocacy and action (see below).

Following the co-design workshop, the team recognised that they needed to better-understand challenges facing farmers, both in their selection of technologies and management practices for food production, and for their marketing strategies. These insights would be important not only for us, but also for policy-makers and others in the supply chain who are keen to support farmer innovation. With this aim in mind, the research team built a database of local agro-ecological farms within 50 km of Brighton and Hove, primarily less than 20 Ha in size (similar to that used by Laughton et al. 2017). A decision was made to focus on non-animal agriculture on the basis of better health outcomes for consumers and greater efficiency of land and resource use, as compared to animal

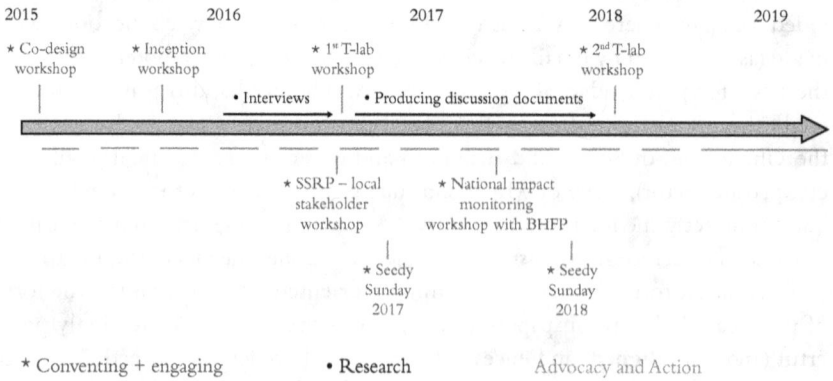

FIGURE 5.2 Key moments in the UK T-Lab.

agriculture. This nevertheless excluded the majority of farms on the downland surrounding the city, which focus on sheep and cattle (although a later project was able to explore the dimensions of animal agriculture – see "Delivering food security and biodiversity conservation through rewilding and community agriculture" below).

Primarily through semi-structured interviews, we gained significant insights into the constraints facing farmers and the challenges for local, sustainable agrifood systems (covering issues such as crop types, technologies and practices, experiences of policy support and marketing strategies). There was very limited policy support, with only one farm in our sample receiving the single farm payment (under the EU Common Agricultural Policy). Some additional findings problematised the initial framing of the research and led us to reflect upon the terminology we had adopted:

- We identified a general questioning of the notion of 'sustainable', with varying emphases and priorities – environmental, social and economic – adopted by different farmers.
- There were also differing definitions of 'local' (varying from the nearby village – closer than Brighton and Hove – to national markets).

T-Lab workshop 1

These findings were presented to a workshop in December 2016, which comprised two parts: one which focussed on the challenge of connecting research, policy and action for food systems in Brighton and Hove more generally, and the second which focussed on the transformations project specifically. Running the two events on sequential days enabled us to situate our own interests within the broader 'system' and to be aware of some of the multitude of potentially transformative initiatives (and research projects) already underway. These two events were held in the 'space maker space' – a room created for local groups to meet, especially to visualise the future of the city.

The first workshop broadened out academic participation to include an interdisciplinary group of researchers from across the University of Sussex who were proposing to conduct research on local agri-food systems as part of the Sussex Sustainability Research Programme (SSRP) – a recently established fund that the University of Sussex had set up to foster collaboration across campus. In addition to presenting highlights from the research findings, four candidate projects were presented, two of which involved authors Adrian Ely and Rachael Durrant and eventually received funding:

- "People, pollinators and pesticides in peri-urban farming" – a citizen-science project that investigated how food was being grown in urban and peri-urban areas (primarily allotments), including how growers control for insect pests, with a view to better-understanding the role of different kinds of pollinators in the urban context.

- "Delivering food security and biodiversity conservation through rewilding and community agriculture?" – an interdisciplinary project that examined the ecological and social dimensions of a range of approaches to land management involving large herbivores in the South East of England, including agro-ecological farming, conservation grazing and re-wilding.

These two projects provided further opportunities for the local hub project work to be interpreted within the wider context of Brighton and Hove's food system. They continued until their conclusion at around the same time as the end of the formal 'Pathways' transformative knowledge network (TKN) project.

The morning's facilitated discussions aimed to understand how transdisciplinary research such as ours, or such as that associated with SSRP, could better effect change. During this discussion, one participant (a researcher) said that they did not think more research was needed, proposing that it was rather action that was required. They questioned whether research outputs from this, and other, projects could sufficiently effect change to bring about a more sustainable food system for Brighton and Hove. Discussion around this issue raised some tensions between research, action-based research such as this project, and practitioners who only engage in action.

The research findings were reported in more detail to a similar (but augmented) group of stakeholders the following morning (the main element of our first T-Lab workshop). In order to deliver this in an engaging way we employed an external professional facilitator, who used the 'Evaluation H' method (see below) to explore the question "How easy is it to supply sustainably-produced food to the city?" Following on from this, a mapping exercise built on the discussions of positive and negative factors, with participants split into two groups, one for positive (encouraging) factors and one for negative (limiting). The groups were initially invited to add to the factors that had been identified so far, their attention being directed towards 'neglected' factors. After that, participants were invited to consider the various factors and how they were addressed (both in terms of strengthening them or helping to overcome them) by existing policies, systems and research, and then asked to note down changes in the above (new policies, system changes or research) that could further contribute to making it easier for small and medium-sized food producers to supply sustainably produced food into Brighton and Hove.

Up until this stage, we had been planning to help build consensus across different views, within an area where there was a plurality of perspectives and contestation about priorities (e.g. the actual and potential role of locally produced food). Ideally, we hoped to develop ideas for social innovations that might drive transformation. What we actually drew from the workshop was a renewed and revised agenda for research, building on that which emerged from the co-design workshop, but with a greater emphasis on the two challenges that participants (especially producers) prioritised. These were access to land for local and eco-logical food production and coordination of markets and logistics/distribution systems between producers, retailers and consumers. The plan to produce two briefing papers, one on issues associated with access to land and the other on mar-ket coordination strategies, is what emerged, largely on the basis of a new net-work map/PIPA produced by the research team on the afternoon of the second day. In the interim, the Council had announced plans to sell currently publicly owned, tenancy land into private ownership, which led to some public mobili-sation against the proposals (Vowles 2016). Partly as a result of this, the 'access to land' paper was subsequently reframed to address potentials for a more local and sustainable food supply, delivered through agro-ecological food production on Brighton and Hove's Downland Estate, which became the focus of our second T-Lab workshop.

Shortly after the workshop, Adrian Ely was invited to join an expert panel for the City Food Strategy. He also worked with Brighton and Hove Food Partner-ship to organise a national workshop (in September 2017) at the University of Sussex that helped to inform a plan to measure the impact of taking such a city-wide perspective on food.

T-Lab workshop 2

The second T-Lab workshop involved a total of 23 people and used less for-mal approaches than the H-evaluation used previously. The event was held in a rented space in a building often used by civil society organisations working on food in the centre of Brighton. After an ice-breaker, the research team went on to give a short presentation on the preliminary findings of the research into the potential for agro-ecological food production on the Downland Estate. This provoked a lot of discussion. There was some criticism of the presentation of one of the statistics (based on research by another Sussex colleague) as "sensationalist" and we were also critiqued for the small number of tenant farmers that had been interviewed. However, these critiques mainly led to productive debate and the tensions that were raised did not lead to any particular point of view dominating the discussion.

Next, facilitated small group discussions (involving a diversity of actors in each) were used to map the following (with regard to the role of the Downland Estate in contributing to a sustainable food system for Brighton and Hove):

- Negative/limiting factors
- Positive/encouraging factors
- New ideas.

Many of the issues raised in the first T-Lab workshop (including logistics and marketing, training needs for farmers) were repeated spontaneously on differ-ent tables at the second T-Lab, which is encouraging (to the extent that we are identifying widely viewed challenges and potential solutions). Discussion of new ideas led to recommendations (generally shared) around the need for a democratic process to identify the 'purpose' of the Downland Estate, the potential value of a survey of soils and other characteristics of the estate (to aid in zoning decisions), and the idea of a research and innovation hub to support transformations to sustainability in the city/biosphere region. The role of the Downland Estate was a politically controversial issue, and there was a desire among some participants to get this on the Council's agenda in advance of the next local elections in May 2019. We failed to do this, primarily because of lack of resources and a political environment of austerity in which cuts to public services and issues of poverty and homelessness became core election issues. However, the issue later became the focus of a Council consultation.

Lessons from the entire T-Lab process

Through these key moments in the T-Lab process, we focussed down on more and more specific priorities associated with the transformation underway – e.g. identifying small farmers in the co-design workshop; access to land as one of the priorities in the first T-Lab workshop; and the Downland Estate as a focus for action in the second – as directed by a network of academic and non-academic participants that broadened out to include increasingly divergent perspectives. As such, a transdisciplinary approach was certainly used, even though we did not work directly with non-academic partners in conducting the research. Such an approach to co-production was difficult as it required regular meetings, sharing information, strategic discussions and going to great lengths to co-ordinate diaries. In particular, where participants were not generally aligned with our view of the transformations required (and may have been among the more powerful), this was even more burdensome. Beyond that, the skills possessed by team members, and the kinds of research that we aspired to do, have not always met the expectations of our participants in terms of what is 'required' or 'needed'. For example, where some have looked to us to provide evaluations we have instead provided input to monitoring and evaluation plans. Others have placed a premium on quantitative knowledge based in the natural sciences, rather than the kind of work that we are more used to undertaking, thereby raising questions about our possible contribution.

The recommendations from the second T-Lab workshop could be seen as aspects of 'designing innovation' (one of the overall aims of a T-Lab process – see Chapter 4). However we were at the very early stages and had not yet reached the stage of 'prototyping'.

Impact, outcomes and pathways

The project is best seen within the context of the broader efforts of researchers at the STEPS Centre, and the University of Sussex. By working together over the timeframe of the project, they have provided evidence to support transformation towards enhanced sustainability in the local agri–food system. At the same time, this is difficult to measure, characterise or attribute as a result of the diffuse nature of this work. Whereas the evidence collected from project surveys provides a picture of change, it does not provide proof of change that is attributable to the project work itself, except in some cases where there is at least circumstantial (and some documentary) evidence for a contribution to these changes. The kinds of changes documented by the project include changes in relationships and networks, policies and practices, as well as knowledge, attitudes and skills, among the various stakeholders, assessed (subjectively) on the basis of the baseline survey and the final survey.

With respect to changes among the research community at the University of Sussex, the SSRP has supported collaborations across the natural and social sciences, including the two projects listed above that benefited from participation in our first T-Lab workshop. It could also be argued that the project work, combined with SSRP initiatives, has contributed to better linkages between research, policy and action. As evidence for this, the research team received approaches for collaboration from actors previously unknown to us (private sector and civil society). Members of the project team also made efforts to collaborate with colleagues at the University of Brighton (e.g. through joint funding applications) but have to date not been as successful. Additionally, we can observe changes in our knowledge and understanding of the actors involved in the problem space. In looking back at the original PIPA network that was constructed at the inception workshop, it is clear that our knowledge has increased considerably since then. In terms of our mapping of relevant actors at a local-to-regional level, we have added the land agents who serve the local authority and several statutory bodies including the South Downs National Park Authority, Natural England and Sussex Wildlife Trusts; at a national level we have added civil society groups such as the Sustainable Food Cities Network, Ecological Land Cooperative and Food Research Collaboration. Indeed, initiating, enhancing and maintaining alliances across the various stakeholders above have perhaps been our greatest contribution to change.

In terms of changes among the general public, the mobilisation against proposed changes to Council-owned farmland in 2016 was notable. These proposals were to a) sell currently publicly owned, tenancy land into private ownership, and b) develop a large area of the Downland Estate that is designated as a Nature Reserve into housing in 2018–2019. In terms of changes among civil society groups, strengthened links between the University, the Council-led 'Brighton and Lewes Downs Biosphere' and the Brighton and Hove Food Partnership have contributed to discussions about links between local production and consumption in the City Food Strategy (BHFP 2018, aim 4, including 4.1.5). In particular, Brighton and Hove Food Partnership developed a longer-term partnership with the project team as one of us became involved in the design and implementation of the city food strategy (BHFP 2018). Moreover, in terms of the social enterprise sector, retail and restaurant niches focussing on local and sustainable food also seem to have strengthened (although this is difficult to evidence), while a private online platform facilitating local producer-consumer supply chains (Food Assembly) was first established in 2015, and then subsequently shut down in 2018 (Farm Drop 2018). We were informed by one of the participants at our second T-Lab workshop that a local farmer had decided to dedicate part of his farm to diverse agro-ecological production for supply within a 15 mile radius, inspired by the ideas we were trying to push.

In terms of politics and governance, a number of local protests (mentioned above) took place during the course of the project, which led the City Council to run a committee-based enquiry into the Downland Estate. Since then, a wider recognition of the need to think strategically about the land around Brighton and Hove has grown among key decision-makers (primarily the City Council and the South Downs National Park Authority), which manifested in the development of a new Whole Estate Plan for the City Downland Estate (see Box 5.1). The Council adopted a progressive, participatory and consultative approach to this planning process from 2020 onwards (in line with the recommendations from our second T-Lab workshop), which aimed to "set out a vision for how our downland could be managed over the next 100 years" (BHCC 2020).

At the national level, the austerity policies of the Conservative government (2016 to the end of the project) led public policy to seek new sources of funding in order to address budget deficits (e.g. leading to the proposals to sell public land). The Brexit referendum vote in 2016 also had an impact on government at local levels and an overwhelming effect on the changes at the national level. The potential room for manoeuvre provided by Brexit (in terms of the UK setting its own policy, following the Common Agricultural Policy) precipitated a number of policy consultations and long-term strategies relating to environment and food being put in place. This, in turn, created uncertainty among some groups (especially farmers, according to evidence from our T-Lab workshops) as there was little clarity on the details and timeline of implementation.

In terms of observing shifts in the alignment of actors, some of those who were thought to be resistant to change were – by the end of the project – more open than expected. It is not clear whether this is a result of our misunderstanding at the outset, or a shift in their knowledge, attitudes and skills. For example, some farmers at the second T-Lab workshop were open to some kind of re-allocation of land (e.g. sub-letting) to agro-ecological farmers on the basis that it contributed to sustainable food systems (although the economic aspects of this were not clarified). Some robust arguments were put forward (e.g. by agro-ecological farmers) that it was possible to grow vegetables on what had traditionally been thought of as 'marginal' land, and some of the participants, including conventional farmers and policy-makers, appeared to accept these arguments. In addition, some of the actors who had been expected to be resistant (e.g. large conventional arable producers) seemed to accept the arguments put forward by the project team (i.e. that there was significant potential for agro-ecological farming to contribute to the city's food supply, including addressing food poverty) and learnt from the contributions of one of the agro-ecological producers and other commercial ecological farmers in the area.

Research methods

We used a combination of web-based research, semi-structured interviews and strategic engagement. During T-Lab workshops, our external facilitator adapted the "Evaluation H" method as described in Box 5.2 (see also STEPS Centre 2017).

BOX 5.2 EVALUATION H

Background

Evaluation H derives from the H-form/'Rugby Post form' Evaluation method developed by Andy Inglis in 1997 to assist local people in Somalia in monitoring and evaluation (Guy and Inglis 1999).

Beyond a standard 'continuum' or 'line' method that allows participants to position themselves (or their perspectives) on a line of possibilities, Evaluation H has an additional dimension. It encourages participants to directly and specifically identify the positive or negative factors that influence their position on the line. They can be clustered, and, through a facilitated process, used as a focus for discussing what needs to happen to build upon and strengthen positive factors, or to overcome or address negative factors, in order to support an overall objective.

What's involved?

The facilitator of the exercise poses a question to the group, which is related to the issue being explored, with the question written at the top of a wall, table or large sheet of paper (the work surface). A horizontal line is drawn across the centre of the work surface, providing a continuum for opinions, e.g. good to bad, easy to difficult, important to not important. Participants are each given sticky notes and pens, and asked to consider their response to the question posed by the facilitator and where on the continuum reflects/ represents their response. Participants are also asked to write the factors (positive and negative), which influence why their response falls at the position on the continuum they have identified. Once all participants have added their sticky notes to the work surface, each of the responses is discussed with every participant having the opportunity to explain their perspective. The factors identified can be positive or negative, and are usually attached to vertical lines at either end of the continuum (hence the 'H' or rugby post

---

(Continued)

name). Ideally the factors are then clustered to identify any common themes that arise and then each distinct cluster can be analysed, i.e. what needs to happen to overcome or address this negative factor, or to build upon and strengthen this positive factor.

Broadening out and opening up

The Evaluation H method is useful for identifying different perspectives along a continuum. As long as a broad range of perspectives are present and feel free to contribute, this is effective at 'broadening out' discussions around an issue. Ideally, the method brings plural perspectives on the issue to an equal status but can also highlight 'outliers' or more marginal views. The dialogue which explores participant's responses then opens up in an attempt to address the plurality of framings. As such, this method can be particularly effective if participants represent different sectors, backgrounds, or types of involvement in the issue being explored, particularly if these different stakeholders do not interact often. Discussion of each participant's responses allows each diverse perspective to be explored, bringing different framings of issues to the surface and illuminating multiple diverse ideas, opportunities, strategies or recommendations. Dialogue emerging from discussion can also help to address dynamics between perspectives, including tensions, commonalities, gaps or opportunities.

Fits and limits

A strength of the Evaluation H method is that it can engage a range of stakeholders, sectors and backgrounds on an even plane, where each participant is held as equal and their responses given equal importance (although this is dependent on appropriate facilitation). This allows each participant to give their perspective in their response to the question without feeling judged or marginalised by other participants. Conversely, a potential weakness of the method is that participants may not feel comfortable, willing or able to give their perspective or reflect on their response with others (especially if the exercise is poorly facilitated).

Re-framing the project – problems and priorities

Our theory of change did not explicitly talk about re-framing. However, within a general pathways approach it sought to illuminate and highlight different framings and – through research and engagement activities – to bridge between them. Thus, through bringing in new evidence and ideas, it contributed to various reframing processes (discussed further in Chapter 11).

The framing of the problem space that was initially chosen did not change fundamentally, but evolved throughout the course of the project. This framing was worded in terms of the "unsustainability of the food system in Brighton and Hove, because of limitations to local food supply and environmentally damaging production and consumption practices". However, during the course of the three years, the initial focus on localisation of supply and innovation for sustainable food production and consumption gave way to more focussed work in the area of market linkage strategies, access to land and land use. In line with local discussions and mobilisation on these issues, this led to a further focussing of attention onto the Downland Estate. Hence, whereas our first project briefing on 'Market Co-ordination' (Taylor 2018) addressed linkages between urban food consumers, local food producers and the urban hinterland with reference to other UK cities, our second project briefing on 'Land' (Wach and Ely 2018) addressed the issues of access to land and land use in and around Brighton and Hove, and our third and final project briefing on the City Council's 'Downland Estate' (STEPS Centre 2019) was an overt attempt to re-frame local debates about the Whole Estate Plan. The project's increasing topical focus was therefore complemented by an increasingly situated framing of the research.

In terms of how this might have led other stakeholders to question established framings and adopt different or altered framings, our approach was slightly different at each stage, with different project outputs. The approach taken in the writing of the first output (Taylor 2018) was to present evidence from other UK cities where market linkages had been reconfigured as a result of public policy or civil society action, as a way to demonstrate what is possible. The second output (Wach and Ely 2018) used a similar approach in an attempt to reframe the widely held notion that the potential of the downland surrounding Brighton and Hove was limited – by geomorphological constraints – to landscape provision, livestock production and (to some extent) arable farming. It did this by using the case of a local community-supported agriculture (CSA) scheme to illustrate its potential for fresh vegetable production. However, it also attempted to reframe this area, which encompasses the Downland Estate, as part of the city (due to it being included in the City Food Strategy Action Plan and its ownership by the City Council). The third output – the report from the second T-Lab workshop – took a different approach, aiming to persuade decision-makers and other stakeholders to move beyond seeing the Downland Estate primarily as a source of revenue for the City Council – and towards a broader view of its value. Rather than using research to highlight the potential of the Estate by reference to examples, the briefing called for the City Council to consider adopting a more democratic/participatory process to identify the 'purpose' of the Downland Estate.

Our attempts, and those of others, to call into question the predominant framings of the potential of the land surrounding Brighton and Hove, as well as the value and "purpose" of the Council-owned Downland Estate, seems to have had some impact – though this is hard to evidence directly. The potential is that reframing the area in this way could lead to more attention from local authorities, greater feelings of ownership or engagement by other local organisations or citizens, and a greater appreciation of the role of local farmers for environmental management practices (e.g. those who use less fertilisers, with resultant benefits for water quality). Our suggestion for a broader framing of this area of land revolved around a recognition of its multi-functionality and the ecosystem services it provides, including local food supply, as well as public access and education (Wach and Ely 2018, STEPS Centre 2018). Some of the participants at the second T-Lab may have started to adopt these broader framings – partly as a result of us convening the meeting, engaging them over these issues, and highlighting the history of the 'Downland Initiative' Feasibility Study (Smiths Gore and University of Reading 2006). However, this was happening alongside financial constraints on the City Council, making it more difficult to translate intention into action.

On reflection, by adopting the "seeding ideas" approach (Ely et al. 2017) – acting as knowledge brokers and giving examples from elsewhere – we were able to shake up 'received wisdoms', provide examples from other local authorities that differed from the local approach and also adopt different assumptions to those implicit in market economics (e.g. prioritising the need to address local food poverty and exploring the potentials for the Downland to contribute to this.) While these assumptions are obviously of questionable validity, they make room for new narratives that could provide a focus for future mobilisation. Approaches such as this use of (from some perspectives perverse) arguments – e.g. about the potential food productivity of Downland, or of the data that we presented on pesticides, which was critiqued as 'sensationalised' in our second T-Lab workshop – seemed to unsettle current framings more effectively than striving for consensus.

Looking ahead, there have been various re-framings of sustainability challenges at the national level which have had little to do with our work so far, but may interact with it in the future. In particular, the UK's commitment to leave the European Union has sparked a renewed interest in food security and in particular vegetable and fruit growing. This illustrates the potential role of political processes in creating windows of opportunity for reframing debates. While the uncertainty and political upheaval created in the aftermath of the 'Brexit' referendum has been challenging, individual actors and alliances who have engaged in our work have attempted to turn it into an opportunity. The complications of Brexit have also included a recognised need for local authorities to plan for food security (Lang et al. 2018).

Innovation and alternative pathways

A form of innovation that is of particular relevance to this project is social innovation, which we see as entailing new combinations of resources (people, knowledge, technologies, ways of working) that has an explicit aim to enhance social or environmental outcomes. It might involve new knowledge (e.g. derived from our research project), but does not necessarily. As such, social innovation plays a vital role in the production, distribution and consumption (including re-purposing and recycling) of food, and many examples of these feature in the City Food Strategy and Action Plan (BHFP 2018). What's more, through our work we have provided support to a number of social innovations that pre-existed the project, including most notably Seedy Sunday and Brighton and Hove City Food Strategy Action Plan. For instance, we organised a workshop in 2017 on monitoring and evaluation of the City Food Strategy Action Plan, which resulted in the formulation of impact plan; on behalf of Seedy Sunday we undertook a survey in 2017, gave talks in 2017 and 2018, organised an information stand at the annual seed swaps in 2017, 2018 and 2019, and contributed to a seed policy panel in 2018.

While we are not at the stage of prototyping particular new social innovations that have emerged from the project, proposals for these did emerge from the second T-Lab workshop (STEPS Centre 2018). A key outcome of T-Lab 2 was that a policy review involving a participatory democratic process was needed to identify the 'purpose' of the Downland Estate, and that a clear vision and political leadership was required to take it forward to implement a new approach to its management. This could be seen as a bridging innovation. Furthermore, participants articulated the need to map the ecological potentials within the Downland Estate – drawing on and collating existing data on (*inter alia*) soils, involving soils, morphology, climate, delivery of biodiversity outcomes, natural capital and infrastructure – in order to inform decisions over where opportunities for food production (and other) activities may exist. This is a 'research need' more than a bridging innovation. Nonetheless, it was clear that there were continuing differences of opinion and a general paucity of data and research on the downland surrounding the city and its potential for producing different kinds of food. There was also an ambition, associated with the Biosphere, for the Downland Estate to be a site for innovation in the move towards more sustainable food systems. The proposal for a 'research and innovation hub', which seemed widely welcomed, could be seen as another bridging innovation – one which responded to various aspects of the local context.

Networks, alliances and collective agency

The T-Lab process brought together various groups, enabling new relationships that have been strengthened over subsequent months (especially with Brighton and Hove Food Partnership). This enabled new, and in some cases stronger, personal and professional relationships to develop between the research community, civil society groups, funders, private sector, media and government actors involved in the problem space. Successive workshops involved progressively greater numbers of people and 'broadened out' (Stirling 2008) to include a more diverse set of actors. This was reflected in a trend towards progressively less generally 'aligned' groups in the co-design workshop, T-Lab 1 workshop and T-Lab 2 workshop – see Figure 5.3.

In connection to this, the group that we convened at the second T-Lab workshop included some who had not engaged with each other before. Nevertheless,

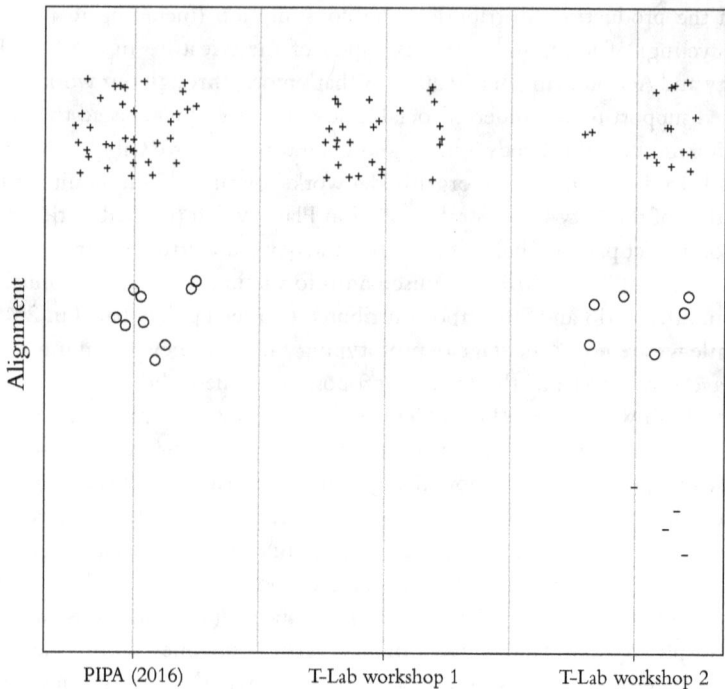

FIGURE 5.3 Number of actors and alignment, as estimated in UK PIPA, T-Lab 1 workshop and T-Lab 2 workshop. Aligned actors are represented by "+", non-aligned by "−" and ambivalent by "0".

they were united in a desire to see a sustainable future for the Downland Estate, and – given the very different approaches to production – behaved in a surprisingly collaborative way, even if there were obvious tensions. Although we did not see the spontaneous formation of a self-identifying group, there were calls for something to 'come out of' the event and for the recommendations to be taken forward. Despite the fact that the research team were not able to follow up sufficiently on this at the time, discussions continued, and fed into other work at the University and elsewhere (see Ely and Wach 2018). More recent moves by the local authority (BHCC 2020) to embark upon a consultation process for the Downland Estate take forward some of the ideas discussed in our T-Lab.

Specific insights and contributions from the UK hub

By the time the project came to a formal conclusion in early 2020, the UK hub work had delivered three specific sets of insights:

1 Alignment and power

In comparison to other hubs (e.g. Argentina), our T-Lab moves from a more aligned, less powerful group towards a less aligned, more powerful group. This was partly a strategic choice and partly a result of the momentum that we had developed over the previous years of research.

2   Alignment against as opposed to alignment towards

In terms of 'transformative pathways' and their open-endedness, the T-Lab process (from co-design through to T-Lab 2) illustrated that it is relatively easy to identify groups who are against the dominant pathway. However, they may themselves favour very different transformations. The focus on local food was relatively unquestioned, e.g. but the choice to frame agro-ecological production as a specific solution was not favoured by all. Moreover, while we engaged with numerous actors in a process of negotiating and proposing social innovations for alternative pathways, we completely side-stepped the need to destabilise the conventional (dominant) pathway that was constraining the alternatives that we favoured. In this sense we did not 'challenge power', even though we came together as being opposed to it.

3   Windows of opportunity and wider transformations

The second T-Lab workshop opened up interesting questions about 'windows of opportunity' and how T-Labs can become entangled and embedded in more formal policy processes. It remains to be seen how this takes place (in relation, for instance, to the long-term impacts of the Whole Estate Plan and the City Food Strategy).

This also raised issues regarding the responsibilities of researchers to the knowledge partners with whom they engaged. We unfortunately did not have the resources (in terms of time) to fully engage with these external processes or to be the main driver of the proposals that came out of the T-Lab. But we adopted an approach that saw the T-Lab as co-owned by a number of stakeholders, so that it became embedded into other ongoing processes. This is an interesting take on 'transformative agency' – the researchers acknowledge their own relative lack of agency but intervene in a way that blends in with the ongoing transformation, rather than seeing our intervention as discrete.

References

Balázs B., Smith, A., Aistara, G. and Bela, G.Y. (2016) Transformative Social Innovation: Transnational Seed Exchange Networks. TRANSIT: EU SSH.2013.3.2-1 Grant agreement no: 613169.

Bangs, D. (2008) *A Freedom to Roam Guide to the Brighton Downs from Shoreham to Newhaven and Beeding to Lewes*, Farlington: Bishops Printers.

BHCC (2020) Protecting our downland for future generations, https://www.brighton-hove.gov.uk/news/2020/protecting-our-downland-future-generations, accessed 18/11/2020.

BHFP (2012) *Spade to Spoon: Digging Deeper, A Food Strategy and Action Plan for Brighton and Hove*, Brighton and Hove Food Partnership.

BHFP (2018) *Brighton and Hove Food Strategy Action Plan 2018–2023*, Brighton and Hove Food Partnership, http://bhfood.org.uk/wp-content/uploads/2018/11/Final-FULL-WEB-Food-Strategy-Action-Plan.pdf, accessed 11/9/2019.

Brighton and Lewes Downs Biosphere (2014) http://biospherehere.org.uk/.

Defra (2012) *Agricultural and Horticultural Survey 2009 and 2010*, Department of Environment, Food and Rural Affairs. London.

Durrant, R. (2014) *Civil Society in Sustainability Transitions of Food Systems*, DPhil Thesis, University of Sussex.

Durrant, R., Barnes, J., Kern, F. and Mackerron, G. (2018) The acceleration of transitions to urban sustainability: A case study of Brighton and Hove. *European Planning Studies*, 26(8), pp. 1537–1558.

Ely, A., Van Zwanenberg, P., Wach, E., Obaya, M. and A. Cremaschi (2017) Seeding ideas: Knowledge brokering and recombination for agricultural transformations, https://steps-centre.org/blog/seeding-ideas-knowledge-brokering-recombination-agricultural-transformations/, accessed 11/9/2019.

Ely, A. and Wach, E. (2018) *Endings and beginnings: Project-Based Work within Wider Transformations,* https://steps-centre.org/blog/endings-and-beginnings-project-based-work-within-wider-transformations/, accessed 11/9/2019.

Farm Drop (2018) Farm drop blog: "We are sad to announce that the Food Assembly closed its doors in the UK on Friday the 28th of September 2018", https://www.farmdrop.com/blog/foodassembly/?utm_source=foodassembly&utm_medium=email1, accessed 11/9/2019.

Guy, S. and Inglis, A.S. (1999) 'Tips for trainers: Introducing the "H-form" – A method for monitoring and evaluation, in Gujit, I. and Braden, S. (eds), *Learning from Analysis, Participatory Learning and Action Notes*, Issue 34, London: International Institute for Environment and Development, pp. 84–87.

IAASTD (2009) *Towards Multifunctional Agriculture for Social, Environmental and Economic Sustainability*, International Assessment of Agricultural Knowledge, Science and Technology for Development.

Lang, T., Millstone, E., Lewis, T. and McFarlane, G. (2018) *Why Local Authorities Should Prepare Food Brexit Plans*, London: Food Research Collaboration, https://foodresearch.org.uk/publications/local-authorities-food-brexit/, accessed 11/9/2019.

Laughton, R. (2017) *'A Matter of Scale' A Study of the Productivity, Financial Viability and Multifunctional Benefits of Small Farms (20 ha and less)*. Land Workers' Alliance and Centre for Agroecology, Coventry University.

Leach, M., Scoones, I. and Stirling, A. (2010) *Dynamic Sustainabilities*, London: EarthScan.

Olsson, P., Folke, C., Galaz, V., Hahn, T. and Schultz, L. (2007) Enhancing the fit through adaptive co-management: creating and maintaining bridging functions for matching scales in the Kristianstads Vattenrike Biosphere Reserve Sweden. *Ecology and Society*, 12(1): p. 28. [online] URL: http://www.ecologyandsociety.org/vol12/iss1/art28/.

Scoones, I., Newell, P. and Leach, M. (eds) (2015) *The Politics of Green Transformations*, Abingdon: Routledge.

Smith, A. (2006) Green niches in sustainable development: the case of organic food in the United Kingdom. *Environment and Planning C: Government and Policy*, 24: pp. 439–458.

Smith, A. and Ely, A. (2015) Green Transformations from Below? The Politics of Grassroots Innovation, Chapter 7 in Scoones, I., Newell, P. and Leach, M. (eds), *The Politics of Green Transformations*, Abingdon: Routledge, pp. 102–118.

Smiths Gore and University of Reading (2006) *Downland Initiative Feasibility Study*, https://www.brighton-hove.gov.uk/sites/brightonhove.gov.uk/files/SP023%20Downland%20Initiative%202005.pdf, accessed September 2018.

South Downs National Park Authority (2012) *State of the National Park 2012*, http://www.southdowns.gov.uk/about-us/state-of-the-national-park-report-2012, accessed 23/12015.

STEPS Centre (2017) Evaluation H: Methods "vignette" on the STEPS Centre Methods site https://steps-centre.org/pathways-methods-vignettes/methods-vignettes-evaluation-h/, accessed 11/9/2019.

STEPS Centre (2018) The Downland Estate: Contributing to more sustainable food systems for Brighton & Hove – Report on a workshop held on 12th July 2018, https://steps-centre.org/wp-content/uploads/2018/09/Downland-Estate-Workshop-July-2018-Report.pdf, accessed 11/9/2019.

Stirling, A. (2008) 'Opening up' and 'closing down': Power, participation and pluralism in the social appraisal of technology Science. *Technology and Human Values*, 33(2): 262–294.

Taylor, R. (2018) *Market Linkage Strategies for Local Food Systems: Lessons for Brighton and Hove*, https://steps-centre.org/publication/market-linkage-strategies-for-local-food-systemslessons-for-brighton-hove/, accessed September 2018.

United Kingdom Census (2011) *2011 Census for England*, Northern Ireland and Wales, Newport: Office for National Statistics.

Van Zwanenberg, P., Ely, A. and Smith, A. (2011) *Regulating Technology: International Harmonisation and Local Realities*, London: Earthscan.

Vowles, N. (2016) Concerns raised over council's biggest sell-off of downland in 20 years, The Brighton Argus 9 November.

Wach, E. and Ely, A. (2018) *Brighton and Hove's Farmland: Potentials for a More Local and Ecological Food Supply*, Brighton: STEPS Centre, https://steps-centre.org/publication/brighton-hovesfarmland-potentials-for-a-more-local-and-ecological-food-supply-2/, accessed September 2018.

White, R. and Stirling, A. (2013) Sustaining trajectories towards Sustainability: Dynamics and diversity in UK communal growing activities. *Global Environmental Change*, 23(5): pp. 838–846.

Willis, G. (2017) Uncertain harvest: Does the loss of farms matter? Campaign to Protect Rural England.

Winter, M., Lobley, M., Chiswell, H., Howe, K., Wilkinson, T. and Wilson, P. (2016) Is there a future for the small family farm in the UK? A report to the Prince's Countryside Fund.

6

BIOLEFT

A collaborative, open source seed breeding initiative for sustainable agriculture

Anabel Marin, Patrick Van Zwanenberg and Almendra Cremaschi

Introduction

In this chapter we discuss the research and engagement process that led to the development of Bioleft. We characterise Bioleft as a multi-actor 'transformation laboratory' that develops and prototypes institutional and technical novelty in order to create an alternative, open and collaborative, innovation system for seeds. Originating as an experimental research and action project involving two social scientists, Bioleft has now become an initiative driven by a transdisciplinary team of more than 20 people in both Argentina and Mexico. Bioleft comprises social scientists, plant breeders, agronomists, agricultural extension workers, farmer-breeders, representatives of farming associations and a small seed firm. Our approach, as with the other initiatives reported on in this volume, has been based on ideas of co-design and the transdisciplinary production of knowledge and action (Kates 2001; Marin et al. 2016; Miller and Wyborn 2018). Consequently, although originating in a research setting, Bioleft has become an initiative co-owned by a diverse group of people that includes academic researchers. It now bears more resemblance to an emerging non-government organisation or social enterprise than a research project.

Our initiative grew out of concerns about the direction of change within the Argentinean agricultural sector, which has become dominated by high input, intensive, large-scale commodity crop production (Phelinas and Choumert 2017). We focussed on seeds, a key input that shapes the possibilities and configuration of agricultural systems. Global seed markets have become highly concentrated over the last 30 years, in response to the emergence of new business models made possible by genomics-based technologies and the worldwide diffusion of strict intellectual property rights, especially patents and patent-like restrictions over seed material. Just three giant multinational corporation (MNC) agro-chemical

DOI: 10.4324/9780429331930-9

firms now dominate the global seed market (MacDonald 2019). Those firms focus their breeding efforts on large commercial seed markets, and on address-ing commercially significant production constraints (Fess et al. 2011). Minor crops, marginal agro-ecological environments, niche markets such as for agro-ecological production, and the needs of small farmers are largely neglected (Fal-con and Fowler 2002; Osman et al. 2008; Smale et al. 2009). This is likely to result in an acceleration in the long-term decline of crop diversity, unsuitable seed varieties (for many farmers), and a much narrower variety of agricultural systems and practices that the seed sector is able to support (FAO 2019; Hubbard 2009). Market concentration also results in the loss of domestic technological capabilities in seed breeding in some countries, and therefore of agricultural au-tonomy and control over food sovereignty (Brieva et al. 2008; Marin et al. 2015; Perelmuter 2008).

The global transformation of the seed industry has impacted Argentina in a significant way. Independent domestic firms and the public sector are respon-sible for an increasingly smaller proportion of seed breeding, undermining the provision of diversity (Marin et al. 2015; Perelmuter 2008). Domestic firms and the public sector also find it more difficult to deliver their varieties to farmers, given that marketing and distribution channels are increasingly dominated by the MNC agrochemical firms. As a consequence, the seed requirements of family farmers are unmet, while producers working in sectors, such as agro-ecological or organic production, informally try and develop suitable varieties within their own networks (see Bioleft.org for testimonies). Argentina nevertheless retains domestic capabilities in breeding. Some firms that were not acquired by the large agro-chemical MNCs during the 1990s and 2000s have been very successful and the public sector, despite significant budget cuts, still possesses plant breeders en-gaged in producing important innovations (Marin et al. 2015, van Zwanenberg et al. 2018). A key objective for Bioleft has been to try and connect those existing dispersed capabilities and to create new ones by taking advantage of new tech-nological and social opportunities to develop the architecture of an alternative seed innovation system.

Towards more sustainable seed innovation and agriculture systems: our framework

Our approach to developing Bioleft was inspired in part by socio-technical tran-sitions theory, which puts 'system innovation' at the centre of processes of trans-formation (Köhler et al. 2019; Smith et al. 2010). This interdisciplinary body of literature gives a prominent role in transformation processes to experimentation with novel social and technological practices that develop within spaces that are protected, at least temporarily, from competition with well-established ways of producing and using the goods and services that experimentation is seeking to provide in different ways. The argument is that these so called 'niche-based' ac-tivities provide a source of diversity – of ideas, knowledge, and practice – which established, mainstream systems, such as those concerned with the development, production and use of seeds, may draw on to solve problems, or which may themselves get translated into new emergent systems (Geels and Schot 2007; Smith 2007).

The literature argues that temporary protection within niche spaces (for example, in the form of subsidies) allows the costs and performance of novel social and technological practices to be improved, as well as space and time to build networks, and to try and modify the unfavourable environments that tend to favour incremental innovation over system transformation (Kemp et al. 1998). For example, niche-based actors may try to construct new markets for their ideas, influence user preferences, lobby for supporting regulations, persuade financiers to back their new technologies or represent their novel practices as solutions to wider cultural and political changes that are causing problems for mainstream ways of providing the goods and services in question. As Geels and Schot (2007) put it, niche entrepreneurs are 'creating the technology and its environment in the same process'.

Within this framework Bioleft can be considered as a niche-based laboratory for experimenting with and developing alternative practices, knowledge and technology to support more sustainable seed innovation systems. Transitions frameworks helped us to appreciate that our activities need to go beyond just designing, testing and improving alternative approaches to seed breeding. We have needed, for example, to try and obtain temporary protection for our experimental practices as we were learning whether and how they can work effectively, in our case in the forms of committed individuals willing to share their time and energy in order to experiment with us and external financial support beyond the original research project. Transition perspectives also helped us to appreciate the importance of building networks with a wide range of people, not only from the worlds of plant breeding and agricultural extension, but also, for example, from government departments of science and technology and agriculture. Likewise, we have sought to develop wider awareness about why we think an alternative seed breeding initiative is important, and of connecting with other like-minded initiatives in the area of sustainable agriculture. We have also sought to create alliances with open-source seed initiatives in other countries which share the objectives and approach we have been experimenting with. This is important in terms of both learning and gaining influence within mainstream seed innovation systems at both local and international levels. The following sections of this chapter outline in more detail how we have approached trying to collectively define a shared vision and approach and to enrol diverse people in Bioleft.

Our methodological approach

In developing Bioleft we drew on ideas about transformation labs (T-Lab), as with the other initiatives covered in this volume. Those ideas emphasise the importance of social interaction between diverse participants in order to learn about sustainability challenges, identify innovative solutions, and then to put some of those ideas into experimental practice. The diversity of participants is important in order to help ensure that a range of different perspectives, experiences and knowledge can be brought to bear on understanding problems and potential solutions.

This approach was inspirational for us because it encourages researchers to become involved in action, and to do so by working with other stakeholders. T-Lab ideas also helped us to think about the centrality of social as well as technological innovation in transformative change, and about social innovation in a structured way. This literature draws attention to the importance of techniques to encourage transdisciplinary learning about complex systems and the problems they generate, and to test the potential of different ideas for achieving system change.

A specific method we used, in conjunction with ideas about T-Labs, was Q-method, which is an approach to systematically study subjective viewpoints on a topic (Eden et al. 2005). With Q-method a small, nonrepresentative but diverse group of people are asked to rank a series of statements about a topic. The method then looks for patterns among rankings and reduces individual rankings to a few clusters, which represent broadly shared ways of thinking about the topic. Among other things, the technique can help identify themes or issues that are critical to differentiating between different views, as well as those about which there is consensus across different perspectives (Barry and Proops 1999).

We ran a pilot Q study in order to inform the remit and running of our first T-Lab workshop. The idea was to map a range of different views about the sustainability problems associated with mainstream seed systems. The exercise covered perspectives on the relationships between intellectual property rules and seed market concentration, on questions of access to seeds, seed innovation and biological and rural socio-economic diversity. We interviewed 11 people for our pilot study, including plant breeders from both private and public sectors, seed firm representatives, academics and civil servants.

Key moments in the T-Lab process

An early key moment, prior to our first T-Lab workshop, was a decision about the planned remit of that event. We decided to focus workshop discussions on the sustainability challenges faced by the agricultural sector that are associated with increasing seed market concentration, and to propose an open-source breeding system for seeds as a way to address some of these challenges. A key aim of the T-Lab event would be to explore the viability of this novel idea with a range of stakeholders involved in the development, use and governance of seeds.

A second key moment, again prior to our first T-Lab workshop, followed the completion of our pilot Q-study. We had expected those findings to help us plan the event, but they prompted us to alter its remit. This was because most of the participants we interviewed for the Q-study believed that seed intellectual property rights were not a significant cause of problems such as loss of agricultural biodiversity and diminishing domestic technological sovereignty. Other factors were seen as more immediately relevant. Consequently, we decided that there would be little purpose focussing the T-Lab event on discussing whether and how an open-source breeding system for seeds would be a way to address sustainability challenges, if our stakeholders did not think that intellectual property rules were fundamentally a problem. We therefore broadened the remit of our planned workshop to focus, more generally, on exploring an unrestricted range of possible problems with, and solutions to, seed market concentration.

A third key moment was the first day-long T-Lab workshop itself, held in March 2017. Nineteen people participated, including representatives from Via Campesina, peri-urban agro-ecological producers, seed breeders from the public and private sector, government officials, academics, specialists in intellectual property law, journalists, trade associations and a member of Congress's agriculture committee. We learnt through this experience that it was illuminating to learn from this large and diverse group of actors, given that they held very different perspectives about the challenges faced by the agricultural and the seed sectors in Argentina and their possible solutions. Nevertheless, given that sheer diversity of opinion, it was very difficult to collectively identify potential solutions that addressed some of those challenges.

We began the event with a presentation of our pilot Q study findings, a brief video produced by the research team, which illustrated a range of effects associated with market concentration and property rights regimes in the seed sector, and a panel discussion. The participants were then split into small groups and asked to try and arrive at a consensus about the most important sustainability challenges associated with the structure and governance of the seed system. The groups collectively identified eight challenges, not all of which were necessarily directly related to the seed sector, nor were they all problems that social innovation could necessarily address. As organisers we chose three of those problems for group discussion in the afternoon, on the grounds that it might be possible to begin to address them through social innovation. These concerned an absence of agricultural diversity; a lack of recognition and support for informal seed improvement; and weak protection and support for domestic seed technological development.

At a subsequent plenary session, discussion focussed on the idea of creating a network of actors working on or interested in participative breeding. This proposal was supported by university-based plant breeders, scientists from the public sector research service, and rural NGOs and social movements present at the workshop. The suggestion was that such a network could be used to experiment with a range of initiatives linked to improving support for participative breeding, as summarised in Box 6.1.

Following this event, we pursued some of the ideas proposed, initially trying (but failing) to raise funding to support an agro-ecological NGO to develop a seed library and to organise training in participatory breeding. We then continued to organise meetings with small groups of stakeholders in order to explore

---

BOX 6.1 FIRST T-LAB WORKSHOP

The T-Lab was organised around two guiding questions:

1   What are the most relevant challenges faced by the agricultural and seed sector in Argentina, as a result of increased seed market concentration?
2   What interventions might address and begin to resolve those challenges?

Several actions were proposed, oriented to support participatory seed breeding:

1   To map participatory crop improvement initiatives at global and national level in order to learn from existing practices and explore networking opportunities.
2   To develop capabilities and good practices in participatory crop improvement, based on a broad conception of the agriculture production system.
3   To obtain certification for the outputs of participative breeding.
4   To create a market for the products of such seeds, when used in practices such as agro-ecological and fair trade production.
5   To create an open-source licence or pledge for germplasm produced through participative breeding.

---

how we might support some of the proposed interventions. A central – and formidable – challenge involved thinking about which kinds of initiatives or interventions were most likely to make people sufficiently enthusiastic to actively participate, in the absence of funding. Eventually, we decided to focus on our original idea, also discussed and supported at the T-Lab workshop, namely the creation of an open-source seed licence. This was our fourth key moment in the T-Lab process. The rationale for that decision was the interest and enthusiasm of a group of plant breeders from the Faculty of Agronomy at the University of Buenos Aires, after a presentation to the group about the open-source ideas we were exploring.

We recognised at that time an important issue that was to be crucial for our work thereafter. Specifically, single T-Lab events, such as workshops, were not sufficient to advance and push our practical idea (nor was it easy to persuade busy people to give up an entire day or two for a workshop). We therefore started a T-Lab *process* in 2018, which included short meetings and presentations with different kinds of stakeholders and possible partners to discuss ideas and to enrol people. Our objective was to create a core team and an extended network to develop and prototype tools to support an open-source licence. We were particularly interested at this stage in enrolling breeders and farmers working with alternative forms of agriculture.

This new way of working resulted in a fifth key moment, which was to develop a digital platform in parallel with open-source licences, with the idea that both could support an open-source seed innovation initiative. The initial rational for a digital platform was as a means to document and register informal seed varieties that were already being used and exchanged by family farmers and others, in order to collect evidence that could be used to discourage future attempts at biopiracy (for example, a firm using intellectual property rights (IPRs) to restrict the use of a seed variety that is already widely used but undocumented). Experience from other countries that have avoided piracy of native varieties suggested that evidence of past use of seeds was an effective tool. We subsequently realised that to the extent that a digital platform could be used to enable the exchange of information between breeders and farmers, it could also be a tool to support participatory breeding. We began to co-develop the idea of digital 'field books' for registering and exchanging data on seed performance. The co-development of these field books, which need to include variables that can be practically collected by farmers and that are also useful for breeding, and which have to be adapted to the requirements of each crop, is a challenging task. Addressing that challenge was the sixth key moment of the ongoing T-Lab process through which Bioleft is being developed.

Impact, outcomes and pathways

Bioleft is contributing to new pathways of seed development and therefore, indirectly, also to alternative pathways of development for the agricultural sector, such as those based on agro-ecological or other low input practices. Well adapted seeds are key to improving the productivity and viability of these alternative approaches to practising agriculture. Such alternatives, despite being the systems typically utilised by many family farmers (FAO 2018; IAASTD 2009) and widely recognised as crucial for diminishing agriculture's environmental impact (IPBES 2019), are ill-served by the mainstream seed sector.

To support the creation of those new pathways Bioleft has developed and is improving two tangible outputs: a set of material transfer agreements inspired by open-source ideas, and a digital platform. The first of these aims to ensure that germplasm and its embodied knowledge can circulate freely for future breeding purposes. The second aims to connect users and providers of seeds, and to create information about seed characteristics and performance that can be used to support collaborative breeding. A third expected and important output of Bioleft that we are developing, through both the diffusion of the digital platform and the enrolment of actors who are interested in using it, is a data set of information about users and seed performance that will be a very valuable asset to support decentralised breeding. This will require policies for the governance of this data which Bioleft is also co-designing with stakeholders.

New seed varieties registered with open-source licences and released for collective improvement are also tangible outputs of Bioleft. In 2018, we registered our first seed, named *Ubuntu*, a salt tolerant variety of *Melilotus* (a forage crop) bred for agro-ecological production systems by a breeder at the University of Buenos Aires and a member of Bioleft's core team. That variety was transferred, in small quantities, to representatives of the Federation of Organizations for Family Farming, and the Organization of Indigenous Nations and Peoples of Argentina. Subsequently, between 2019 and 2020, 20 additional seed varieties were released with an open-source licence: a maize variety, a second fodder crop variety, and 18 varieties of tomato. The latter were obtained from a University of Buenos Aires project that had recovered tomato varieties from the first two thirds of the 20th century. One hundred sixty of those recovered tomato varieties were multiplied and 18 selected during a public tasting experiment. Seeds from these varieties were then transferred to 300 producers using Bioleft's open-source material transfer agreement.

We have also produced other kinds of outcomes. One is a transdisciplinary core team of people and a larger community beyond that core team that is willing to contribute to the development of collaborative approaches to seed innovation for more sustainable agricultural systems. The other is the development of new knowledge and skills in three important areas: (a) participatory and co-design methods for social innovations aimed at transformation processes; (b) the design and use of legal tools for open innovation; and (c) collaborative breeding processes. In relation to the last of these, beyond the knowledge gained from day-to-day work developing Bioleft, two PhD students are also researching processes of collaborative breeding within Bioleft as part of their doctorates. One focusses on differences and conflicts over knowledge between scientists and farmers in respect of collaboration in participatory breeding processes, and the second on the challenges of expanding from participatory evaluation of seed varieties to more integrated forms of participatory breeding.

Re-framing processes around seeds and sustainability

Processes of reframing the way in which people think about and approach seed and agricultural sustainability problems and solutions, have been important for our developing initiative (as discussed further in Chapter 11). This has occurred both within the process leading up to the creation of Bioleft, and then subsequently as we have experimented with new seed breeding practices.

For example, in the early stages of creating the initiative, it was clear that most people critical of existing seed system practices were focussed on immediate problems with proposed changes to the national seed law that were seeking to strengthen domestic intellectual property rights over seeds. Those problems were largely related to issues of price and farmers' access to seeds. Responses were framed in terms of efforts to resist those proposed changes. We sought to encourage a broader, longer-term view of the problems posed by existing seed innovation practices, and of possible solutions. In particular, we sought to encourage reflection on the potentially problematic effects of existing seed innovation trends on crop diversity, the diversity of agricultural systems that new seeds were able to support, on the structure and ownership of the seed industry and on patterns of future agricultural development. Bringing in experience from other countries, where stricter intellectual property rights are more established, was an important means of fostering that longer term and broader perspective. In terms of solutions to that wider set of problems, we also sought to shift discussion away from the defensive approach of trying to lobby Congress over reforms to the seed law, and explore a more offensive strategy such as our emerging proposal to create a parallel open-source system. Much of our earlier work in the project involved trying to persuade many initially reluctant actors that our alternative way of thinking about and addressing our shared focal problem might be viable.

Once Bioleft had been established, we have been involved in an on-going process of reframing as expectations between the various actors directly involved within Bioleft have differed, and as we have collectively tried to align those expectations or at least reach workable consensus. Although all of the people directly involved in Bioleft share the core idea that existing seed innovation systems, dominated by a few large companies, cannot support a more sustainable agricultural system, and that a more decentralised, and open and democratic breeding system is required, there is less consensus, unsurprisingly, about how to build such a system. With what specific objectives, using which tools, through what processes and involving which actors? And how 'open' should seed licences be? How much information can or should farmers register in relation to the performance of the seeds they are testing in order to contribute to the process of collaborative breeding? Should Bioleft charge for certain products or services? Which form of governance is best suited to ensure wide participation and demo-cratic decision making, but at the same time preserve the spirit of the initiative? These are some of the questions we continue to discuss and negotiate, and that to the extent to which we reach some agreement within the team we advance in the direction of creating common expectations. In part, disagreement reflects dif-ferent interests and perspectives of those involved, but there are also competing ways of thinking about, or framing these issues in relation to disciplinary back-ground and between academics and practitioners (especially between scientific breeders and farmers). We do not need to fully agree at every stage with regard to every issue in order to continue developing Bioleft, but we have noted that it is the implementation of ideas in practice that helps to develop shared expectations about what is possible and acceptable. Throughout the whole process, negotia-tion is crucial, as is a willingness to let go of top-down control and direction.

Our collaboration with actors outside of the Bioleft team has also involved efforts to articulate, discuss and sometimes reframe objectives and expectations For example, experience working with the seed breeding group at the University of Buenos Aires working on recovered tomatoes has been a good example of the need to create workable alignments around shared ideas and aims, and the effort involved in doing so. Looking to the future, it will be important to create space to discuss and negotiate ideas about open-source innovation with actors within the dominant seed innovation regime. For example, many domestic seed firms adopt a business strategy based on being first movers in seed innovation, which is entirely compatible with some open-source ideas, at least in terms of the free circulation of germplasm for plant breeding. We think there are strong possibilities to work with such actors, although this will require challenging mainstream assumptions about intellectual property and innovation.

Innovation and alternative pathways

Bioleft was created and developed under the assumption that innovation is one of the main drivers of transformation. The initiative is developing and testing a novel, disruptive way to develop and exchange seeds and information; one that, in clear contrast with the market driven mainstream seed innovation system, is based on cooperation, collaboration and solidarity, and not only on profits (which are possible within this alternative system, but not via the exclusive appropriation of seed germplasm). A key challenge for us has been to think about how seed innovation, in the absence of the legal ability to exclusively appropriate new knowledge (embodied in a new seed variety) can nevertheless work. The key inspiration here is open-source software, and Bioleft, like other open-source seed initiatives in other countries, is exploring how those ideas can be adapted and applied in seed systems.

In order to prosper in the Argentinean context – where the actors and institutions that help to constitute and reproduce dominant agricultural systems are extremely powerful – we were interested in whether a disruptive idea like Bioleft could act as a 'bridging' innovation, linking actors with different ideas, and perspectives on, and priorities about, food and agricultural sustainability. It is not too difficult, for example, to imagine innovations such as an open-source breeding initiative that both promise to support greater diversity in agricultural production with the development of domestic technological capabilities, thus 'bridging' across the priorities of different institutional actors, and creating actionable consensus. This seemed important because we wanted to create alliances between actors that possess different resources, able to bring in and link the skills, knowledge, political support and markets that will be needed if more sustainable and socially just, but disruptive, pathways of change are to be politically and practically viable.

Initially we tried to interest people in open-source seed breeding ideas who held very different views of the problems posed by seed market concentration and agricultural intensification, such as the domestic seed industry trade association (which represent both large and small seed firms), but here we failed. We did however find that the idea of an open-source seed breeding initiative resonated with university-based seed breeders, rural NGOs, agro-ecological producers, and scientists from the government's agricultural research service. We subsequently found that farmer-breeders, organic farmers who produce for export on medium-sized farms, small seed firms in the organic and biodynamic sector, and farming associations representing small family farmers, were also interested. This coalition of actors and institution provided the basis upon which we began discussing and developing Bioleft. There are three reasons why we think we managed to interest those different groups of actors, even though they might not necessarily agree on what a more sustainable agricultural system might look like, or what the priorities are for achieving a more sustainable agricultural system.

First, the open-source idea behind Bioleft is appealing because all those groups want to ensure that useful seed varieties and traits bred by the public sector and by farmers themselves are not captured by large seed firms in the future, which would restrict their widespread use for breeding, irrespective of any divergent views about what a more desirable set of future agricultural practices should consist of. Second, open-source seed innovation is interesting to actors who want to sell or provide new seeds, to those who are primarily interested in ensuring unrestricted access to seeds, and those interested in expanding crop biodiversity. Third, an institutional innovation like Bioleft is compatible with the existing mainstream seed breeding system and with the associated legal structure based on strict intellectual property rights. It can be accommodated without major changes to the *status quo* even though, as we would argue, it is quite a radical idea and suggests a transformative change in the ways seeds are created, shared, sold and used.

The key more general point here and one that we think is interesting is that innovations that can 'bridge' divergent perspectives on sustainability play an important role in forming alliances between different interests, and thus help to reconfigure social relations around socio-technological systems in ways that can open up space for more sustainable pathways of change.

Networks, alliances and collective agency

We have put considerable effort into forming alliances with a range of people and institutions as we have developed Bioleft, and of embedding Bioleft within wider networks. This has been key to making the initiative begin to work. At the beginning of the project, with only a handful of social scientists as part of our core team, and some limited funding, it was clear we lacked the capacity to take the idea of an open-source breeding initiative very far. This was especially so given that none of us were central actors in either the mainstream Argentinean seed system or the various social movements that sought to challenge that regime (although we had good contacts in each of these, mainly through previous research work).

We therefore sought to expand our core team to include people with different sets of skills and knowledge, and that were involved in wider seed and agricultural networks of various kinds. Over the period from 2015 to 2019 we slowly added diverse people both from within and outside academia to our core team, with expertise in agronomy, intellectual property law, journalism, plant breeding, agricultural extension, anthropology, economics, and software programming as well as farmer-breeders, representatives of farmers organisations, and a manager of a small seed firm (see Figure 6.2). We have also worked intermittently with designers, a visual artist and a musician. Adding people gradually has been important so as to ensure that we develop a consolidated group, and that we have been able to take advantage of development opportunities as they arise.

It is striking just how broad our core team is, in terms of backgrounds and expertise, and we have learnt that establishing a venture, such as Bioleft, from scratch really does require such diversity. This might not be news for entrepreneurs starting a new business or non-profit organisation, but from the perspective of traditional academic-led research it has been an eye-opener, despite the contemporary emphasis on the importance of transdisciplinary work. Early on in the initiative, it was obvious that we would need people with expertise in agronomy and intellectual property law in order to be able to understand plant breeding, to communicate with and enrol breeders, and to develop an open-source licence in a way that worked within the framework of domestic legislation and practice. We subsequently realised that communication would also be vital, in part so as to gain support from different kinds of communities (and so we employed a journalist, who was already working on ideas around commons, and worked closely with a filmmaker). By 2017 we also managed to persuade a senior university plant breeder, an extension worker and two farmer-breeders to work with us, which has been key, not only for their expertise, but also their access to plant breeding and farming networks.

People on our core team have either given their time voluntarily (which has been a little easier for those employed by universities, with relative flexibility as to how they allocate time) or were paid for part-time work, or have worked with us as part of a funded doctoral programme. We raised a small amount of additional funding, beyond the end of the initial project, which has been vital to enable some of our team to be paid, and for our fieldwork costs. Critical to our ability to enrol a transdisciplinary group is that people have been very enthusiastic about and ideologically committed to the ideas behind an open, collaborative form of production (and so willing to gift their time to the initiative or exchange it for less money that they could earn elsewhere). We have also run Bioleft in a relatively non-hierarchical manner so that people who participate in the core team feel they have agency to influence how the initiative develops, which has helped enthuse people, and persuade them to continue working with us.

Beyond developing our core team, we have also put a lot of effort into creating a wider network of support with potential allies, and of linking Bioleft to existing, broader seed and agricultural networks. Those potential allies and wider networks include domestic actors, such as government departments, seed banks, alternative farming associations and rural social movements and existing networks of public sector plant breeders interested in, say, breeding in fodder crops (as shown in Figure 6.1). They also include international bodies such as overseas

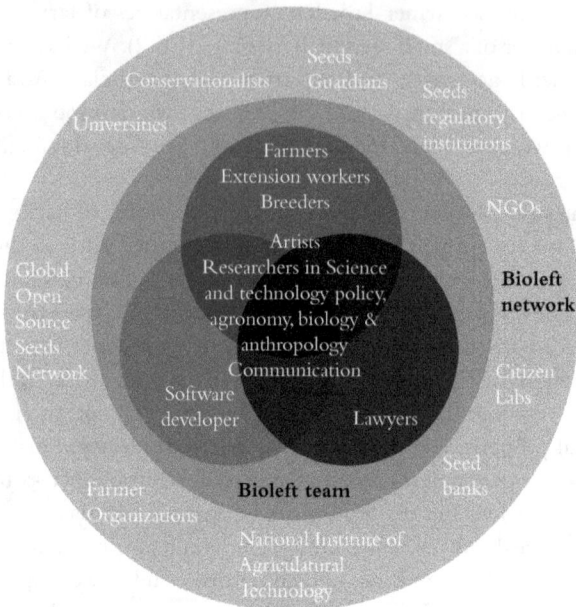

FIGURE 6.1 Alliances and network expansion.

universities and global funding agencies working on sustainability issues, and a global network of open-source seed initiatives, which one of us from Bioleft currently chairs.

In building that wider network of support we learnt two things. First, it was more productive, in the early stages of the project, to try and enrol people and institutions who shared our overall perspectives on the problems with existing seed systems, and the values implicit in open-source solutions. Very early efforts to try and work with more diverse groups did not work well, as described earlier in this chapter. Yet, once Bioleft was operating, in the sense that we had begun releasing new seed varieties, working with institutions such as the National Institute for Agricultural Technology, the National Seed Registration Authority, and some medium-sized domestic seed firms, was more productive because we were able to demonstrate the ideas behind Bioleft. Figure 6.2 shows the sequence of our engagement strategy followed in this respect, with an initial attempt to talk to and collaborate with a heterogeneous group of people and institutions, followed by a narrowing down to a more aligned group, and finally broadening once more.

The second issue we learnt was that given few resources on our part, in terms of both funding and core team members, it was important and useful to try and find, and take advantage of, synergies with other, existing initiatives and networks on seed breeding in order to advance our project. For example, by col-laborating with existing public sector breeding initiatives, for example, on open

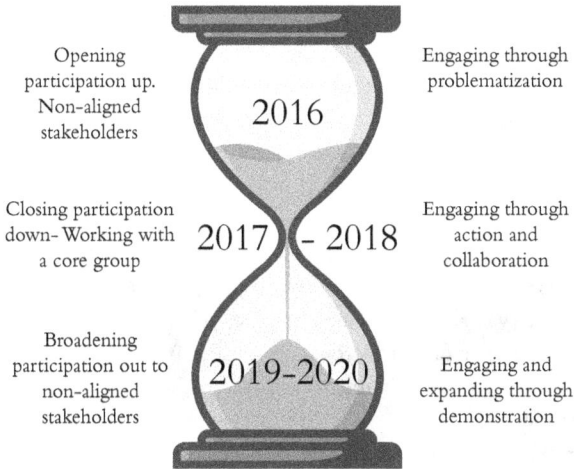

FIGURE 6.2 Bioleft engagement strategy.

pollinated maize and tomatoes, we could begin to test whether our open-source licences might work in practice, as well as enlarge the community of people working with Bioleft.

During the early phases of developing Bioleft we were not very influential within the Argentinean seed system. While actors within the mainstream seed system (for example, established seed firms, seed trade associations and agencies within the Ministry of Agriculture) did not view us as a direct challenge to the *status quo,* for the reasons we described earlier in this chapter – for example, we were not campaigning to change existing intellectual property law – ideas about open-source innovation were nevertheless met with scepticism. In part this was because it was not clear that there was a viable business model behind the idea of Bioleft. At the same time, many actors who have traditionally resisted mainstream seed systems were distrustful of our initiative. Here campaigners had typically sought to preserve farmers' rights to save and reuse seed, and were hostile to any system of property rights. Since Bioleft proposed to use contract law and existing intellectual property law to mandate sharing people were suspicious.

Our agency to influence other actors and nurture change, as a group of people collaborating in the development of Bioleft, is in part individual, and in part the collective actions of our team and other actors within the networks which we are part of. At an individual level, influence varies depending on the different kinds of expertise, authority and contacts that members of our core team possess – in relation to any given topic or issue. For example, one plant breeder, who became part of our core team in 2017, was very well regarded and influential, both within the national plant breeding community, but also within parts of national government with whom he had previously interacted closely. His presence as part of Bioleft was key to ensuring that other plant breeders turned up to events and became interested in working with us, and in opening avenues to contacts within government and other public sector institutions, and persuading those actors to take the initiative seriously.

The collective agency of our initiative is more difficult to identify and understand. In part, it appears to be a product of the combination of appropriate kinds of expertise, contacts, and then actions, of the core team as whole, as well as the ways in which we have managed, or otherwise, to work together and with people in our wider networks. For instance, we were only able to work effectively with an open-source software company – which we had contracted to work with us – once we also employed a programmer within our core team. The programmer was able to understand the kinds of things that the breeders and farmers within our group were interested in and to then translate these in interaction with the software firm, in ways that other members of the team had been unable to do successfully.

In another example – where we failed to persuade others to work effectively with us – we co-organised a seed fair in 2018 in the north of Argentina with organisations belonging to two national associations representing family farmers, hoping to enrol those organisations into Bioleft. Even though we had planned the event with representatives of the national associations, who were enthusiastic about Bioleft, only a handful of representatives of farmers' organisations participated, and with their own agenda, which bore little resemblance to our plans. A lack of prior interaction with family farmers' organisations, and some misunderstandings and poor communication within our networks contributed to those difficulties.

Another way in which we can understand the source of Bioleft's collective agency, and we think an important one, is as a result of the practical demonstration of our ideas. By releasing new open-source fodder crop varieties, maize varieties and ancient tomato varieties with an open-source agreement, and generating media coverage about those initiatives, we have encouraged plant breeders, farming organisations and an interested public to join the initiative and experiment with us in ways that merely writing or talking about a new idea could never match. For example, the government agency responsible for registering seed varieties is willing in principle to find a way to allow 'informal' seed varieties released with a Bioleft licence to become legally registered – something that would undoubtedly be far more difficult if Bioleft was just an idea on paper. Of course, writing and talking about new ideas remains important in trying to persuade the academic community, policy-makers and other stakeholders about how best to think about problems, and about how they might act on them. But by doing so, alongside socio-technical experimentation, those activities become a more powerful source of agency.

Specific insights from the Argentinean case

We conclude by highlighting some of the key things we have learnt about the process of developing Bioleft. First, is that both social and technological innovation are central to processes of system transformation. The sustainability transitions literature has always emphasised that while new kinds of technological artefacts may provide opportunities to solve social problems in a more sustainable way, those artefacts cannot be meaningfully separated from the novel or reconfigured social processes that – in combination with new artefacts – constitute an innovative technological practice. Attention in sustainability and innovation policy nevertheless often tends to focus mostly on creating material novelty, as if unsustainable material artefacts, such as chemical pesticides, are the fundamental problem, rather than the social institutions and practices that have evolved to create and support the use of those artefacts. Our experience with Bioleft underscores how new ways of organising activities, with new more sustainable logics and principles, and that motivate and mobilise different kinds of actors, are for us the key innovation in thinking about reconfigured seed systems. Novel artefacts, in the sense of new kinds of seeds, and then perhaps in the longer term and indirectly, reconfigured agricultural production practices, flow from those new social practices.

A second thing we have learnt is that the kinds of social innovations Bioleft has been experimenting with need to be disruptive in order to offer a more sustainable pathway of change; they need to try and build an alternative, based on a different, imagined future. Doing so is difficult, not least because the kinds of actors that need to start doing things differently, such as plant breeders, agricultural extension staff, regulators and farmers, work and operate within existing structures and institutions for organising seed breeding and production. A novel idea for doing things in a more sustainable way not only needs to appeal to a relatively wide range of actors with different perspectives, interests and institutional locations (a 'bridging innovation', as we have described it in this chapter) but perhaps more importantly, it is much easier to pursue and develop such ideas if they avoid fundamentally challenging those existing structures and institutions, so that they do not get destroyed from the outset by existing interests. The dilemma here is that novel ideas that do not fundamentally challenge existing structures and institutions often offer little in terms of sustainability. Open-source ideas are a very good example of a social innovation that might be able to finesse that dilemma. They are quite profound in their implications, and offer, at least symbolically, an imagined future that appeals to many people, but they can also operate alongside existing institutions and practices, and do not directly or at least immediately undermine them.

Third, we want to emphasise the importance of transdisciplinarity in building a team of people that are able to explore and begin to develop a research-led social innovation. This is crucial, not only to obtain the wide range of capabilities involved in this kind of action-oriented research, but also to gain access to the diverse communities and networks that putting any innovation into working practice will need to negotiate with and involve. By bringing plant breeders, extension workers, seed firms and farmers into our core research-action team, our initial ideas were tested, contested and expanded to accommodate the views and concerns of these communities. For example, we had to adapt our ideas about the design and content of open-source clauses in order that public sector breeders were able to transfer their varieties with our contracts in ways that fulfilled the requirements of their institutions. We also had to pay much more attention to issues of accessibility and user interfaces when developing our digital platform in order to enable communication with different types of farmers. And in experimenting with participatory breeding, the extent to which knowledge generation can effectively be decentralised and performed collaboratively is an issue that we could not begin to address properly in the absence of the diverse views, knowledge and experience of our transdisciplinary team. As emphasised earlier in this chapter, the ability to demonstrate how an initiative works, even if only as a prototype, is a critical source of agency, for example, in terms of persuading people and institutions to support us and work with us.

Fourth, in building the core team of Bioleft it has been very important, for us, to move from processes of co-design and co-production, as emphasised in the sustainability science literature, to a process of co-ownership. Novel solutions to sustainability problems perhaps not only have to be developed jointly, but they also need to be appropriated by all actors. An imagined future needs to be shared. This, of course, has its difficulties, not least the practical and time-consuming need to constantly negotiate how an initiative like Bioleft should develop, and to relinquish some degree of power over that process.

Fifth, as the socio-technical transitions literature emphasises, and as we have discovered in practice, putting novel ideas into working practice requires that existing institutions also evolve to accommodate those new ideas, which requires the ability to persuade others of new ways of conceptualising problems and the ability to exert political influence. So, in building networks of support for Bioleft it has been crucial not only to consider enrolling actors that can help to build the initiative from within, for example, by bringing in complementary capabilities, but also from the outside, by bringing in people who have the capacity to lobby and influence existing institutions. For instance, new seeds, bred by farmers can only be exchanged within an open-source system if existing regulatory institutions do not penalise the activities performed by small- and medium-sized farmers, on the grounds that those farmers are not registered as seed traders and if the seeds they develop are not stable, unique and uniform as existing regulations require. In aiming to deal with this problem we have had to lobby and persuade the National Seed Institute to consider changing wider regulatory rules to accommodate Bioleft activities.

Finally, we have also learnt that the contexts and cultures in which we have created our initiative are important to take into account when thinking about why and how ideas like Bioleft have been feasible to develop, and whether or not the process and design might work in the same ways in different settings. Argentina is a country where civil society is very active and demanding, and where there is a low level of trust in government. This leads some groups of actors to support grassroots initiatives that could address some current sustainability challenges. As researchers, we took advantage of this and worked as intermediary actors between farmers, breeders and institutions, helping to create a civil society-based initiative with our role as bringing people together, obtaining resources and combining knowing and doing.

References

Barry, J. and Proops, J. (1999) Seeking sustainability discourses with Q methodology. *Ecological Economics* 28(3), 337–345. doi: 10.1016/S0921-8009(98)00053-6

Brieva, S., Ceverio, R. and Iriarte, L. (2008) *Trayectoria de las relaciones socio – técnicas de los derechos de propiedad intelectual en la agricultura argentina: los derechos de obtención de semillas (DOV) en trigo y soja desde principios de los años '70 a la actualidad.* http://xxijhe.fahce.unlp.edu.ar/programa/descargables/brieva_ceverio_iriarte.pdf

Eden, S., Donaldson, A. and Walker, G. (2005) Structuring subjectivities? Using Q methodology in human geography. *Area 37*, 413–422.

Ely, A. and Marin, A. (2016) Learning about 'Engaged Excellence' across a transformative knowledge network. *IDS Bulletin* 47(6), 73–86.

Ely, A., van Zwanenberg, P., Wach, E., Obaya, M. and Cremaschi, A. (2017) Seeding ideas: Knowledge brokering and recombination for agricultural transformations, https://steps-centre.org/blog/seeding-ideas-knowledge-brokering-recombination-agricultural-transformations/, accessed 17/1/2020

Falcon, W. P. and Fowler, C. (2002) Carving up the commons-emergence of a new international regime for germplasm development and transfer. *Food Policy* 27. www.elsevier.com/locate/foodpol

FAO (Plant Production and Protection Division). (2019) *What Are Seed Systems? What Are Seed Systems?* www.fao.org/agriculture/crops/thematic-sitemap/theme/compendium/tools-guidelines/what-are-seed-systems/en

Fess, T. L., Kotcon, J. B. and Benedito, V. A. (2011) Crop breeding for low input agriculture: A sustainable response to feed a growing world population. *Sustainability 3*(10), 1742–1772. doi: 10.3390/su3101742

Geels, F. W. and Schot, J. (2007) Typology of sociotechnical transition pathways. *Research Policy 36*, 399–417. doi: 10.1016/j.respol.2007.01.003

Hubbard, K. (2009) Out of hand: Farmers face the consequences of a consolidated seed industry. In *Farmer to Farmer*. http://www.farmertofarmercampaign.com/OutofHand.FullReport.pdf

IAASTD (2009) *Agriculture at a Crossroads: Synthesis Report, International Assessment of Agricultural Knowledge, Science and Technology for Development.* Nairobi: United Nations Environment Program.

IPBES (2019) *Global assessment report on biodiversity and ecosystem services of the Intergovernmental Science-Policy Platform on Biodiversity and Ecosystem Services.* Bonn: Intergovernmental Science-Policy Platform on Biodiversity and Ecosystem Services.

Kates, R. W., Clark, W. C., Corell, R., Hall, J. M., Jaeger, C. C., Lowe, I., Mccarthy, J. J., Schellnhuber, H. J., Bolin, B., Dickson, N. M., Faucheux, S., Gallopin, G. C., Grubler, A., Huntley, B., Jager, J., Jodha, N. S., Kasperson, R. E., Mabogunje, A., Matson, P., Mooney, H., Moore, B., Riordan, T. and Svedin, U. (2001) Environment and development: Sustainability science. *Science 292*(5517), 641

Kemp, R., Schot, J. and Hoogma, R. (1998) Regime shifts to sustainability through processes of niche formation: The approach of strategic niche management. *Technology Analysis & Strategic Management 10*(2), 175–198. doi: 10.1080/09537329808524310

Köhler, J., Geels, F. W., Kern, F., Markard, J., Onsongo, E., Wieczorek, A., Alkemade, F., Avelino, F., Bergek, A., Boons, F., Fünfschilling, L., Hess, D., Holtz, G., Hyysalo, S., Jenkins, K., Kivimaa, P., Martiskainen, M., McMeekin, A., Mühlemeier, M. S., Nykvist, B., Pel, B., Raven, R., Rohracher, H., Sandén, B., Schot, J., Sovacool, B., Turnheim, B., Welch, D. and Wells, P. (2019) An agenda for sustainability transitions research: State of the art and future directions. *Environmental Innovation and Societal Transitions 31*, 1–32. doi: 10.1016/j.eist.2019.01.004

MacDonald, J. (2019) Mergers in seeds and agricultural chemicals: What happened? February 15 edition of Amber Waves: The Economics of Food, Farming, Natural Resources, and Rural America, Washington DC: United States Department of Agriculture, Economic Research Service.

Marin, A., Ely, A. and van Zwanenberg, P. (2016) *Co-design with Aligned and Non-aligned Knowledge Partners: Implications for Research and Coproduction of Sustainable Food Systems COSUST Special Issue: Co-Designing Research on Social Transformations to Sustainability.* https://core.ac.uk/download/pdf/74226465.pdf

Marin, A., Stubrin, L. and da Silva Jr., J. J. (2015) *KIBS Associated to Natural Resource Based Industries Seeds Innovation and Regional Providers of the Technology Services Embodied in Seeds in Argentina and Brazil, 2000–2014.* http://www.iadb.org

.Miller, C. A. and Wyborn, C. (2018) Co-production in global sustainability: Histories and theories. *Environmental Science & Policy.* doi: 10.1016/j.envsci.2018.01.016

Osman, A. M., Almekinders, C. J. M., Struik, P. C. and Lammerts van Bueren, E. T. (2008) Can conventional breeding programmes provide onion varieties that are suitable for organic farming in the Netherlands? *Euphytica 163*(3), 511. doi: 10.1007/s10681-008-9700-y

Perelmuter, T. (2008) Las semillas en disputa: un análisis sobre del rol de la propiedad intelectual en los actuales procesos de cercamientos. el caso Argentino. *Revista Museos. Es 4*, 1–20.

Phelinas, P. and Choumert, J. (2017) Is GM soybean cultivation in Argentina sustainable? *World Development 99*, 452–462. doi: 10.1016/j.worlddev.2017.05.033

Schot, J. and Geels, F. W. (2008) Strategic niche management and sustainable innovation journeys: theory, findings, research agenda, and policy. *Technology Analysis & Strategic Management 20*(5), 537–554. doi: 10.1080/09537320802292651

Smale, M., Cohen, M. J. and Nagarajan, L. (2009) *Local Markets, Local Varieties: Rising Food Prices and Small Farmers' Access to Seed.* Washington, DC: International Food Policy Research Institute

Smith, A. (2007) Translating sustainabilities between Green Niches and socio-technical regimes. *Technology Analysis & Strategic Management 19*(4), 427–450. doi: 10.1080/09537320701403334

Smith, A., Voß, J.-P. and Grin, J. (2010) Innovation studies and sustainability transitions: The allure of the multi-level perspective and its challenges. *Research Policy 39*(4), 435–448

van Zwanenberg, P., Cremaschi, A., Obaya, M., Marin, A. and Lowenstein, V. (2018) Seeking unconventional alliances and bridging innovations in spaces for transformative change: The seed sector and agricultural sustainability in Argentina. *Ecology and Society 23*(3), art11. doi: 10.5751/ES-10033-230311

7

KENYA

Making mobile solar energy inclusive

Victoria Chengo, Kennedy Mbeva, Joanes Atela,
Rob Byrne, David Ockwell, and Aschalew Tigabu

Introduction

The Africa Sustainability Hub (ASH) has been running since 2015 and has aimed to showcase a model of transformative partnership that harnesses research and policy on the kinds of sustainable technologies and innovations which could inform Africa's actions in the post-2015 Sustainable Development Goals (SDGs). In a crowded global research environment, the hub is a platform of international, trans-disciplinary action-oriented work with a strong focus on practical responses – including the development of new concepts, tools and methods. ASH has accumulated experience in low carbon transitions and expertise in low carbon innovation, as well as environmental policy and governance. ASH has also established strategic linkages with a wide array of stakeholders and actors, including the research community, civil society, government and development partners.

For the 'Pathways' transformative knowledge network (TKN) work, ASH has been pursuing action research focussed on enabling sustainable and equitable access to Solar Home Systems (SHS) for all via mobile-based payment systems, including those who cannot participate in micro-financing schemes. ASH, hosted at the African Centre for Technology Studies (ACTS) together with the other members of the Hub – the Africa Research and Impact Network, African Technology Policy Studies (ATPS) network and the Stockholm Environment Institute (SEI) – has continually aimed at gathering socially inclusive evidence on various sustainability pathways and sustainable technologies and innovations for low-carbon energy transitions that meet the needs of the poor. There has been a focus throughout on research that interrogates whether dominant business models create 'pathways' (towards enhanced access to clean lighting and cooking solutions for the poorest in Africa) (Ockwell et al. 2019).

DOI: 10.4324/9780429331930-10

The basis of the ASH work is built on fundamental sustainability questions in Africa's energy transition journey. Despite efforts around renewable energy alternatives, these technologies have been limited in their penetration into the everyday life of society and especially the poor. For example, bio-digesters in Kenya and Rwanda had been installed at a rate of just 0.3% of the technical potential by 2010, mainly for cooking (Tigabu et al. 2015). This and several other projects are usually characterized by failures to attend to the social aspects of local cultural practices around energy consumption (standing up to cook, using specific-sized pots, etc.), or linked energy services (heating and lighting homes, repelling insects, etc.). With regard to lighting/electricity, even though there is increasing grid connectivity aided by the key government programmes such as the Last Mile Initiative, affordability and reliability of these connections remain a challenge to most people especially in rural areas (Atela et al. 2020). The off-grid solar home systems market has been growing fast, with the Kenyan solar energy market becoming one of the most advanced in Eastern Africa; however, the country is still not sufficiently exploiting its solar energy resources and associated utility pathways (Muok et al. 2015). As of 2015 (at the inception of this project), the leading mobile SHS firm in East Africa (M-KOPA) had just 180,000 households across Kenya, Tanzania and Uganda as customers (Fox 2015). The solar energy has mainly been promoted to replace some of the lighting options such as kerosene, but has not focussed on other utility options such as cooking, where a number of sustainability concerns still exist, given that most people, i.e. more than 70% of Kenyans still using biomass for cooking (Karanja & Gasparatos 2020).

In most of the energy transition efforts, large amounts of resources have been spent on assisting those at the bottom of the economic pyramid to transit from inefficient to efficient energy use, but with numerous sustainability concerns (Ockwell et al. 2019; Negro et al. 2012; Bhattacharyya 2012). We see the key issue here as the relatively techno-centric approaches to promoting the various renewable options in ways that create a path dependency of business models combined with a poor understanding of the socio-cultural and political contexts of these technologies in Africa (Gigante 2016). A pathway to a low carbon economy must be socially responsive and inclusive. More broadly, these technologies need to be integrated into the political economy of low carbon development at both national and regional levels (Newell et al. 2014).

This gives a broad problem space of the access to and payment of SHSs, in particular for low income households, with a goal of distributing and financing models that enhance the equitable access to SHSs. The technological innovations towards renewable energy access in Kenya have continually evolved, bringing about dynamic and varying framings of the problem space and associated transformation.

There has been a broad social recognition of the existence of a problem concerning pro-poor access to solar PV. However, according to the general public, there has been a limited social imaginary of the diversity of possible sustainable and equitable pathways, closing down futures across civil society. This is reflected in the wider media interest in pro-poor solar PV, which has only been addressed in generalities. There has also been a significant research gap around pro-poor solar PV initiatives, with a focus on just a handful of sites (Millan & Atela 2017), without attendance to mobile-payment systems. Likewise, the private sector has only approached pro-poor solar PV initiatives with a limited focus, generally failing to leverage research to assess model effectiveness, in particular around alleviating energy poverty.

The emergence of Pay-As-You-Go (PAYG) micro-finance enterprises is an extension of the pico-solar market, which has developed within the already prominent solar PV market in Kenya that has been present since the late 20th century (Muok et al. 2015). Unsurprisingly, the benefit structure of the technology and business models has generated conflicts – should the entrepreneur or the low-income customer benefit, or both? And how, if at all, should SHS articulate with government strategies for grid-based electricity systems?

There has been little research on this problem space, but the Africa Sustainability Hub has had a long-standing reputation of mediating between research and policy dimensions, providing evidence-based research and policy analysis to enable the engagement of diverse actors. This means that ASH continues to support inclusive low carbon innovations in the space of a Kenyan population with low electricity access, high costs and low reliability. It has been our hope all along that providing a robust evidence base upon which to explore this challenge will facilitate the generation of innovative approaches.

Theory, research and action

ASH started this research process with a Participatory Impact Pathways Analysis (PIPA) exercise to outline the key stakeholders concerned with pro-poor mobile payments for solar PV. This exercise outlined the sorts of actors involved in the problem space, as well as their relative power to effect change and their alignment to ASH's proposed solution. As can be seen in Figure 7.1, the PIPA (carried out at the inception workshop in April 2016) identified a high number of concerned government actors, who alongside the private sector were identified as the most powerful stakeholder sectors.

Like other hubs, ASH applied the transformation laboratory (T-Lab) approach throughout the research, which involved a diverse cross-section of stakeholders. This aimed to generate rich and diverse insights into what needs to be done or changed to enable equitable and sustainable access for all to solar PV systems via mobile-based payment systems. The T-Lab process in particular was seen as critical to the project because of its key focus on transformation. This challenges the dominant approach of holding discussions that usually end up as 'talk-shops'. Additionally, the Kenya hub from the outset planned and integrated cross-learning with the China Hub (Chapter 8).

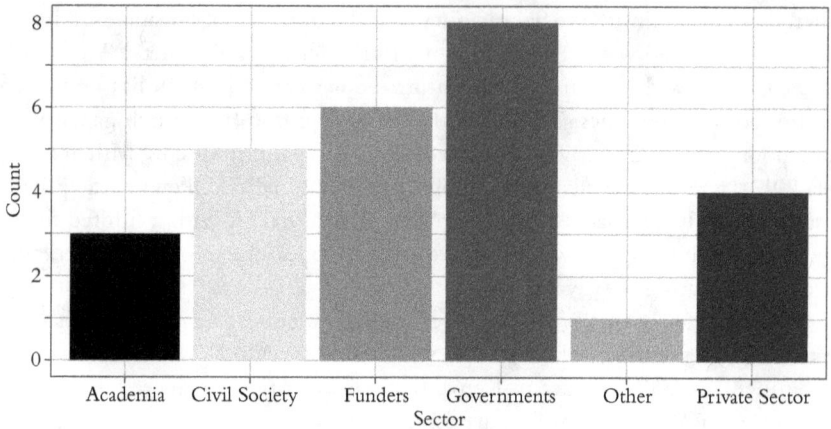

FIGURE 7.1 Envisaged stakeholder engagement in the PAYG solar market, based on a PIPA exercise (April 2016).

To achieve the aim of generating an evidence-base on whether mobile-based payment systems for SHSs as an innovation can be transformative, a broad process methodology was outlined. This process aimed to start with a baseline field study that included mapping out the problem space and initiating a process of participatory engagement, "opening up" pathways to transformation, interacting to cross-pollinate perspectives, and closing down on possible futures to guide to the core issues. Eventually, a build-up of insights from the first T-Lab workshop in Kenya evoked a process of iterative evaluation that led to the presentation of a synthesis of the evidence base, in which stakeholders would enrich the process.

Key moments in the T-Lab process

The T-Lab process was identified as a useful methodology for this problem space because of: a) its complexity; b) conflict over the space; c) an urgency for solutions; and d) the chance to build a practical transformation. Its complexity derives from the diversity of divergent actors, often with similar overall missions but differing policy solutions. This has emerged as a central conflict, with governmental preferences for on-grid expansion clashing with a private sector focussed on fiscal policy. Nonetheless there is a strong sense of urgency, with government stakeholders taking seriously their obligations to low-income households, and a vibrant private sector keen to do business and enhance access to energy.

While there is a general consensus on the need to scale access to electricity, especially to low-income households, there has been little effort towards making existing initiatives complementary. For instance, the national government funded and supported a project to instal SHSs in public schools but was ambivalent about developing robust policies to support the broader solar sector. This was primarily so due to the fact that it involved a project implemented to support the rollout of solar laptops in schools (Standard 2016). On the other hand, the private sector has been working on enhancing access to electricity through mobile payment systems, but the government has not made any explicit engagement to support such projects, within a broader antagonism to solar energy. This was a central paradox that ASH aimed to unravel at the T-Lab workshops, facilitating dialogue on how the different approaches can be made more mutually beneficial.

ASH integrated the T-Lab process into her other existing initiatives, in particular those related to energy access and the broader political economy of low-carbon transition. The hub aimed at using the T-Lab process to unearth the barriers and opportunities to transformative change in access to energy, thus informing the design of other projects.

T-Lab workshop 1

The first T-Lab workshop for the Africa Sustainability Hub was held over two days in early 2017 in Nairobi, Kenya, engaging 18 participants/actors drawn from across different sectors such as the government, academia, NGOs, private sector, technology agencies, end users, and the media. These actors were identified based on broad criteria including institutional diversity, experience and capacity, influence and networks.

Open discussions were first held as an attempt to frame the overall problem by bringing stakeholders into the same space. This was followed by a process of opening up the discussion using two rounds of the *World Café* method (Estacio & Karic 2016). This is a creative, simple, effective, and flexible process for leading a collaborative dialogue with a large group of participants, where knowledge is shared within smaller groups. Participants are invited to discuss a topic of mutual interest in three or more rounds of conversations, with each member of the group moving to a different new table at each round. This method is effective in bringing together individual ideas into one comprehensive message.

The first *World Café* allowed for a more detailed discussion among groups of participants, thus generating more insights into the sustainability challenges facing mobile enabled SHS, but also allowed for building consensus on various issues towards closing down. The second *World Café* generated options for addressing these challenges and the institutions and actors relevant to pursuing these options through a Participatory Impacts Pathways Analysis (PIPA) process. After each group outlined their understanding of the problem and attendant solutions, they moved around other tables at timed intervals to make inputs on the different aspects. This allowed for a final deliberation at the end of the workshop to identify divergent and convergent perspectives, upon which concrete steps of engagement could be outlined. Concurrently, PIPA exercises were deployed throughout the workshop. The outcomes of such options were documented in various forms (written and digital outputs) thus forming the basis for the subsequent T-Lab workshop.

Overall, the first T-Lab workshop provided a number of preliminary insights into the problem space, explored in detail in the technical report that emerged from the event. This included an appreciation of the broader policy landscape for solar in Kenya (and a list of policy documents relevant to solar energy in Kenya – see Table 7.1) and an exhaustive menu of sustainability challenges and concerns facing mobile-enabled SHS. The workshop identified no less than seven perspectives on transformation, illustrating the breadth of discussions. A community of practice emerged from these discussions and was sustained throughout the T-Lab process.

TABLE 7.1 Policy documents relevant to solar energy in Kenya (2016)

Policy	Focus
Kenya's constitution, 2010	Clean and safe environment as a basic right
Kenya Sustainable Energy 4 All action agenda	Clean and sustainable energy for all social groups with 80% from renewable sources such as solar
Kenya Climate Change Action Plan 2013–2017	Targets renewable energy, e.g. solar wind to meet as one of the priority low carbon development pathway.
Kenya Nationally Determined Contributions	Prioritizes renewable energy, e.g. solar wind to meet mitigation commitment under the Paris Agreement
Kenya Climate Change Act, 2016	Supports energy conservation, efficiency and use of renewable energy
Feed-In-Tariffs Policy on Wind, Biomass, Small-Hydro, Geothermal, Biogas and Solar Resource Generated Electricity, Revised in 2012	Provides tax incentives for imports on renewable energy
Second Medium-Term Plan (MTP) of Vision 2030	Supports investments in renewable energy, i.e. 70% of energy investments from renewable sources
Kenya Green Economy Strategy and Implementation Plan (GESIP), 2016	Prioritizes solar energy and other renewables as part of green economy transition
Least Cost Power Development Plan (LCPDP), 2011–2031	Highlights that solar is suitable for off-grid but not on-grid electricity generation
Energy Act, 2006	Supports a diversity of energy sources including renewables to meet Kenya's energy demand
Rural Electrification Master Plan	Aims to connect all Kenyans to electricity
National Environment Policy, 2013	Supports clean energy such as solar – supportive to clean environment

Enhancing the reach and scale of the mobile solar payment systems was found to be critical to having a bigger impact footprint. It was crucial to bring in sector players and stakeholders across different levels of the private and civil society actors, to broaden engagement up and outward from their initiatives. In the same breath, engaging universities, innovation centres and technical education facilities helped to tap into home-grown research knowledge and innovations, to enhance the mobile payment systems and increase the transformative footprint. Broadening out to include regulatory agencies such as the National Environment Management Authority (NEMA) allowed the hub to shape effective policy and innovation interventions around specific issues such as e-waste. The end user involvement beyond usage was noted as critical in enhancing the transformative impact of the mobile solar payment systems. Constant engagement with device distributors and other private sector actors such as solar solutions providers and the end users helped to sensitize the local communities to the products and broaden the discourse to include access to clean energy. It was found that this enhanced the acceptability and ownership of the initiatives. Towards this end, efforts to enhance interventions through inculcating innovation systems among the community of practice provided solid ground for the preparation of the second T-Lab, as well as allowing the hub to translate transformative narratives into concrete interventions that can be evaluated and measured.

Initial insights from the first T-Lab focussing on the case of M-KOPA (M meaning 'mobile' and KOPA meaning 'to borrow') revealed that the mobile PAYG approach, within a period of less than five years, had so far connected about 330,000 homes (mainly the rural poor) in East Africa to solar power and about 500 new homes were being added every day. The second T-Lab was therefore designed with M-KOPA in mind, to suggest piloting the changes suggested, analysing more pay-as-you-go systems, and having more field research. The T-Labs are a process rather than just events, and it was important to engage stakeholders throughout the process. The hub developed different outreach and publicity platforms and approaches, including writing articles in a leading daily newspaper.

At the mid-point survey (carried out between the two T-Lab workshops), three key developments were identified. The first was a change in attitudes, whereby most, if not all, of the participants expressed interest in mutual collaborations, or at the very least engaged in learning the problem space. The second was a more specific set of participant to participant engagements, such as a county government official negotiating with a PAYG merchant on the use of the products in their county. Third, there was a growth in the understanding of various socio-economic contexts and applications, as well as a commitment in principle to exploring them within their own specialist systems. It was established that bringing otherwise disconnected stakeholders together helped bridge perspectives although more structural changes would take time.

T-Lab workshop 2

The guiding approach of the second T-Lab workshop in June 2018 was around combining rigorous academic ideas and analysis with real-world challenges and stakeholders. Particularly important was the recognition and identification of the private sector in the solar energy transformation in Kenya, with an emphasis on the challenges and transformative impact of PAYG services to low-income households in Kenya. Participants were drawn from various sectors including the private sector, civil society, the government – both national and county government entities, academia, research organizations, the media and even M-KOPA, who deliberated on the various perspectives of transformation and sustainability in the context of the SHS space.

After the first T-Lab workshop ("seeing the system" stage), it had been realized that certain issues had to be looked into in-depth to make the whole transformation process successful. In designing the "innovation" stage, the key questions were generated. These questions were not just limited to understanding the broader benefits, governance and horizons and gaps of the space, but they were also concerned with the specific forms of innovations needed, the actually existing policies on the ground, the challenges of scaling up the space and delving into the participants' understanding of a transformative space.

One outstanding feature for the second T-Lab workshop was its focus on the specifics pertaining to the innovation needed. This specificity in research would later see participants in this T-Lab workshop generate specific socio-technical innovation ideas, specific governance approaches, etc., all of which were centred on improving the space.

The methods of engagement in the workshop unfolded constructively, incorporating individual presentations, breakouts, plenaries and *World Cafés*. These created a platform for a great deal of knowledge transfer and idea generation as the expert and diverse groups shared perspectives.

Lessons from the T-Lab process

The project demonstrated the importance and significance of combining innovative and rigorous academic ideas and analysis with real-world challenges and stakeholders. Even seasoned actors in the sector found the workshops insightful and revelatory at times. The T-Lab approach broadened out the research process by including diverse actors with different expertise and experiences within the space, and diversity and heterogeneity of factors was a major feature of both T-Lab workshops.

The T-Lab process moved through four discrete phases. In trying to produce a collective sense of the need for change, there were thorough engagements and interactions between stakeholders at the T-Lab workshops. This was both to keep stakeholders aware of what changes were needed in the space, and to help elicit the views and ideas that underpinned T-Lab agendas. From this, ASH was able to make visible alternative views about the space through stakeholder consultations. These alternative views also helped in "designing the innovation", with some possible solutions given in the second T-Lab workshop. A consensus was then encouraged by managing the different fields of view of the stakeholders, merging their ideas and different schools of thought.

Interestingly, an alignment between research organizations, civil society and academia with the private sector (more than expected from the initial PIPA) was noted. The private sector was seen to have accomplished a lot in the space despite numerous challenges such as a lack of policy support, import taxes, cost effectiveness and the quality of products/standards. The national government and policy-makers were more reluctant in their support of the private sector in the space. This sparked positive criticism of the policy-makers who were challenged to identify good initiatives in the private sector and support them.

Co-production through the T-Lab process was evident from the workshop participation which was drawn from a wide variety of stakeholders ranging from national and sub-national government entities including regulatory bodies; the private sector involved in the mobile-enabled solar trade and energy practitioners; major universities such as Strathmore which hosts an energy research centre, a UK university represented by a research student and other research organizations; civil society; the media; and PAYG business representatives and end users. This brought together perspectives and competing interests, especially between both the national and county governments and the private sector. Overall, this positively affected the knowledge produced by enriching the diversity of stakeholders and industry players.

Contribution of the T-Lab to outcomes and pathways

The Transformation Pathways project managed to spur dialogue among the various stakeholders in the energy sector, with many of them (including ASH) committing to follow up on aspects of the project closest to their interests. Other than creating alliances, there was recognition of the role of the private sector in the solar energy transformation in Kenya: the T-Lab was a revelatory experience which led to the realization of how challenging and transformative the PAYG initiative had been to the majority poor in Kenya. Although the national government was making some strides in enhancing energy access through grid extension, the private sector was seen to have accomplished a great deal, despite the numerous challenges listed above. As of January 2018, MKOPA had connected over 600,000 homes to affordable solar power (as noted in the second T-Lab workshop report). While the hub did not note a significant change in the stakeholders it did not engage with, alternative views about the space emerged through consultations between the stakeholders. These alternative views also helped in 'designing the innovation' – a series of proposals discussed later in this chapter.

Most participants were very appreciative of the process and described it as transformative in itself, given that it provided a forum for academia, research and policy and industry actors to put their perspectives on the table for a more collective solution moving into the future. The forum opened up opportunities for various stakeholders involved to understand and acknowledge the various transformative work going on in the solar industry, including a diversity of products such as SHS units, solar roofs, solar panels and new stoves. Most participants were therefore of the view that engaging people from different fields helped to unlock the potential for shaping transformation.

Bringing together some of the end users of the PAYG systems saw them discuss some of the challenges they face in the use of the product (e.g. tariff costs/charges associated with the PAYG service providers' customer care calls). These and other challenges identified by the users saw the push for a transformation within the space. In addition, an 'alliance' was formed by the stakeholders joining forces to counter the government's laxity to give the solar industry the due recognition and action it deserves. Beyond the project phase, the ASH research team has also continued to engage the community of practice established through the T-Lab process in other various initiatives that support transformative energy innovations through policy support and capacity building at the subnational government level.

Research methods

The research team had previously used policy analysis, dialogues and social scientific methods to address similar problems. Here, a primary method used was the T-Lab, incorporating the PIPA. During the research scoping, the hub identified key stakeholders with interest and influence in the mobile enabled SHS around policy, business and technology. This initial PIPA was used to form the trajectory for what pathways could be engaged with to enhance the uptake of research outputs.

By building a learner-centred model, stakeholders were engaged throughout. The application and use of *World Cafés* ensured that knowledge sharing and idea generation occurred throughout the process. Personal experiences with the PAYG models were shared, questions were directed to experts, and most importantly, transformative success stories were benchmarked.

The research team built on this with the use of *World Cafés* in which three core structured questions were tackled in rounds of interactive discussions – participants were split into small groups alongside a moderator for each group. The moderators then summarized the key points gathered in the discussions while the group members expounded on the key points and responded to questions from other groups. After all the groups had presented, a compilation of ideas, priorities and actions were made. PIPA exercises were also implemented to provide further insights.

Re-framing sustainability challenges

Throughout the research process, the ASH research team was attentive to the tension between the government's focus on grid solutions and other stakeholders' focus on off-grid solutions. The first T-Lab workshop went a long way in diffusing these tensions as the different stakeholders present were in agreement that the system being discussed had a potential impact in alleviating problems around access to clean energy by low-income households. The process introduced many civil society groups to the problem space, and the research community were able to develop future research programmes based on the work. Further, the private sector actors acknowledged that they would be in a position to expand their scope of definition of impact of the PAYG products to include more socio-economic indicators. There was also a change in the problem recognition within the government. The county and national representatives were keen on supporting mobile payment systems, including pledging to explore with other government ministries how to support the innovation.

The shift from the first to second T-Lab included a clearer focus on the questions that arose from stakeholder engagement in the first T-Lab. This included questioning who the beneficiaries of mobile-enhanced SHS were, how these benefits and barriers were defined across the different stakeholders, and the technologies of governance and innovation that supported the space. The research team was also keen to find out whether there had been notable transformations since the first T-Lab.

A change in the participants' perception on the initial problem was also noted. Aside from the diverse transformational views between the government and the private sector regarding mobile-enabled solar PVs, it was interesting to note that the government, through a World Bank partnership, was spearheading the Kenya Off-Grid Solar Access Project (KOSAP) (KPLC & REA 2017), targeting 14 of 47 electrically marginalized areas. KOSAP serves as an off-grid electrification strategy (though it is not a comprehensive policy) designed to benefit "household, public and community institutions, enterprises and community facilities that cannot access electricity through the national grid and whose use of electricity will replace kerosene and other fuels". Even though the KOSAP project acknowledges the potential of the mobile-enabled PAYG SHSs, it was criticized for alienating the private sector. In light of this, the private sector was encouraged to support the government better in its efforts to advance solar energy access in Kenya.

Innovation and alternative pathways

The baseline study and T-Lab workshops allowed for refining the research questions and opening new lines of enquiry. However, within the broader project research questions, what was apparent was the need to take a comparative approach between the first and second T-Labs. A coherent network of T-Lab participants was created which established a stakeholder map to help refine future research on the same system.

The KOSAP project generated significant debate over whether the government was seeking to undermine or complement investments in SHS by the private sector. Though hailed as a good initiative, the private sector viewed the project as an insecurity. Nonetheless, the second workshop found that this could be the best platform for harmonizing the various transformational views between the government and the private sector. The two could forge partnerships, since the private sector has been in the space for long enough to gain expertise and the government bears the capacity to finance the project and ensure the advancement of socio-technological innovations. A complementary rather than competitive relationship between these actors is needed.

A major observation by researchers has been the poor coordination of activities and actions around renewable energy. Through this process and her networks, ASH established an innovative bridging platform to enhance skill development, capacity building and coordination of renewable energy access and mainstreaming efforts within the devolved county governments in Kenya, as well as in the SHS space. This platform known as the 'County Energy Access Platform' will be comprised of two major components: a virtual hub and a face-to-face forum for knowledge sharing. The platform will support research work, empower county governments in the development of county energy plans, and map out resources and gather energy information. While several renewable energy initiatives exist, there are questions as to the governance of those initiatives. Thus, the County Energy Access Platform will take a transformative approach and coordinate platforms beyond workshops to help counties build technical knowledge. Like other institutional innovations proposed or emerging from the 'Pathways to Sustainability' TKN, the County Energy Access Platform could bridge between different scales and framings in order to enhance uptake of more sustainable technologies and practices. The T-Lab community of practice pledged to support ASH through the platform.

Additionally, the ASH – through the community of practice – will also be keen on influencing policies and embed the pathways thinking via the emerging large energy projects working in Kenya. The idea it to use the thinking drawn from the T-Lab experience to spur a more opened up thinking around renewable energy – not just about access but also about utility options that speak to the energy needs of various social groups especially the poor. One key opportunity the hub is building on is the Modern Energy Cooking Services (MECS) programme – a £40 million (US$50.5 million) UK Aid-supported initiative aimed at promoting modern energy cooking services in the Global South. The hub is supporting this project in Kenya by strengthening the pathways to sustainability thinking through a more inclusive stakeholder engagement strategy that enables bottom-up approach to promoting clean cooking as a niche for strengthening socio-technical sustainability given the vast majority of the poor who still depend on biomass for clean cooking. The programme works through a multi-partner programme of activities – led by Loughborough University in the UK to catalyse the transformation of clean cooking that enables long-term use of MECS to generate inclusive environmental and development benefits for the poor by enabling technological, institutional and market innovations.

Networks, alliances and collective agency

Based on the stakeholder/network mapping in the original PIPA exercise, the first step in this research was to develop an informal network, which allowed for a maintenance of engagement throughout the project. The first T-Lab workshop brought some of this group – which became a community of practice – together. The second T-Lab engaged users of the PAYG models in discussing the challenges faced in the use of the products (including around user experience). These and other challenges identified by the users produced a push for transformation within the space. As is evident from the descriptions above, a number of alliances emerged from the networks involved in the T-Lab process. However, these were not investigated (or the associated changes in collective agency) in detail during this study.

Specific insights from the Kenyan context

This research generated a host of insights. The first T-Lab looked closely at the increased access to PAYG solar PV platforms, how to enhance access to similar investments, expanding the PAYG product range, and ways of increasing knowledge sharing. More broadly, widening the stakeholder engagement with the schemes was brought out to be of key importance.

Integrating more service providers by creating opportunities and platforms was identified as a vital next step. This would create a better environment for innovation, in particular with regard to the product packages available to end users. Further, enhancing access to investment incentives from national and county governments would be crucial for attracting actors in the private sector including solar energy service providers who could venture more into mobile solar service provision.

An organic review of government policies taking advantage of the devolved system is critical to enhancing the transformative reach and impact to the end users, where facilitative measures and interventions by national and county government actors could be used for advancing the actions of sector stakeholders including solar service providers, mobile solar payment actors and civil society. Across Kenya's energy policies, the distribution of functions and powers between the national and county governments creates two distinct, albeit connected spaces in which PAYG solar services can now operate. This structure informs the governance approaches that could potentially elevate the mobile-enabled PAYG SHS space. County governments are responsible for developing individual county plans, as well as reticulation of energy services and regulation of said services. Given the barriers to the integration of the mobile-enabled PAYG SHS sector into the national policy regime, the autonomy afforded to county government in terms of energy services is a great opportunity for the PAYG enterprises. The potential for partnerships between enterprises like PAYG businesses and county governments in expanding energy access is great, particularly with the drafting of the County Integrated Development Plans by each of Kenya's 47 counties.

Additionally, it is important to harness frameworks including legal and policy mechanisms that increase the space for engagement and innovation, helping to enhance traction and penetration of innovative renewable energy solutions including the mobile solar payment mechanisms among target communities. The *M-KOPA* solar energy company (among many other companies) comes out as a great case study that has transformed the energy innovation ecosystem in Kenya especially for the off-grid and low-income households. The system relies on the *M-PESA* (where M stands for mobile, *PESA* means money) technological platform, offered exclusively to *Safaricom* mobile network customers (*Safaricom* is a leading mobile network provider in Kenya, partially owned by the national government). The mobile money system leverages the increasing number of households owning mobile phones and being able to access financial services, especially in rural areas with limited banking services (Chengo et al. 2019).

The packages offered by the mobile solar payment service providers ought to be more product-oriented on top of focussing on household items, thus encouraging income generating activities, which would enhance the transformative capacity of the products. In this regard, expanding the product range in addition to the scope of users in order to spur income generating activities is necessary. This can be done through augmenting products that come with the device from household-oriented items to production-oriented items, while engaging critical players such as grassroots SMEs to spur transformation through poverty alleviation. Evidence from studies on the impact of these technologies within Kenya indicates that developmental benefits associated with solar electrification are linked to the use of "connective" devices (Byrne et al. 2014). The economically productive impact of off-grid solar PV in Kenya is generally marginal; however, the use of solar-generated electricity to power appliances such as televisions, radios or charging cellular phones increases the interconnections of people to markets and the cultural hubs of urban centres. Rolffs et al. (2015) claim that despite the growth of the sector and dissemination of mobile-enabled SHS, there has been relatively little impact on the energy access figures in Kenya, despite the country being one of the largest per capita markets for SHS in the world.

Enabling knowledge sharing by having cross-sector players engage is important in expanding the breadth and depth of these initiatives. This could spur innovative solutions among different actors in the value chain that would enhance the end user experience, involving clean energy entrepreneurs, innovation hubs and solar energy providers, institutions of learning, policy-makers and the end users in taking advantage of the knowledge and research that has been done in solar energy services to spur collaborative actions and initiatives which would have a bigger transformative impact.

It can be argued that clean energy entrepreneurs and sector players could also engage alternative funding mechanisms in order to enhance their involvement in renewable energy access and in particular solar energy solutions.

In terms of actors that are key to these innovations, interventions around the sustainability of solar PV systems through the T-Lab approach involved engaging state actors at national and county levels. This includes a range of state departments such as environmental control agencies, safeguard agencies, energy regulatory bodies and climate change departments among others who are critical in regulating both domestic and international solar processes.

On the other hand, in the Kenyan context, non-state actors such as advocacy groups, the private sector, SMEs, NGOs, grassroots movement also have an enormous role in contributing to sustaining the transformations of mobile enabled systems. The private sector players are critical in supporting economic transformations and associated challenges through diversifying credit sources for poorer households, diversifying solar products to match the needs of all, including the poorest of the poor, in each setting. Also critical is the involvement of local grassroots end user communities who are the consumers of these products. Further, the media could also play a key role in bridging the information gap that exists between the users, producers, policy-makers, and distributers of solar PV systems to enhance transformation.

The Transformative Pathways to Sustainability research project brought out insights into the conflicts within transformative spaces, and the importance of decentralizing policy-making. Bridging the gap between policy-making processes and transformative initiatives in the SHS space thus becomes critical. The private sector needs to push for redress of policy frameworks to support the SHS space through existing forums such as the Kenya Private Sector Alliance (KEPSA). In one way or another, through KEPSA, initiatives spearheaded by the private sector would gain legitimacy and attract support from the national government.

Given that many other policy initiatives term the private sector as crucial to the successful expansion of the energy sector, and that the national government has been attempting to alienate the private sector through the KOSAP Project, factors that would create a complimentary environment between government and private sector, as opposed to a competitive one, need to be researched further.

The gap between policy-making processes and initiatives on the ground remains a subject of debate which can also be probed further. It is time to shift focus from the national government policy frameworks to those within county governments in Kenya which are better placed to address the pertinent issues on the ground around energy access. Nevertheless, it is the mandate of the national government to develop policies and other relevant statutes to which the county policy frameworks have to align with.

References

Atela, J., Leary, J., Brown, E., Chengo, V., Adhiambo, S., Khaemba, W. and Chepkemoi, M. (2020) *Techno-policy Assessment of Modern Energy Cooking in Africa*. The case of Kenya. MECS-UK Working Paper (under review).

Bhattacharyya, S. C. (2012) Energy access programmes and sustainable development: A critical review and analysis. *Energy for Sustainable Development* 16 (3): 260–271.

Byrne, R., Ockwell, D., Urama, K. and Ozor, N. (2014) Sustainable energy for whom? Governing pro-poor, low carbon pathways to development: Lessons from Solar PV in Kenya, https://steps-centre.org/publication/energyaccess/

Chengo, V., Leary, M., Atela, J., Mbeva, K. and Tigabu, A. (2019) Understanding the sustainable development prospects of mobile enabled solar systems in Kenya, Climate Resilient Economies Working Paper no. 006/2019. African Centre for Technology Studies. Nairobi: ACTS Press

Estacio. E. V. and Karic, T. (2016) The *World Café*: An innovative method to facilitate reflections on internationalisation in higher education. *Journal of Further and Higher Education* 40 (6): 731–745. doi: 10.1080/0309877X.2015.1014315

Fox, B. (2015) 'Can 'pay as you go' solar light up rural Africa?' *African Business*, 66–67

Gigante, A. A. (2016) Reviewing path dependence theory in economics: Micro–foundations of endogenous change processes, MPRA Paper 75310, University Library of Munich, Germany

Karanja, A. and Gasparatos, A. (2020) Adoption of improved biomass stoves in Kenya: A transect-based approach in Kiambu and Muranga counties. *Environmental Research Letters* 15, 024020

KPLC & REA (2017) Kenya Off-Grid Solar Access Project (K-OSAP), Kenya Power and Lighting Company & Rural Electrification Authority

M-KOPA (2014) Company Overview, http://solar.m-kopa.com/about/company-overview/

Millan, L. and Atela, J. (2017) The untapped potential of solar energy in Kenya: Factors limiting the integration of solar PV into the electricity grid. *Climate Resilient Economies Working Paper 005/2017*. African Centre for Technology Studies. Nairobi: ACTS Press

Muok, B. O., Makokha, W. and Palit, D. Solar PV for enhancing electricity access in Kenya: What policies are required? Policy Brief. *The Energy Institute*, 2015.

Negro, S. O., Alkemade, F. and Hekkert, M. P. (2012) Why does renewable energy diffuse so slowly? A review of innovation system problems. *Renewable and Sustainable Energy Reviews* 16 (6), 3836–3846

Newell, P., Phillips, J., Pueyo, A., Kirumba, E., Ozor, N. and Urama, K. (2014) The political economy of low carbon energy in Kenya. IDS Working Paper 445. Institute of Development Studies, Brighton, United Kingdom: 38 pp. Available online at: http://opendocs.ids.ac.uk/opendocs/bitstream/handle/123456789/4049/Wp445.pdf?sequence=5

Ockwell, D., Atela, J., Mbeva, K., Chengo, V., Byrne, R., Durrant, R., Kasprowicz, V. and Ely, A. (2019) Can pay-as-you-go, digitally enabled business models support sustainability transformations in developing countries? Outstanding questions and a theoretical basis for future research. *Sustainability* 11, 2105. doi:10.3390/su11072105

Rolffs, P., Ockwell, D. and Byrne, R. (2015) "Beyond technology and finance: Pay- as-you-go sustainable energy access and theories of social change. *Environment and Planning A* 47 (12), 2609–2627. doi: 10.1177/0308518X15615368

Standard (2016) First batch of school laptops arrive in Nairobi, all Class One pupils to have devices by December, August 5 2016, https://www.standardmedia.co.ke/education/article/2000210973/first-batch-of-school-laptops-arrive-in-nairobi-all-class-one-pupils-to-have-devices-by-december, accessed 18/8/2020

Tigabu, A. D., Berkhout, F. and Van Beukering, P. (2015) The diffusion of a renewable energy technology and innovation system functioning: Comparing bio-digestion in Kenya and Rwanda. *Technology Forecast for Social Change* 90, 331–345. doi: 10.1016/j.techfore.2013.09.019

8

CHINA

The economic shock of a green transition in Hebei

Lichao Yang and Chulin Jiang

Introduction

China's past three decades of rapid economic growth have brought many out of poverty and expanded energy access considerably. China is today the world's largest energy consumer by volume (IEA 2013). But much of this expanded energy access has been achieved by burning coal: in 2012, around 76.5% of energy production and 66.6% of energy consumption in China came from coal (China Statistical Yearbook 2013), a highly polluting and carbon-intensive fuel. The period has therefore also seen grave costs to the environment and public health. Recent scholarship found that the Beijing-Tianjin-Hebei (BTH, referred to in Chinese as Jing Jin Ji) region experiences severe urban air pollution episodes throughout the year, and especially during the winter heating season. One of the major contributors is coal burning (see, e.g. Wang et al. 2015; Zhang et al. 2017). Beyond such striking, direct effects on human health, China's energy mix lies at the core of a litany of interlocking health, environment and social challenges, from pressures on water supplies to worker safety – and, perhaps most prominently in the international arena, global climate change (Zhang et al. 2017).

Climate change will have highly uncertain and potentially hazardous effects in China, particularly on energy, water and food security. For example, there is the potential for severe water shortages and more flooding disasters. Decades of export-oriented growth mean China's eastern seaboard cities are particularly vulnerable to climate change and sea-level rise, with warming potentially increasing the frequency and level of inundation in delta megacities, such as those in the Pearl River Delta, due to storm surges and floods from river drainage, potentially affecting residents and damaging critical infrastructure in heavily

DOI: 10.4324/9780429331930-11

industrialized low-elevation coastal areas (McGranahan et al. 2007). These hazards – like many others, from desertification to water scarcity – are known to have uneven social effects (Zoleta-Nantes 2002) and will disproportionately affect the poorest in society. Therefore, efforts to move China away from high-carbon energy pathways and towards large-scale low-carbon energy access are crucially important aspect of achieving a transition that addresses climate change and meets the needs of the poor.

The second largest producer of CO_2 (and another direct contributor to particulate air pollution) is the cement industry. Since 2007, there has been a wave of cement plant closures in the provinces surrounding Beijing. This has led to a rapid increase in structural unemployment, in particular for the large number of rural, informal labourers that lack labour contracts. This process of plant closure has escalated since 2013 when the State Council issued a demanding policy on pollution control, which was followed by a series of implementation rules throughout the Beijing-Tianjin-Hebei metropolitan region. By focussing in on the laid-off workers in a local area within this region, this study engages in the social dimensions of green transformation in order to provide a more holistic picture of the transformation for sustainability (Jiang et al. 2018). Currently, social impacts are rarely taken into account in the process of green transformation in China, and a positive step would be to include social impacts into governmental decision-making, something we explored in our T-Lab.

In China, cities represent a higher level division of administrative than townships. Our T-Lab activities took place in a particular township (anonymized here as Township L) within a city (anonymized here as City S) within the Beijing-Tianjin-Hebei metropolitan region. At the outset of the project in 2015, there was not a wide recognition of the problem by different groups. Among the general public, laid-off workers' interests have been largely neglected. Therefore, there has been no reported resistance against being laid-off without any compensations in any form from the laid-off workers, which failed to appeal to public attention. Likewise, within civil society it was overwhelmingly environmental NGOs that engaged with green transformation-related issues. These NGOs were not interested in protecting the economic interests of any particular group of people and therefore the problem was rarely acknowledged in civil society. Within the global research community various aspects of China's systemic green transformation have been analysed, including innovation (Tyfield et al. 2015), political economy (Schmitz 2016) and narratives (Geall and Ely 2015). However, the social impacts of the country's rapid transformation, and in particular social justice implications for poorer and marginalized groups, have largely remained unstudied.

There has been significant conflict within China over this issue. During the last decade, China has released a series of environmental policies which are more restrictive in terms of environmental protection. The implementation of these policies has forced the traditional heavy industries to shut down, especially in the provinces and regions close to Beijing. Tens of thousands of workers were laid-off in this process and their interests were not addressed by policy-makers. This led to a major conflict between the implementation of environmental policy and the interests of lower-class people who were laid-off. Despite this conflict, there has been some media interest; however, this was only reported in a small number of English websites, with few case studies. While there is not a collective sense of urgency for change, there is an opportunity for transformation, starting at the individual level as people become conscious of the issues. The problem is complex, with a lot of stakeholders with different needs, interests and concerns. Further, there is no clear solution and as of yet (at the time of writing – November 2019) there have been no major initiatives to provide alternative solutions.

The hub has been working with the problem since August 2015, when Yang Lichao visited L Township for the first time. Before the first T-Lab, we organized three visits to L Township in August 2015, October 2015 and September 2015. These visits included both participant observation and conducting 55 in-depth interviews with various local actors on this issue. This allowed us to form links with key actors including local government officials, laid-off workers, NGOs, media, scholars and plant owners.

More recently, the government has openly recognized the problem. The Party Secretary at the L Township was anxious to explore pathways towards sustainable livelihoods for laid-off workers in his region, and central government has issued a political command of "creating employment opportunities for local people" (Hao 2018) for both the district and city level. This acknowledgement has been relatively centralized, and according to our fieldwork conducted in 2015 and 2016, local government officials rarely communicated with other actors and stakeholders about this issue.

Theory, research and action

In our initial investigation of the problem space, we conducted Participatory Impact Pathways Analysis (PIPA) to characterize the actors and stakeholders related to the problem, and to assess the alignment and power of these actors. Government (at national and local levels) were seen as the most powerful actors (see Figure 8.1). In terms of their alignment to the research team's vision for transformation, this started off as being lower than other actors such as academia, civil society or private sector.

It is difficult to influence policy-making in China. We therefore invited multiple stakeholders involved in the problem, based in part on the PIPA exercise, to engage in our T-Lab. We wanted to stimulate awareness raising by placing local government officials in a space where they could directly communicate with the other stakeholders, in particular the laid-off workers.

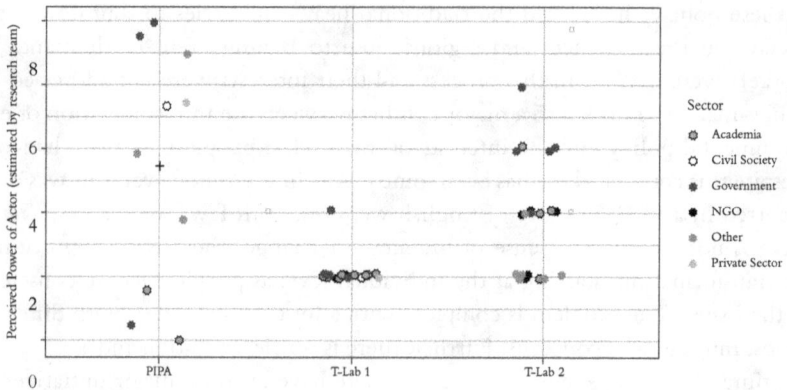

FIGURE 8.1 Plot showing the differences in perceived power of stakeholders mapped during the PIPA exercise and engaged during T–Lab workshops 1 and 2.

While a comparison of the stakeholders we initially identified (in the PIPA) and the stakeholders we worked with at the two key T-Lab workshops would suggest that there was less power in the participants in our workshops (see Figure 8.1), there were a number of key decision-makers involved in the T-Lab process. In our first T-Lab, we invited the township governor and other major decision-makers in various regional sectors; in the second, we also invited the township government officials who were directly responsible for environmental protection and civil affairs. During our first T-Lab workshop in October 2016, we foregrounded the voices of laid-off cement factory workers and ensured that they were heard and their stories shared. Participants realized that there were a lot of groups that had been neglected during the process of laying off workers and it was agreed that China's green transformation should consider not only environmental and economic factors, but also social factors. It was agreed that it was important to consider the potential impact of any reforms on different stakeholders during the policy-making process.

Our project design was not to enact direct policy change through interventions, in part due to China's specific political background. However, we expected to stimulate and foster changes in knowledge, capacity and awareness of multiple stakeholders, mainly through T-Lab. We observed that we had raised the awareness of local government officials and had moved actors to both internalize the issues at hand and interact with one another.

Key moments in the T-Lab process

Our guiding question in the design of the T-Lab has been: what new district government policies can be used to support laid-off cement workers in L Township?

By promoting dialogue and understanding among the different groups, the T-Lab workshops aimed to develop more sustainable pathways that would benefit different stakeholders. During the workshops, participants analysed and discussed: the impacts of green transformation on different people; their major concerns with the green transformation process; the challenges and opportunities that green transformation has brought to different actors; women's triple roles; and the major changes between pre- and post- green transformation. The discussion covered both the big picture of the impacts on different groups and the individual households at a micro-level. Some specific suggestions were proposed in the first T-Lab workshop, such as providing occupational training to laid-off workers so that they could learn new skills. We observed some change in the government actors during the interviews since the first T-Lab workshop. For example, the bureau of human resources and social security provided training opportunities to the laid-off workers after they had taken part in our first T-Lab workshop. They organized some training programmes over 2017–2018, including welding and domestic services, which have directly helped some laid-off workers find employment.

While the T-Lab could not create any job opportunities for laid-off workers in itself, it did provide an opportunity for different stakeholders to work on the same issue together, with different stakeholders sharing their own experiences and perspectives. In particular, the T-Lab process inspired local government officials to include social impacts in their considerations in the policy-making process. The project therefore primarily focussed on creating a sense of the need for change. Through the T-Lab process we worked towards engaging more stakeholders and actors and brought them together in a safe space for them to develop consensus about awareness of the problem and the challenges/opportunities they are facing.

The T-Lab process (especially the direct involvement of officials in processes of deliberation) was a new approach for our research team, and we learnt from the process as participants ourselves. For instance, we found that our initial plan for a two-day workshop was unsuitable as it is unrealistic for government officials to spend two days participating. Considering the primacy of government officials as stakeholders, we amended our workshop design and decided to hold the workshop for just one day. The T-Lab process ended up being a learning experience for all concerned.

T-Lab workshop 1

Our first T-Lab workshop involved 19 participants, of whom 6 were from academia, 4 were from civil society, 5 were government officials, 2 were from NGOs, 1 was from the private sector and 1 was from the media (see Figure 8.1). We conducted the workshop in S City, Hebei Province in October 2016.

BOX 8.1 POLICY/PROJECT IMPACT SIMULATION EXERCISE

Simulation involves the imitation of real-world processes and may be used in education and training, clinical healthcare or entertainment. Simulation is very useful for educational purposes, particularly often used in training workshops. We used a policy/project impact simulation exercise in the first T-Lab workshop of the China hub. The method had previously been developed within the "Good governance" project in Southwest China by Action Aid, and also used in development projects in Guizhou, China by Partnerships for Community Development.

In the exercise, all participants are assigned roles in a hypothetical community. They stand shoulder to shoulder in a straight line, and hear the facilitator read out examples of imaginary policies that will be applied in that hypothetical local context. Then, based on their assigned role and situation, participants react to each policy by either taking steps forward (if they would expect to benefit from the policy) or backward (if the policy would be personally detrimental to them). After some time, the different individuals – who started at the same position – have accumulated varying positive or negative impacts, readily visible through their position in the room. This method revealed individual experiences of change due to different policy/project implementation, including different impacts on women and men. The China hub's adapted policy/project impact simulation allowed all participants to have a vivid view of various people in a community that looks exactly like the one they come from/live. We incorporated gender perspectives into the simulation, and also integrated it into the narrative (forward/backward) exercise that illustrated how particular policies had winners and losers.

We used three facilitation methods in our first T-Lab: interviews with different stakeholders; policy/projects impact simulation (see Box 8.1); and narrative sharing from laid-off cement workers. Through the first T-Lab, we found that the government officials had never really faced the laid-off workers' concerns directly. The T-Lab helped them to really sit together with the workers, so they were able to communicate, hear their voices and experience their emotions, beginning the process of transformation at the individual level. The laid-off workers reflected that it was a great experience to have the opportunity to be heard and to be understood. The T-Lab had helped them to build up a safe space to share their stories. They reported that "they were amazed that some people really cared about their lives". As most of the participants had never participated in a stakeholder meeting, it took time to get used to talking with one another equally. For instance, the government officials had never attended a meeting together with these different types of people and, therefore, they initially looked uncomfortable to openly discuss in the small groups. This T-Lab provided an opportunity to build up a channel for communication. In our evaluation of the first T-Lab workshop, we agreed that we would have liked to invite more female participants, particularly female laid-off workers, and better prepare the policy / projects impact simulation to give a more explicit gender-focus (see Box 8.2).

To move between the two T-Lab workshops, we started by collecting partici-pants' expectations for the second workshop. This included introducing more cases of green transformations, conducting field visits; conducting a case study and pro-viding the research results/outputs to decision-makers. We initially went back to S City for a three-day field trip in December of 2016 to re-interview participants and other laid-off workers. We were trying to figure out the main reasons for the relative silence of laid-off workers' after the factory shutdowns, and the laid-off workers' re-silience in terms of their livelihoods. The research report was written up and shared for the second T-Lab workshop. We then prepared and submitted research proposals to the Forum on Health, Environment and Development (FORHEAD), and ex-changed insights from our research on different forums and platforms engaging in environmental policy and green transformation. We conducted follow-up field trips in late June and early July 2017 to investigate what actions and measures participants took following the first T-Lab. While we did not observe any direct policy changes, we did observe a general raising of awareness in local government officials, which allowed us to focus on further awareness raising in the second T-Lab.

BOX 8.2 THE TRIPLE ROLE APPROACH TO GENDER ANALYSIS

- Draw a "time line" picture that reflects a day in the life of a man/woman. The picture should show the main work or responsibilities that the per-son carries out from the time he or she gets up in the morning, to the time he or she retires in the evening.
- Table for daily routine work done by women and men:

Work done by women	Time of day	Work done by men
e.g. fetch water/wash	5:00am	Sleep
e.g. kitchen work begins	6:00am	Dress and wash self
...	7:00am	...
	...	

- Categorize the activities as (a) reproduction; (b) productive; (c) socio-cultural
- Identify other roles that are not listed and add these to the chart.

Women	Men
Reproductive and household roles	Reproductive and household roles
Productive roles	Productive roles
Socio-cultural/community roles	Socio-cultural/community roles

(Continued)

Then we asked participants to think about:

- Do both men and women participate in reproductive and household roles?
- Are any of the roles in this category performed by both men and women? Who had the greatest responsibility for reproductive and household roles? Men or women?
- Do both men and women participate in productive roles? Are any of the roles in this category performed by both men and women? Who has the greatest responsibility for productive roles?
- Do both men and women play a role at the community level? Are there roles in this category that are performed by both men and women? Who has the greatest responsibility for community roles?
- Which roles in the community carry the most status? Are these performed mostly by men, by women, or by both men and women?
- Which roles are the least respected? Are these roles performed mostly by men, by women, or by both men and women?
- How have men's and women's triple roles changed in green transformation? Are there any gender differences?
- What are the challenges and opportunities men and women have in green transformation?
- How should the government and NGOs support men/women in establishing new livelihoods?

T-Lab workshop 2

The second T-Lab workshop was conducted in April 2018 in the L Township district of S City, Hebei Province, with the specific purpose of "creating the collective sense of a need for change". We engaged 20 participants, of whom: four were from academia, one was a government official, five were from NGOs, five were laid-off workers and one was from the private sector (see Figure 8.1).

We expanded on the work done in the first T-Lab workshop by focussing on seeing the system and preparing for a designed innovation. A great deal of the work was on creating the collective sense of a need for change, awareness about the problem and engaging stakeholders (instead of challenging public policy and bringing the change directly). We spent more time getting to know the different stakeholders by conducting field work and paying them visits. It was a significant breakthrough to be able to interview a governmental official from a key government sector, the District Air Pollution Prevention and Control Office. This is a steering team which mainly coordinates the environmental protection work in L Township district. The interview led to their participation in the second T-Lab workshop, during which they were able to engage with other stakeholders.

Moving between the two T-Lab workshops, we found that most of the participants in the initial workshop could not attend the second. Indeed, most of the participants of the second T-Lab workshop were new to multi-stakeholder interactions using a participatory approach, which meant that more time was needed to create a safe space for them to interact. To build this mutual trust, we conducted collective activities, and as a result, they were able to share their stories and opinions in terms of their lives and green transformation. For instance, the female laid-off workers who had been engaged reflected that they were happy to be heard in front of multiple stakeholders and that the T-Lab workshop had provided an opportunity for them to share their lives and expressed their concerns. In addition, they got the chance to have direct engagement with the local authority so that they could understand the development plans of the town where they live. Such information enables villagers to make more informed decisions around their family development. As the first T-Lab allowed us to accumulate experience in multi-stakeholder interactions, during the second we were more skilled in facilitation and promotion of participation.

Lessons from the T-Lab process

Compared with the initial PIPA assessment, which found a broad spread of alignment across potential stakeholders, the two workshops primarily engaged with highly aligned actors. The power of the actors in the workshops was also markedly lower than the average power of actors in the PIPA, which reflected our concentration on local rather than central actors. In terms of specific sectors, academics were seen as more powerful as time went on, and more powerful governmental actors were engaged with in the second T-Lab. A more powerful set of governmental actors, the District Air Pollution Prevention and Control Office, was invited to participate in the second T-Lab workshop, with great success.

We specifically designed the second T-Lab workshop to include more female participants, and in particular female laid-off workers. Therefore, we invited four women laid-off workers and highlighted gender perspectives in the second T-Lab workshop. The main method used in our second T-Lab was gender analysis. Gender analysis is a socio-economic analysis that uncovers how gender relations affect a development problem (Cai et al. 2017). The aim is to show that gender relations will probably affect the solution or to show how they will affect the solution and what could be done. Gender analysis is an important approach to ensure gender equality and women's empowerment.

We incorporated gender analysis into the project design stage, e.g. by identifying the specific needs of women. We highlighted the gender perspectives and gender analysis tools in this workshop and invited more female laid-off workers to participate, ensuring that women's voices were heard. Through the participation of women, we tried to explore women's specific needs in the process of large-scale lay-off.

A key method in our gender analysis was the Triple Roles Approach. The purpose of this was to identify the different roles and gender divisions of labour in the household pre- and post-green transformation. We divided the participants into four mixed groups and let them fill in the chart of "an ordinary day of my family/household" using the Triple Roles Analysis Framework (Box 8.2).

Using this approach, all participants were able to recognize the triple role of women and realize that women have specific gender needs in this process of transformation. In addition, women undertook more responsibilities post-green transformation. In particular they had to take paid work in factories, restaurants, hotels and other informal service sectors. They undertook more productive roles as well as reproductive roles. The participatory discussion concluded that we should ensure inclusive and equitable quality education and promote lifelong learning opportunities for all, because women are undertaking the roles as bread-winners as well as the men.

All of our project activities, including both T-Lab workshops, engaged with a diverse set of actors drawn from those identified in the PIPA. This included local government officials, scholars, media workers, NGOs, laid-off workers and the cement factory managers and owners. Some small businesses that relied on the cement factory to survive, such as restaurants and hairdressers, should also have been involved in the project. Therefore, we interviewed them and also tried to invite them to participate in the T-Lab workshops.

Beyond the workshops themselves, we were able to co-produce knowledge during follow-up field visits and direct communication with those actors. Both of the T-Lab workshops enabled key stakeholders to interact, and we were able to share our research in different academic seminars.

Contribution of the T-Lab to outcomes and pathways

From the beginning of this project, we identified that the problem was not recognized by civil society, the research community, the media or the private sector. Although it was recognized by the government, there had not been high-level discussions and critically, the major stakeholders had not been involved. The locked-in strategy of the government was to provide new working opportunities for laid-off workers by optimizing the investment environment and attracting enterprises from other regions to invest in L Township. However, this had not been successful, and there was little exploration of alternative pathways. The T-Lab process was therefore a window of opportunity to spark discussion between government stakeholders and a diverse set of actors. We believed if enough input were provided by all actors involved, better solutions or alternatives could be found.

The T-Lab workshop could not help the government attract enterprises or create any job opportunities for laid-off workers. However, it provided an opportunity for multiple stakeholders to think about the problem space and reframe it. It was the first time for the system actors to experience this sort of participatory workshop. As a result, the participants gained awareness of the problem, and created the collective sense of a need for change. They worked together and reframed the problem.

We conducted follow-up field work and observed and recorded the changes following the T-Lab workshops and the interviews. We did observe some change in the government sectors during the interview since the first T-Lab workshop. For example, the Bureau of Human Resources and Social Security provided training opportunities to the laid-off workers (which had been proposed in the first T-Lab workshop), including in welding, and domestic service trainings for women, which has helped some laid-off workers find jobs.

It is hard to identify the extent and nature of change over the short life of a project, or to attribute causality. However, since we are the first group to address this problem and work on it, we believe that our activities have contributed to this change.

Re-framing sustainability challenges

Over the course of the T-Lab, there has been a significant shift in how participants have been thinking about the problem space. The T-Lab workshops increased all stakeholders' awareness of the potential social impact in environmental policy implementation. Local level government officials increased their knowledge and interest in learning about social concerns and crucially, the participants started thinking about how to bring changes for themselves. For example, through the Triple Roles activity, male and female villagers identified their specific challenges in the process of green transformation and clarified their specific needs and presented them to local government officials and others.

The T-Lab workshops provided an opportunity for different stakeholders to work on the same issues together, giving them the chance to reframe the problem at both an individual and group-level. This is key as we believe that real change should be bottom-up, from the individual to group/institutional level, and from the group/institutional to social level.

Innovation and alternative pathways

An important aspect of the work the T-Lab did was to encourage us to provide more information for local governments in helping them mapping out new transformation strategies. Through the process, we helped foster connections with experts in different sectors, such as economists and legal experts. We found that social innovations require the input of all stakeholders, and that building multi-stakeholder workshops with majority-aligned groups can be useful for finding new solutions to complex challenges.

It was important for us to spend time getting to know the different stakeholders throughout the process. We found that bringing together diverse actors contributed a wider set of embodied resources to the project. The diversity of actors involved in the T-Lab workshops and the safety of the spaces we constructed were instrumental in bringing together local government officials and other stakeholders. This meant that government officials, who are often under pressure to provide new working opportunities for laid-off workers using limited/ineffective strategies, were able to communicate with other actors.

The project produced stronger relationships between us as academics and both government officials and local communities. These networks have developed since the project's inception through bringing in auxiliary stakeholders, such as restaurants and hairdressers that relied on the cement factory to survive. Both these new actors included in the project, and the central stakeholders led to the formation of new alliances.

Specific insights from the disciplines, culture and context of the China hub

The purpose of a T-Lab is – in general – to generate innovations that can overcome lock-ins to unsustainable practices and create seeds of change with the potential to have a transformative impact on the broader society towards sustainability (Olsson 2016). In our case, we applied this approach to an ongoing transformation involving the closing down of polluting factories, but focussed on the challenges of ensuring this was done in a socially just way. We did make the participants aware of this problem and – through the first T-Lab – created a collective sense of a need for change. The participants realized that alternative pathways (especially supporting the laid-off workers) should have been considered before the shutting down, and the policy-making should be more inclusive

Transdisciplinary research involving academics from different disciplines as well as other stakeholders such as policy-makers, workers and civil society is extremely rare in China and very seldom reported in the scholarly literature. As such, the approach adopted in this project was relatively innovative and path-breaking. The relationship between social science research and policy is also very different to that in the other countries that form the hubs of the "Pathways" transformative knowledge network (TKN). This is illustrated by the collaborative rather than adversarial engagement with policy-makers in the China hub (in comparison to others), and the subtle ways in which individual-level interactions contributed to changing perceptions in decision-makers, possibly influencing wider processes of change.

We believe the T-Lab is a process instead of a "one time" or "two times" events, and – as explained – our engagement went well beyond the two main workshops. The work of the China hub attempted to make the multiple stakeholders aware of the problem, and tried to build up the collective sense of a need for change through the T-Lab process. We also highlighted gender perspectives in the project activities, such as promoting gender awareness and helping the participants to analyse gender relations, which will probably affect the solution. As the only hub that adopted gender as a central focus of our work, we believe that our experiences are important for the wider network, and for the Transformations community. While it is only one manifestation of the power imbalances that drive particular directions of (transformative) pathways, gender represents an important consideration in both analysis and intervention in our search for transformations that are caring and socially just.

References

Cai, Z., Fan, X., and Du, J. (2017) Gender and attitudes toward technology use: A meta-analysis. *Computers & Education* 105:1–13.

China Statistical Yearbook (2013) published by Chinese Statistics Press

Geall, S. and Ely, A. (2015) Innovation for sustainability in a changing China: Exploring narratives and pathways, STEPS Working Paper 86, Brighton: STEPS Centre.

Hao, F. (2018) Can a cement-making district reinvent itself? *China Dialogue*, December 20. https://www.chinadialogue.net/article/show/single/en/10966-Can-a-cement-making-district-reinvent-itself, accessed 13/10/2019

IEA. (2013) *World Energy Outlook*, November 12, 2013

Jiang, C., Yang, L., Xie, J., and Ely, A. (2018) Research on 'Green Unemployed Group' from the perspective of resilience. *Guizhou Social Sciences* 347(11):135–142.

McGranahan, G., Balk, D., and Anderson, B. (2007) The rising tide: Assessing the risks of climate change and human settlements in low elevation coastal zones. *Environment and Urbanization* 19(17):17–37.

Olsson, P. (2016) The transformation labs (T-Labs) approach to change. Background Report for the Knowledge Network on "Transformative Pathways to Sustainability: Learning across Disciplines, Contexts and Cultures," Stockholm: Stockholm Resilience Centre.

Schmitz, H. (2016) Who drives Climate-relevant Policies in the Rising Powers? *IDS Evidence Report* 180, Brighton: Institute of Development Studies.

Tyfield, D., Ely, A., and Geall, S. (2015) Low carbon innovation in China: From overlooked opportunities and challenges to transitions in power relations and practices. *Sustainable Development* 23:206–216.

Wang, G., Cheng, S., Li, J., Lang, J., Wen, W., Yang, X., and Tian, L. (2015) Source apportionment and seasonal variation of PM2.5 carbonaceous aerosol in the Beijing-Tianjin-Hebei Region of China. *Environmental Monitoring and Assessment* 187(3):143.

Zhang, L., Sovacool, B. K., Ren, J., and Ely, A. (2017) The Dragon awakens: Innovation, competition, and transition in the energy strategy of the People's Republic of China, 1949–2017. *Energy Policy* 108:634–644.

Zhang, Z., Wang, W., Cheng, M., Liu, S., Xu, J., He, Y., and Meng, F.(2017) The contribution of residential coal combustion to PM 2.5 pollution over China's Beijing-Tianjin-Hebei region in winter. *Atmospheric Environment* 159:147–161.

Zoleta-Nantes, D. (2002) Differential impacts of flood hazards among the street children, the Urban poor and residents of wealthy neighbourhoods in metro Manila, Philippines. *Mitigation Adaptation Strategies for Global Change* 7:239–266.

9

WETLANDS UNDER PRESSURE

The experience of the Xochimilco T-Lab, Mexico

Hallie Eakin, Lakshmi Charli-Joseph, Rebecca Shelton, Beatriz Ruizpalacios, David Manuel-Navarrete and J. Mario Siqueiros-García

Introduction

The question of transformation is complex. It involves uncertain, often unpredictable, outcomes in contested spaces fraught with historical meaning, long-standing and often polarizing perspectives on what is "good" and what is necessary for such spaces, and who will benefit or lose out from any intervention. Such is the case with the Xochimilco wetland in the southern part of Mexico City, in the borough of Xochimilco. This urban wetland is the last remnant of the complex lacustrine system that was the basis for agriculture and livelihoods in pre-Columbian times (Morehart 2018). Xochimilco's fate is intertwined in the history of water exploitation, access and use in Mexico City. Prior to the arrival of the Spanish, natural springs fed the wetland, providing a freshwater system supporting significant biodiversity and enabling a unique agricultural innovation, the *chinampa* system. *Chinampas* are artificial islands of rich organic matter, intentionally built up through the excavation of lakebed soils, which are carefully contained by a border formed by the roots of *ahuehuete* trees, planted in rectangular formation directly into the wetland. This highly productive farming system supplied the pre-Hispanic population with food and transformed the wetland into a significant agroecosystem with deep cultural and economic significance (Morehart 2018).

The *chinampa* system continues to be a source of diverse ecosystem services as well as the basis for micro agro-enterprises that supply vegetables to high-end consumers and city and local markets. However, the wetland agroecosystem is much smaller than in the past. Irregular, urban settlements have encroached on the wetland conservation area and contribute to significant contamination of the wetland's water through illicit sewage discharge, together with waste from tourism, agriculture and other activities (Zambrano et al. 2009). Water quality

DOI: 10.4324/9780429331930-12

concerns have undermined fishing and agricultural livelihoods, and threaten the eco-tourism activities of the area (Mazari-Hiriart et al. 2008; Zambrano et al. 2009). The wetland ecosystem nevertheless is recognized and valued locally and internationally as a cultural and historical site, green water infrastructure, and symbol of Mexico's indigenous past and ecological aspirations for the future (Manuel-Navarrete et al. 2019).

This was the ecological and social domain in which the North America Hub working in Mexico focussed its transformation lab (T-Lab) experiment. The numerous interventions that had been made over the prior three decades had largely been unsuccessful in reversing ecological degradation and creating viable livelihood opportunities for those who depend on the wetland's sustainability. Despite the clear value of the area to local residents, its cultural and historical symbolism, and its stated ecological significance for the city as a whole, efforts to conserve the wetland were failing. Our premise was the possibility that *problem reframing* and *new sources of collective agency* might be necessary to find alternative pathways towards sustainability (Charli-Joseph et al. 2018). We proposed a T-Lab as a novel form of intervention that might serve this function.

The problem space

Sustainability challenges in Xochimilco have been long in the making, and are intimately related to the broader challenges the megalopolis of Mexico City, population 21.6 million (United Nations 2018), faces concerning water, poverty, urbanization and governance. Water is highly political and contested in Mexico City, and characterized by significant inequities (Castro 2004; Jiménez Cisneros 2011). The solutions that have been implemented to address scarcity and flooding in the city have often exacerbated social inequities. Natural springs, perceived as the dominion of *pueblos originarios* (villages of indigenous origin on Mexico City's watershed), have been tapped and piped to supply the economic activities and population of Mexico City's urban centre – an action that has left deep resentment in communities that once controlled the use of such springs, and has exacerbated water scarcity (Aguilar and López 2009, Tellman et al. 2018). In Xochimilco, the water that sustains the wetland is no longer from local natural springs, but rather from treated wastewater from the neighbouring urban borough of Iztapalapa.

As Mexico City's population burgeoned in the 20th century, groundwater extraction from the aquifer below the city accelerated, eventually supplying 60% of the city's demand. This exploitation is not sustainable: extraction vastly exceeds recharge and has triggered massive subsidence of as much as 300 mm/y (Osmanoğlu et al. 2011). Subsidence, in turn, exacerbates flood risk – leaving some *chinampas* in Xochimilco chronically inundated. Subsidence and flooding together add to the precariousness of housing, particularly informal housing, which is unlikely to meet urban construction standards, in what is also an active seismic zone.

The challenges of Xochimilco are also embedded within a larger problem of urbanization and access to adequate housing in Mexico City. A lack of affordable public housing in the urban core has pushed lower-income residents to the urban fringe where cheaper land is more available. Low-income families have used informal networks and strategies to build homes where they can: most often on agricultural parcels, or land reserved for ecological services and watershed conservation (Wigle 2010). The border of the Xochimilco wetland, despite its unstable soils and risk of flooding, as well as the *chinampas* themselves, have become sites of such informal expansion (Connolly and Wigle 2017).

As one can imagine, the chronic pressures of housing, water scarcity and flood risk have become significant burdens for urban governance (Lerner et al. 2018). There is little trust among residents of the city and federal water authorities, and many residents perceive injustices in water allocation across economic classes and between residential areas (Eakin et al. 2016). This tension results in mistrust that periodically erupts in protests and civil actions, some of which turn violent (Castro 2004; Eakin et al. 2020). Water resource management is heavily centralized and largely in the hands of authorities who rely on conventional engineering and infrastructural solutions rather than social interventions (Lerner et al. 2018).

Informal residents in the wetland area not only struggle with exposure to flooding and subsidence, but are also villainized in public discourse for not complying with urban regulations and for discharging their sewage directly into the wetland waters. Government-funded infrastructure solutions are also prohibited by law in those settlements considered "informal" or "irregular". Yet corruption is also in play: public officials are not inclined to enforce regulations during electoral seasons and permit housing construction or even incentivize construction by promising that formal public services will follow, if the candidate is elected (Connolly and Wigle 2017). The fishers and farmers who rely on the wetland's ecosystem services, and struggle to maintain their livelihoods, are also often implicated in its degradation through association with agrochemical contamination, mechanization, illicit land sales and construction. In this context, the younger generation – the children of *chinamperos* – are less and less inclined to pursue farming, leaving less incentive for wetland conservation.

While there is broad recognition that the Xochimilco wetland is faced with persistent, often interdependent issues, different groups have conflicting perceptions of the causes and solutions to these issues. Many residents in Mexico City perceive the area to be polluted and degraded, but simultaneously recognize it as part of the cultural heritage of the city and as a site for recreation. For civil society groups, there is a problem of siloed activism, with uncoordinated groups working on different, specific challenges. While urbanization of the wetland is widely recognized as a problem, the dominant narrative and effort has been focussed on ecological conservation and restoration, rather than on the drivers of urbanization itself. Informal and illegal settlements are typically blamed for environmental "bads", yet it is also recognized that informal urban growth is often incentivized through electoral politics.

In light of the multiple agents involved in Xochimilco, the North America Hub hypothesized that a new foundation for collective action in this complex problem space might be needed for systemic change towards a more sustainable future. This foundation would need to be based on reframing the problem from one that is out of anyone's control and driven by exogenous stressors degrading the system, to one in which all agents could see their role in, and capacity for, enacting change. We hoped that the T-Lab process would help create problem ownership, system understanding and the identification of alternative pathways.

Theory, research and action

Our primary objective was to create a space and process through which a small group of diverse actors from Xochimilco could work towards discovering new collective possibilities for transformative action. Our approach thus foregrounded participatory methodologies that were designed to foster alliances among the participants in the process. The T-Lab was designed as a two-year process in which there would be at least two intensive collective interactions among a group of actors (named T-Lab workshops 1 and 2), along with a series of other activities – individual interactions between single participants and the research team or other small group events. No specific project outcome or innovation was envisioned by the research team; rather, our aim was to provide space and facilitate the activities to let collective agency emerge without our control or direction.

Theory of transformation

Our design of the T-Lab was based on the idea that transformation entails internal, cognitive shifts as well as changes in behaviour and institutions (O'Brien and Sygna 2013). We also initiated the activities with the premise that agency – individual and, critically, *collective agency* – is fundamental to any social-ecological transformation. Collective agency is built from explicit recognition and reflection on individual agency and empowerment in relation to the role of individuals as part of shaping and being shaped by a complex social-ecological system (Bandura 2000; Pelenc et al. 2013; 2015). Transformation thus entails eliciting the values, meanings, skills, expectations and understandings experienced by the actors within a social-ecological system (SES); mobilizing existing agency and connecting actors to novel ideas, new actors, new sources of knowledge and understanding; problem reframing; and finally a collective process of opening-up and defining courses of action and experimentation. This process creates an opportunity to make new connections and alliances, and potentially enables actors to feel empowered to engage with existing power structures and processes with new energy and constructive strategies.

Reframing (for details on our project's efforts in problem reframing, see Chapter 11) is about reflecting on meanings and it includes a set of steps: (a) to recognize what is meaningful, (b) to detach meanings from their material support, (c) to question narratives that support a given set of meanings, (d) to create new narratives and connections between meanings and (e) to find new material support for those meanings. This does not necessarily follow a linear process. However, these steps were iterated multiple times during our T-Lab process. Reframing can contribute to breaking cognitive pathways and mental models that limit one's ability to imagine solution possibilities. But we further intended that reframing would result in social learning and the emergence of new solutions. We think that if reframing is achieved through discussion and accompanied by the formation of new relationships, there is a greater possibility that the internal changes that happen within agents manifest in projects and collective actions that impact material, system dynamics.

Fostering collective agency involves engaging with methods that help actors identify their own agency, reflect on what they value in the SES as well as how their own activities and actions relate to those values, find common values with others and realize complementarity in skills and capacities. In reframing the problem, we emphasize the need to focus less on the current material state of the social-ecological system, and more on shared values and emotions associated with the system. In recognition of the September 2017 earthquake and its effects in catalysing action among participants in the T-Lab, we note that external circumstances and windows of opportunity are also critical in enabling actors to reflect and mobilize relationships and engage in new activities towards social and environmental change.

Research methods: observing change and transformation

By focussing on process, rather than a specific outcome, our entire approach entailed considerable attention to and innovation in participatory methodology and group facilitation. These approaches and methods are described in the sections that follow. T-Labs workshops were structured and organized by the research team, but the content was constantly co-produced; we held preparation meetings with participants prior to the workshops in order to get input into the structure, objectives and desired outputs. Consistent co-production along the process, and of the very process, was key to sustain the participants' commitment. This co-production required continuous one-on-one interactions of members of the research team with individual actors in between group meetings, activities, and T-Lab workshops 1 and 2. Concurrent to both these forms of interaction was intensive work by the research team in analysing the data collected in the individual meetings in order to have material to return to participants prior to group activities.

In parallel, we also implemented and designed metrics to evaluate change in agency and problem perception through interviews with participants and periodically repeated exercises employing a method we called "Agency Network Analysis" or ANA, which articulates cognitive mapping and action networks and that is accompanied by Q-Method analysis (Charli-Joseph et al. 2018). These combined metrics allowed us to measure changes in, e.g. how long-established inhabitants perceive new, often irregular, settlers; instead of viewing them as "others" and a "threat", they might now be viewed as potential collaborators. In addition, we have evidence from pre- and post-Q-methodology evaluations, social network evaluations, and qualitative evidence of empathy. The Q-Method (baseline and change) captured learning as changes in individuals' perceptions, and the divergence or convergence of these perceptions within the group. In terms of empathy, we recorded comments indicating how participants learnt to see the system from the perspective of another. An additional indicator of learning and collective agency was simply the continued participation of the actors, and their growing confidence in their relationships with each other (Shelton et al. 2018).

Measuring "transformation" is far more difficult. We do not know whether or when (potentially years) or in what context transformative change will materialize, nor in what form or the extent to which it might be attributed to the T-Lab. Our goal was to create the collective agency necessary as one important ingredient towards system transformation, and our methods of evaluation focussed largely on that intermediate goal. We did, however, conduct follow-up interviews after the second T-Lab and we continue to think about ways in which to understand the system-level impacts of T-Labs.

T-Lab implementation sequence

The project evolved in an organic and dynamic fashion over the course of the two years. While the first activities were intentionally and carefully designed by the National Autonomous University of Mexico (UNAM) – Arizona State University (ASU) research team, we left open the design of subsequent activities to reflect the nature of the group and the direction it would want to take. During this second period, the research team played the role of sustaining, documenting and feeding an emergent process (Figure 9.1).

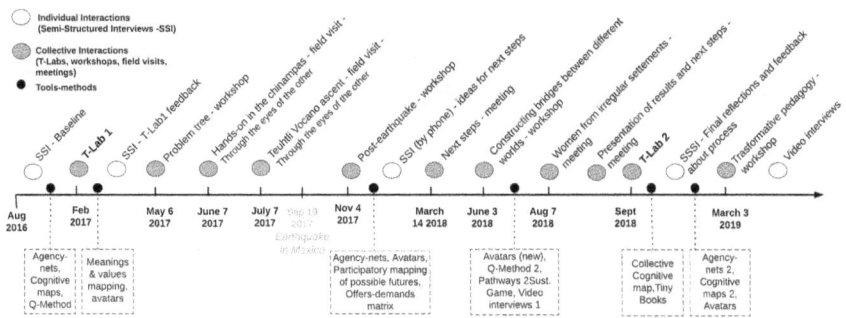

FIGURE 9.1 Individual and collective interactions throughout the process, indicating the first (T-Lab 1) and second (T-Lab 2) T-Lab workshops.

Phase 1: activities leading up to the first T-Lab workshop

Preparations leading to T-Labs are as important as the T-Lab workshop itself and therefore they require the allocation of significant effort and resources. The steps taken and decisions made during this initial phase will determine the entire process and from the outset we conceived of the actual T-Lab workshop as only a culminating moment in a larger process.

To identify and invite individuals to join us in this experiment, we drew from existing literature on sustainability change agents (e.g. Westley et al. 2013) as well as our own intuition. We sought individuals who all together possessed: (a) diverse types of knowledge about the area; (b) influence over other social actors (e.g. through capacity building projects, organized collective work, institutional attribution); (c) capacity and willingness to experiment with different approaches; (d) determination and will to support conservation of socio-ecological attributes of the system; (e) sense of attachment to the place (identity); (f) experience in alternative activities (e.g. organic farming, ecotourism, eco-technologies); (g) solidarity and empathy with respect to other group members and (h) experience working on problems of community development and grassroots innovation. We expected that individuals with these characteristics would be most likely to embrace the open-ended, experimental nature of what we were proposing to do in the T-Lab and would add constructive diversity and/or strategic social connections to the process (Charli-Joseph et al. 2018). We conducted in-depth interviews with 17 individuals identified by these criteria (11 of which resulted in continuing core participants).

A key innovation in this phase consisted of designing and implementing specific methods to elicit the profiles of each agent, articulated in a novel approach

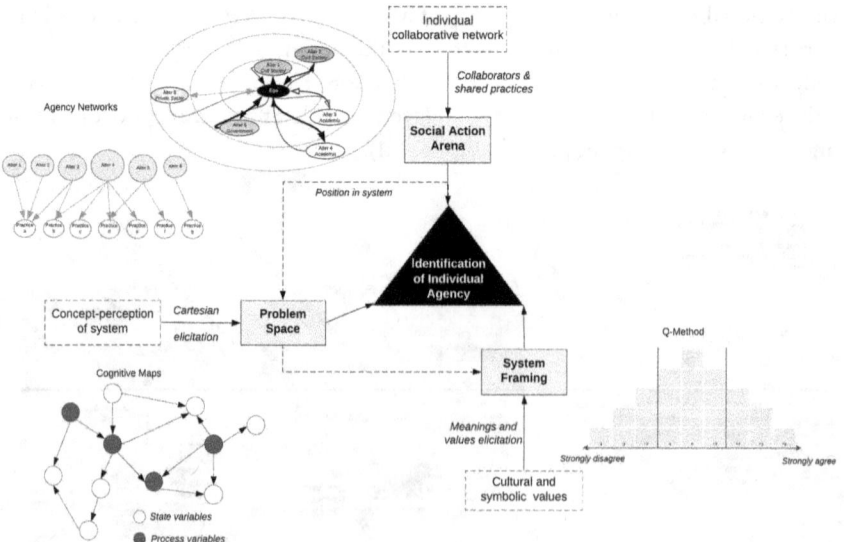

FIGURE 9.2 Profile of actor = ANA + Q-Method.

called Agency Network Analysis (ANA), which enables the visualization of an individual's activities, social interactions and relationship to the social-ecological system (Figure 9.2). The information and baseline data collected through these innovative methods allowed us to strategically design the actual T-Lab interaction.

Phase 2: T-Lab workshop 1

Design

The first T-Lab entitled "A transformative space for the Xochimilco wetland" was conducted over two days in February 2017, in Mexico City, with 11 participants (3 *chinamperos*, 3 residents and activists with informal settlements, 4 members of civil society groups working in sustainable agriculture, rainwater harvesting or ecological restoration and 1 person associated with the federal government). All activities in the first T-Lab were designed to help build trust among participants, and reveal explicit, implicit and underlying meanings, values, and emotions associated with the social-ecological system that constitutes "Xochimilco". It was clear from the interviews that the personal process of accepting loss of geographic or physical attributes of the wetland (e.g. the agricultural land, the *chinampas*, or the problem of water contamination) are a key step in embracing social-ecological transformations (Eakin et al. 2019). We wanted to direct the conversation away from the standard dynamics of non-academic partners requesting more data and information from the universities, and the universities dumping such knowledge on non-academic partners without a real plan for action. We worked to avoid a "blame game" in which the discussion focussed on external actors and how they had created the problems as such discourse may undermine the agency present in the local population. Participants were invited to stay overnight in the retreat where the interaction was facilitated. We hoped that this retreat-style design would encourage casual social interaction over food and drinks.

Facilitation methods

The first day was spent in a series of participatory and tactile activities. For example, each participant created an "avatar" to represent him or herself, with associated "powers" that reflected their particular personal capacities or skills that we had *a priori* selected as potentially associated with collective action and agency (Westley et al. 2013). In small groups, the participants created dioramas of aspects of the social-ecological system that were particularly meaningful to them, discussed what those meanings were and what values they represented, and shared those with the broader group. Collectively, we decided to focus on examining the more abstract underlying values that the participants had articulated. These, then, became the focus of discussion: were they threatened? How could they be preserved? What were barriers to change? What was threatened? As participants became more familiar with each other they shared more intimate narratives of change and stagnation, identified underlying senses of loss associated with the psychological impacts of ecological degradation and livelihood viability (Charli-Joseph et al. 2018; Eakin et al. 2019). The second half-day, inspired by the 3-Horizons approach, was dedicated towards brainstorming strategies for overcoming barriers to change: what would these look like? What would they entail? How might these strategies draw upon the knowledge and capacity existent among the group? What should be the next steps?

Reflections

The first T-Lab accomplished many things but perhaps most important for our purpose of catalysing collective agency was the facilitation of trust and a spirit of collaboration among the participants, very few of whom knew each other prior to the meeting and acknowledged having shared concerns. However, we found that reflecting as a group about system transformations can be daunting. One challenge was to separate material objects and realities (e.g. the land on which they traditionally farmed) from the participants' values and feelings towards them (e.g. the autonomy that farming provided the household). Centring the conversation on the potential persistence of intangible attributes allowed a discussion of the possibility of inevitable material losses intrinsic to transformations. While some objects must go, we can still preserve or recreate their benefits and associated values. The goal was to reconceptualize the wetland system in terms of a suite of intangible values that seemed to resonate with the group as a whole to then think about possible intervention pathways.

Another challenge was the tendency of the collective conversation to focus on what had already been tried and practised in the past. People had difficulty imagining that any effort to, e.g. sustain "self-sufficiency" would be aimed at a different material manifestation in the system than "maintaining the *chinampas*". Thus, the pathways turned out to be less transformative than we had hoped: a pathway to support the value of "self-sufficiency" was not "imagine an alternative livelihood in case the *chinampas* was no longer viable" but rather "use rain barrel technology to capture clean water for the *chinampa*". This was somewhat different than the more traditional response of "improve the water quality in the wetland", but we did not feel like we were moving the group into a new mode of thought. When we probed participants to explain how these solutions (e.g. "organize workshops to help people use rain barrel technologies") might lead to outcomes that were different than what had been tried in the past, the conversation turned to recognizing existing structural barriers that hinder more transformative change. We ended Day 2 with a recognition that if the internal barriers – those emerging within the community – were not addressed directly, the proposed pathways would likely not have results different than those of the past.

We had initially wanted to avoid conversation about barriers to change, fearing that this would be a disempowering conversation. We realized, however, that if the barriers are not tackled explicitly, the types of interventions proposed by the group would unlikely be different from those in the past. The conversation around barriers seemed to open up new ways of thinking about an issue and revealed some of the deeper cognitive and social factors perceived as impeding change within the community. These barriers then became the focus of action (for instance, how to address lack of self-esteem in the community), rather than the concrete strategies for addressing the manifestation of the problem in the landscape (i.e. how to address water quality). The first T-Lab laid the foundation of a new social network and a shift in framing reflected in a shared language among participants and interest in continuing to engage and meet in the months that followed. We noted the emergence of a greater sense of problem ownership and individual empowerment, and crucially, that solutions must be formed and implemented from the ground up.

Phase 3: continuous engagement

As a way of building momentum towards T-Lab workshop 2 and eliciting what the participants hoped to achieve from the process, we conducted three exploratory exercises, and organized two excursions: to a *chinampa* cultivated by one of the participants, and a walk on a volcanic mountain that overlooked the wetland, on which irregular settlements were developing. These exercises and activities, discussed in greater detail in the "Innovation and alternative pathways" section of this chapter, were designed to help participants assume alternative perspectives on the challenges they perceived, explore possibilities of collaboration, and envision alternative realities.

Prior to T-Lab workshop 2, we convened a small group of core participants to play a role in planning the next steps. It was the first time they expressed their restlessness towards the project's open design and focus on interactions, which contrasts with more traditional, goal-oriented workshops and projects. They also questioned how far we were willing to take our involvement as researcher-activists and wanted to know if they could count on us to participate in the initiatives they proposed. During the meeting, participants decided that any intervention had to address not only the urban-*chinampa* divide, but also recognize and connect with the other groups found in Xochimilco in a more concrete initiative with both short- and long-term goals.

Notably, a major earthquake occurred in Mexico City during this phase of our work (September 2017); this devastating event provided an opportunity to focus the group on concerns of solidarity and collective agency in the midst of "rebuilding" in a fragile and hazardous ecosystem. The earthquake itself appeared to reinforce the nascent idea that the urban residents do not have many alternatives to residing (illegally) within the wetland and thus are not entirely to blame for the encroachment. Building on our prior effort to help all participants identify their "powers", we organized a meeting in which we exchanged ideas about the services and capacities each of us had to offer, and what each of us required or desired in the wake of the earthquake. A new sense of empathy and a new interest in "building bridges" between the wetland stakeholders and the urban residents seemed to emerge from the recognition that all were affected by the earthquake; this solidarity was exemplified in the Pathways to Sustainability Game, described in greater detail in the "Innovation and alternative pathways" section of this chapter.

Phase 4: T-Lab workshop 2

The second T-Lab focussed on a plan of action directed and initiated by the non-academic participants. The action plan was based on a previously collectively articulated cognitive map of the "problem" of Xochimilco. The research team intentionally refrained from taking leadership in this last T-Lab, other than serving as facilitators and conveners and advocating for framing whatever strategy participants decided to pursue in line with transformative pathways to sustainability. We hoped that the accumulated evidence that the group had acquired considerable agency and capacity would be motivating to the participants to act on the values they now knew they shared, and the knowledge they had gained over prior activities in terms of possible action-pathways. First, the research team summarized ideas that had emerged over the course of the two years:

1   the need to create bridges between the two worlds of the urbanizing core and the livelihoods dependent on wetland conservation and agriculture,
2   the need to "reactivate" the agroecological traditions of Xochimilco as a means of halting urbanization,
3   the idea that informal residences could be made more compatible with the ecology of the area through innovations in construction and design.

What emerged as an output of this T-Lab was the desire to develop a project proposal that mimics, in some way, the understanding and empathy that has developed across T-Lab participants and different zones of the wetland. The group specifically wanted to develop a pedagogy for questioning and understanding the complexity of the water problem in Xochimilco through programmes or workshops in which people come together to carry out particular technical projects to improve – on a small scale – water quality or quantity. Their idea was to meet people where they are: find what connects them to the place of Xochimilco and the water issue and, through specific capacity building projects, enhance that connectivity and mobilize action.

Post T-Lab workshop 2

After T-Lab workshop 2, in individual interviews, we met with each participant and again applied the ANA methodology to assess whether: (a) ego-nets had expanded or changed; (b) links between participants had been created or strengthened; (c) practices in the action-nets had changed in terms of relations between collaborators-practices (we expected this to change after the earthquake) and (d) cognitive maps changed in the way they represent the issues in the system (reasons for degradation), or in the perception of the issue itself (this would imply reframing, since even if the cognitive map does not change per se, the way they explain or frame the problem could change). We also applied the Q-Method to assess whether the participants had changed their perspective on what attributes were meaningful to them in the wetland.

Following the proposal of T-Lab workshop 2 for a pedagogical initiative and participants' interests on learning facilitation and participatory tools and techniques, we held a 1-day workshop where participants reflected on transformative learning and planned this initiative. Our team participated on equal terms as the rest of the core participants and we hired external professionals to facilitate the workshop. The outcome was a T-Lab facilitator's toolkit and guide to assist others in replicating our process of fostering collective agency (see Ruizpalacios et al. 2019).

Innovation and alternative pathways

Though innovation was not a key theme in our work, a central aspect of our T-Lab was that it opened the possibility to construct a new pathway in which *chinamperos* and urban dwellers could come and work together. This pathway may be thought as *socially* innovative in itself. These are groups that have positioned themselves as antipodes to each other, both in terms of what Xochimilco means to them and also in terms of who is perceived as responsible for the degradation of the area or unmet needs. By the end of the project, the participants had altered their discourse, and were emphasizing the pursuit of activities that would "build bridges" and solidarity towards common goals.

While the entire process of the T-Lab was oriented towards problem reframing and questioning of prior assumptions, there were several exercises specifically aimed at such social innovation and exploring alternative pathways. For example, we designed an interactive role-playing game that we called the "Pathways to Sustainability Game" (Ruizpalacios et al. 2018) to help the participants move towards the idea of thinking about a strategic intervention and how it might play out in a complex system such as Xochimilco. The game simulated collaboration in a planning context (role playing a committee with a budget for implementation) as well as enabling the players to monitor and reflect on the strategies they pursued as they affect the system over time. In another activity implemented in the months following the earthquake, participants prototyped miniature models of new settlements that would maintain the core values identified in T-Lab workshop 1 (aesthetic, self-sufficiency, and identity) and set new pathways towards desired scenarios where agriculture on the *chinampas* and urbanization might coexist. The models depicted well-conserved *chinampas* and included houses that were smaller, built with lighter materials and eco-technologies. These imagined designs are radically different from the ones currently being built.

Through exercises such as the ones described above, the participants and re-search team began to see that ecosystem health and human well-being are not separate issues, and that residents in the urban areas and in the wetlands may share common ambitions about system change. While the activities of the T-Lab may be only partially responsible for this realization, now there is acknowledge-ment that any action must involve efforts from both sides, and this represents a success in opening new pathways for Xochimilco.

As a result of the second T-Lab, the participants concluded that they wanted to pursue the idea of "bridging" worlds: that of urban/*chinampa*, as well as the highland/lowland parts of the system. As they formulated the focal activities in this pathway of change, they emphasized education: interventions to change perspectives, attitudes and behaviours around the issue of water, concluding that water linked the different parts of the system that have not been in coordina-tion. They envisioned the creation of bridges through outreach and innova-tive education between actors with different roles in the system: chinamperos and non-chinamperos, those in the urban core versus the wetland, and between generations. Essentially, participants recognized the scaling of T-Lab-like peda-gogical process as a main transformative pathway towards sustainability in Xo-chimilco. They advocated for more transformative methods and pedagogy for engagement, drawing the recognition that the arts, as well as technical expertise, might be mobilized towards transformative ends. At their request, we produced a "guidebook" that captures the essence of the different methods and approaches to engagement that we used in the project: *The Transformation Laboratory of the Social-Ecological System of Xochimilco, Mexico City: Description of the Process and Methodolog-ical Guide* (Ruizpalacios et al. 2019) for use not only by the participants in their own activities and advocacy work, but also for public dissemination.

Networks, alliances and collective agency

The aim of the T-Lab process was, in essence, to create conditions that would give rise to a sense of collective agency. Our decision, at the start of the project, to invite individuals to join the T-Lab who had limited, if any, prior connection to each other, was strategic. Our aim was to see if the activities we engaged in would be conducive to forming a new network of individuals with diverse capacities, interests and stakes in the system, but who nevertheless could collab-orate towards a common goal. In this objective, we noted significant changes: the Agency Network Analysis we conducted with the participants illustrated to them and us that many of them saw their social collaborative networks expand.

We established a WhatsApp group and Facebook page that facilitated con-tinued communication among participants during the entire process, not only about project sponsored activities but also about information that individual participants wanted to share with the group, and even for informal social and friendly chatting – building social bonding within the group. At present, as we are writing this chapter (2019), they continue to interact through social media and in person. While they have not focussed on a single, specific project, they have met to support each other in political action. Recently, e.g. after the formal T-Lab project had come to a close, one member of the T-Lab group called other members through social media to a critical situation in the wetland: the wetland's water in one area had simply evaporated, leaving the *chinampas* desiccated. With subsidence and problems in water management, this occurrence is increasingly likely. The T-Lab group mobilized collectively, without our support to address the situation through civic action. Events such as this suggest that the primary goal of the project – to create conditions in which collective agency could emerge among relative strangers – was achieved.

While the T-Lab process ultimately did not incorporate new actors over the course of the two years, the activities that we conducted as a group such as the Pathways to Sustainability Game and discussions following the September 2017 earthquake emphasized to the participants the need to build bridges to communities not well-represented in the T-Lab process. Hence the effort of the group on learning and developing capacities in pedagogies that could "build bridges" across different social and ecological divides that mark the Xochimilco wetland.

Concluding insights

The T-Lab of Xochimilco was designed under the assumption that transformations of social-ecological systems cannot be engineered from outside since such human-dominated systems are extremely complex and not amenable to controlled manipulation. Instead, social-ecological transformations require cultivating changes in the system's main driving component; human individuals and collectives. Consequently, we did not attempt to catalyse a specific, preconceived pathway or strategy of change but rather focussed on creating a space for reflection, reframing and exploration with the hope that such a space might affect transformative processes. Due to the project's own limitations, we could only involve a reduced number of people with limited influence in the whole social-ecological system. While this constrained the possibility of effecting an actual system-level transformation, by selecting participants who were not already intensively collaborating we were able to experiment and learn important lessons about cultivating transformative intentionality through the nurturing of individual and collective components of a system (Manuel-Navarrete et al. 2019). We achieved this experimenting and learning by providing a space in which people could reflect on their agency and what they might be able to do together that they could not achieve alone, or within their siloed networks. Ultimately, transformative spaces must be community-building spaces: spaces that cultivate collective agency (Pereira et al. 2018). In such spaces the relationships of actors to other system elements through livelihood activities are potentially disrupted, and connections are built on shared values, histories and futures. The project was able to create conditions in which collective agency emerged among relative strangers, and was self-sustained by them after the project was concluded.

References

Aguilar, A.G., López, F. M. (2009). Water insecurity among the urban poor in the peri-urban zone of Xochimilco, Mexico City. *Journal of Latin American Geography* 8(2), 97–123.

Bandura, A. (2000). Exercise of human agency through collective efficacy. *Current Directions in Psychological Science* 9(3), 75–78.

Castro, J. E. (2004). Urban water and the politics of citizenship: the case of the Mexico City Metropolitan Area during the 1980s and 1990s. *Environment and Planning A* 36(2), 327–346.

Charli-Joseph, L., Siqueiros-García, J.M., Eakin, H., Manuel-Navarrete, D., Shelton, R. (2018). Promoting agency for social-ecological transformation: a transformation-lab in the Xochimilco social-ecological system. *Ecology and Society* 23(2), 46.

Connolly, P., Wigle, J. (2017). (Re) constructing informality and "doing regularization" in the conservation zone of Mexico City. *Planning Theory & Practice* 18(2), 183–201.

Eakin, H., Bojórquez-Tapia, L. A., Janssen, M. A., Georgescu, M., Manuel-Navarrete, D., Vivoni, E. R., Escalante, A. E., Baeza-Castro, A., Mazari-Hiriart, M., Lerner, A. M. (2017). Opinion: Urban resilience efforts must consider social and political forces. *Proceedings of the National Academy of Sciences* 114(2), 186–189.

Eakin, H., Lerner, A. M., Manuel-Navarette, D., Hernández Aguilar, B., Martínez-Canedo, A., Tellman, B., Charli-Joseph, L, Fernández Álvarez, R., Bojórquez-Tapia, L. (2016). Adapting to risk and perpetuating poverty: Household's strategies for managing flood risk and water scarcity in Mexico City. *Environmental Science & Policy* 66, 324–333.

Eakin, H., Shelton, R., Baeza, A., Bojórquez-Tapia, L. A., Flores, S., Parajuli, J., Grave, I., Estrada Barón, A., Hernández, B. (2020). Expressions of collective grievance as a feedback in multi-actor adaptation to water risks in Mexico City. *Regional Environmental Change* 20, 17.

Eakin, H., Shelton, R., Siqueiros, J. M., Charli-Joseph, L., Manuel-Navarrete, D. (2019). Loss and social-ecological transformation. *Ecology and Society* 24(3), 15.

Jiménez Cisneros, B., Gutierrez Rivas, R., Marañón Pimentel, B., González Reynoso, Arsenio E. (2011). *Evaluación de la política de acceso al agua potable en el Districto Federal. Mexico City*, Programa Universitario de Estudios Sobre la Ciudad, Universidad Nacional Autonoma De Mexico.

Lerner, A. M., Eakin, H. C., Tellman, E., Bausch, J. C., Hernández Aguilar, B. (2018). Governing the gaps in water governance and land-use planning in a megacity: The example of hydrological risk in Mexico City. *Cities* 83, 61–70.

Manuel-Navarrete, D., Morehart, C., Tellman, B., Eakin, H., Siqueiros-García, J. M., Hernández Aguilar, B. (2019). Intentional disruption of path-dependencies in the Anthropocene: Gray versus green water infrastructure regimes in Mexico City, Mexico. *Anthropocene* 26, 100209.

Mazari-Hiriart, M., Ponce-de-León, S., López-Vidal, Y., Islas-Macías, P., Amieva-Fernández, R. I., Quiñones-Falconi, F. (2008). Microbiological implications of periurban agriculture and water reuse in Mexico City. *Plos One* 3(5), e2305. doi: 10.1371/journal.pone.0002305

Morehart, C. (2018). The political ecology of chinampa landscapes in the Basin of Mexico. *Water and Power in Ancient Societies*. E. Holt. IEMA Proceedings, State University of New York at Buffalo. 7, 19–39.

O'Brien, K., Sygna, L. (2013). *Responding to climate change: The three spheres of transformation*. Proceedings of Transformation in a Changing Climate, 19–21 June 2013, Oslo, Norway, University of Oslo.

Osmanoğlu, B., Dixon, T. H., Wdowinski, S., Cabral-Cano, E., Jiang, Y. (2011). Mexico City subsidence observed with persistent scatterer InSAR. *International Journal of Applied Earth Observation and Geoinformation 13*(1), 1–12.

Pelenc, J., Bazile, D., Ceruti, C. (2015). Collective capability and collective agency for sustainability: A case study. *Ecological Economics* 118, 226–239.

Pelenc, J., Lompo, M. K., Ballet, J., Dubois, J. L. (2013). Sustainable human development and the capability approach: Integrating environment, responsibility and collective agency. *Journal of Human Development and Capabilities* 14(1), 77–94.

Pereira, L. M., Karpouzoglou, T., Frantzeskaki, N., Olsson, P. (2018). Designing transformative spaces for sustainability in social-ecological systems. *Ecology and Society* 23(4), 32.

Ruizpalacios, B., Charli-Joseph, L., Eakin, H., Siqueiros-García, J.M., Manuel-Navarrete, D., Shelton, R. (2019). *The transformation laboratory of the social-ecological system of Xochimilco*. Mexico City: Description of the process and methodological guide. Mexico City, Mexico: LANCIS-IE, UNAM. Available at: https://steps-centre.org/wp-content/uploads/2019/09/Guide-T-Lab-Xochi-screen-version-English-NA-Hub.pdf

Ruizpalacios, B., Charli-Joseph, L., Eakin, H., Siqueiros-García, J. M., R. Shelton (2018). Creating bridges in Xochimilco through the 'Pathways to Sustainability'game,https://steps-centre.org/blog/creating-bridges-through-the-pathways-to-sustainability-game/

Shelton, R., Janssen, M., Meinzen-Dick, R. (2018). Measuring Learning from Interventions through Participatory Processes. (CBIE Working Paper Series #CBIE-2018-004). Center for Behavior, Institutions, and Environment.

Tellman, B., Bausch, J. C., Eakin, H., Anderies, J. M., Mazari-Hiriart, M., Manuel-Navarrete, D., Redman, C. L. (2018). Adaptive pathways and coupled infrastructure: seven centuries of adaptation to water risk and the production of vulnerability in Mexico City. *Ecology and Society* 23(1)., 1.

United Nations (Department of Economic and Social Affairs, Population Division). (2018). *The World's Cities in 2018*. Data Booklet (ST/ESA/SER.A/417).

Westley, F. R., Tjornbo, O., Schultz, L., Olsson, P., Folke, C., Crona, B., Bodin, Ö. (2013). A theory of transformative agency in linked social-ecological systems. *Ecology & Society* 18(3), 1–16.

Wigle, J. (2010). The "Xochimilco model" for managing irregular settlements in conservation land in Mexico City. *Cities* 27(5), 337–347.

Zambrano, L., Contreras, V., Mazari-Hiriart, M., Zarco-Arista, A. E. (2009). Spatial heterogeneity of water quality in a highly degraded tropical freshwater ecosystem. *Environmental Management* 43(2), 249–263. doi: 10.1007/s00267-008-9216-1

10

ENABLING TRANSFORMATIONS TO SUSTAINABILITY

Rethinking urban water management in Gurgaon, India

Dinesh Abrol and Pravin Kushwaha

Introduction

Gurgaon, a rapidly urbanising south-western area of the National Capital Region (NCR), is one among the few cities developed by real estate developers in India. The city was originally planned for a population of 1 million. As per the latest urban planning document (Master Plan), this urban settlement, referred to as the Gurgaon-Manesar Urban Complex (GMUC), is expected to have a population of 4.25 million by the year 2031 (Dhillon, 2012, p. 4). From being a "little more than a village" having barren land "with no local government, public utilities, or transportation" in the 1970s, Gurgaon has, since the 1990s, become one of the "fastest growing urban centres in India" (Rajagopalan & Tabarrok, 2014).The immediate trigger behind such a rapid urban transformation was the increased demand for space from transnational corporations for the establishment of their back offices and call centres and the development of housing projects for the benefit of middle-class professionals.

Over the last couple of decades, the city of Gurgaon (recently renamed Gurugram) saw a vast swath of open agricultural lands being converted to hard paved surfaces, either asphalt roads or residential or commercial buildings. Gurgaon is a preferred investment destination due to its proximity to the Indira Gandhi International Airport, availability of newly built office spaces in the city, the social ecosystem built around shopping malls and the places like DLF Cyber Hub (one of the largest hubs of IT activity in the National Capital Region), the Rapid Metro Rail connecting the key locations such as the Cyber City, Udyog Vihar and DLF Phase III where most offices are located. Over the last two and a half decades the city of Gurgaon has seen an influx of working-class and middle-class migrants, growing in numbers by several times.

DOI: 10.4324/9780429331930-13

Increasing urbanisation and influx of migrants (both middle-class and working-class) have been squeezing the distant as well as local sources of water, turning Gurgaon into a water-scarce landscape. The Central Ground Water Board (CGWB) has already declared Gurgaon as a "dark zone" (where ground water depletion exceeds the rate of recharging) (Arora, 2019). The rate of the depletion of the ground water table is more than two metres per year (Hindustan Times, 2017). Illegal extraction of ground water is quite prevalent for construction activities despite its legal restrictions (Singh, 2012). Despite the lack of municipal city planning, the growth story of the city has earned it the name of "millennium city" of India, under the influence of 'market driven urbanization'.

Critics have been constantly raising concerns of planning failures, especially the lack of trunk infrastructures and public services – two major challenges that the rapid urban transformation of Gurgaon is unable to deal with (Goldstein, 2016). Private developers have been allowed to acquire agricultural land and convert it into real estate properties for non-agricultural use. Unique to this

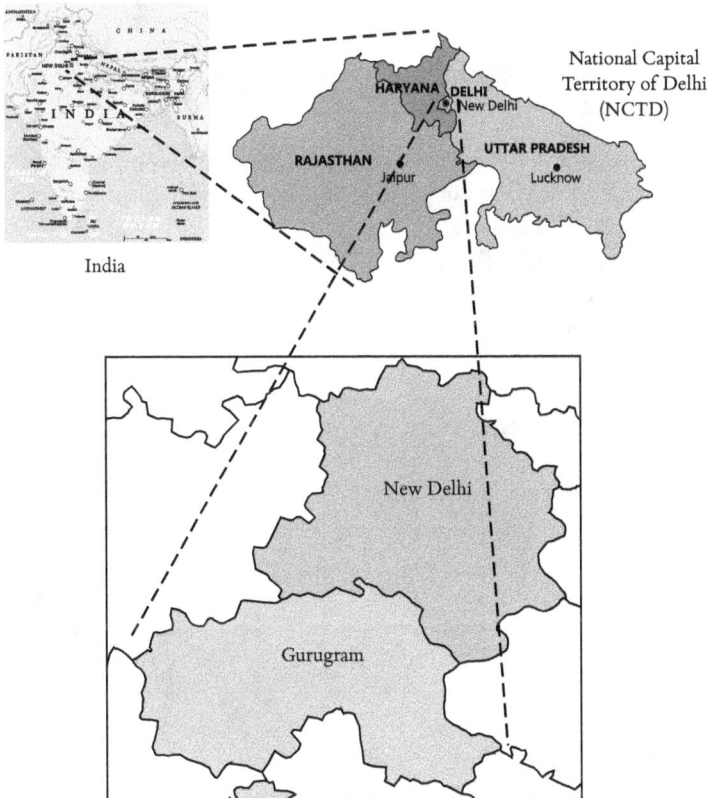

FIGURE 10.1   Map showing location of Gurugram in India and the National Capital Region.

process was the withdrawal of the state from making provisions for "essential public goods and urban planning" and the transfer of this responsibility to the private sector (Chatterji, 2013; Rajagopalan & Tabarrok, 2014). Even with three master plans in just seven years, the city of Gurgaon continued to experience challenges with basic amenities like water, power, roads, regulated traffic and adequate policing about which the residents from all classes have a lot of complaints. Residents' welfare associations (RWAs) and middle-class citizen platforms are trying to deal with some of these problems at their own local level in a piecemeal fashion. The working people have their focus on the immediate livelihood problems. Their challenge of social mobilisation for the formation of socially and ecologically just pathways to urban planning and governance has also not been receiving adequate attention from the political structures and the institutions devoted to the advancement of research and professional education located within the National Capital Region (NCR). This chapter describes and explains the structures and processes which the South Asia hub engaged to develop the transformative spaces with the aim to intervene in the prevailing situation in the domain of urban water management.

Urban water management in Gurgaon: problem space and the challenge of transformation

Planners in Gurgaon have been essentially relying upon the supply of water from sources that are located outside the city (at a considerable distance) to meet the growing demand of water for the urban settlements (Centre for Science and Environment, 2012). Techno-managerial solutions have been popular in this approach (HT Correspondent, 2019; Mishra et al., 2018). Water management, urban planning and governance have mostly addressed the concerns of the dominant classes, i.e. the middle classes and the wealthy. The concerns of the poor and marginalised and their representation in the agenda of the government have been rarely prioritised by the emergent citizens' platforms in Gurgaon. This gap has been evident in the way these platforms tend to approach citizens' urban engagement and make interventions (Roychowdhury & Puri, 2017) (Arora S., 2019). Examples are Gurgaon First, Gurgaon Citizens Council (GCC) and "iamgurgaon".

Water conservation and wastewater management have come to be secondary considerations in day-to-day water management practices of the local administration and in the policy framework of the state government. Natural recharging/replenishment of ground water by protecting the water bodies as well as by promoting rainwater-harvesting systems has a symbolic presence. An efficient system of recycling of wastewater for the entire urban area was absent except for the presence of effluent treatment plants and sewage treatment plants at selected locations. These systems covered only a limited catchment area due to the lack of sufficient collection and transportation infrastructure for the sewage in the city. Within the dominant pathway of water resource management, water has been treated as a commodity, without sufficient consideration to sustainability of sources of supply. This has ultimately led to unsustainable habitations.

The distribution of water across the city is also a challenging task. Usually, government agencies recognise only certain areas in the city as part of the formal water distribution system. These areas are often identified as industrial areas, planned residential areas and commercial areas. The vast majority of unplanned areas where a large percentage of the urban population lives remain unrecognised by the public water distribution system. Most of these unrecognised urban spaces rely upon informal sources of water supply that are often inadequate.

Water supply, distribution and use are a conflicted terrain, with demand coming from different agricultural, industrial, commercial and residential groups. Water has emerged as a business opportunity leading to a growing mismatch between supply and demand, deepening gender, class, caste and community-based inequalities.

BOX 10.1 THE PROBLEMS AND CHALLENGES OF URBAN WATER MANAGEMENT IN GURGAON

The vulnerability of the urban water management system in Gurgaon is understood to be driven by the systemic problems of overexploitation of sources of surface and ground water, growing inequity in distribution of water, rising use of water for non-priority priority purposes and decreasing reliability of the water supply system. Planning, governance and practices under perusal for management of water do not recognise co-evolving inequities (rural-urban, marginalisation of poor people) and the growing vulnerability of water management system.

Mainstream pathways of water management are driven by unsustainable practices of consumption by the middle classes. At the same time, the inability to tackle water and wastewater together is apparent. Lack of protection of local water bodies, low priority given to reuse and recycling, recharging/ replenishment, eco-friendly technology of harvesting and treatment of water and wastewater management are a systemic outcome of the institutional lock-in to mainstream pathways.

The issues of lack of representation, voice and power of the poor and marginalised people in the sphere of water management are also a systemic outcome of mainstream pathways of urban development. Therein exists the challenge of changing the policy paradigm.

There is lack of coordination and cooperation among the protagonists of change due to limited dialogue and experimentation in respect of how to tackle the challenge of sustainable water management.

At the time this project was initiated in 2015, there was broad but shallow recognition of these problems across different publics, without a shared understanding among different groups. A comprehensive and integrated perspective, with reference to a sustainable water management system was absent from the research landscape too. There was also a realisation that the National Capital Region (NCR) was still going ahead with the development of new cities without adequate planning interventions concerning urban sustainability, with alternatives mostly failing to find their place in the urban planning and water governance discourse. In most cases, governing agencies had chosen to underplay the challenges posed by these problems.

BOX 10.2 INSTITUTIONAL CONTEXT OF THE RESEARCH AND ENGAGEMENT

The new pathways for real-world experimentation are in the making. Two important institutions, namely, the Gurgaon Water Forum and the Transdisciplinary Research Cluster on Sustainability Studies (TRCSS), JNU (Jawaharlal Nehru University) have emerged as part of the T-Lab activities, and these institutions are on the way to stabilising themselves through the T-Lab process.

The Gurgaon Water Forum (GWF) is a multi-stakeholder platform of mobilised public groups collaborating on the issues of sustainable urban water management (SUWM) and city development.

The TRCSS, JNU is also gaining ground with the closer involvement of the students and faculty in the field. There is a network of S&T institutions and civil society organisations (CSOs) collaborating with the faculty and students of TRCSS, JNU. Within JNU the TRCSS is now more stable and acceptable to faculty and students.

The GWF and the TRCSS are engaged in the implementation of SUWM solutions. The real-world experimentation has started with the support of stakeholders and government agencies. The GWF is now a well-accepted entity collaborating with public administration.

Community mobilisation has been catalysed using citizen science, citizen dialogue and advocacy, workers' group enterprise and urban studios/labs.

Citizen dialogue and advocacy through community radio has facilitated community mobilisation across various low-income residential areas in the city.

Currently, the GWF is working on the ground in collaboration with activists from close to seven organisations who represent the interests of the middle and working classes. The GWF has brought together the mobilised publics to actively contribute to the formation of Social Carriers of Innovation for Transformations (SCIT), described further below.

Public participation in decision making has been absent, with existing governing mechanisms functioning in a top-down manner where the scope for integrating various kinds of stakeholders are limited. More significantly, despite formulating two official NCR Plans in the past, the last one notified on September 17, 2005 with the perspective year 2021 (National Capital Regional Planning Board, 2020), their adequate implementation is a fundamental challenge for the National Capital Region Planning Board (NCRPB) because of the lack of support and coordination among participating governments of different states.

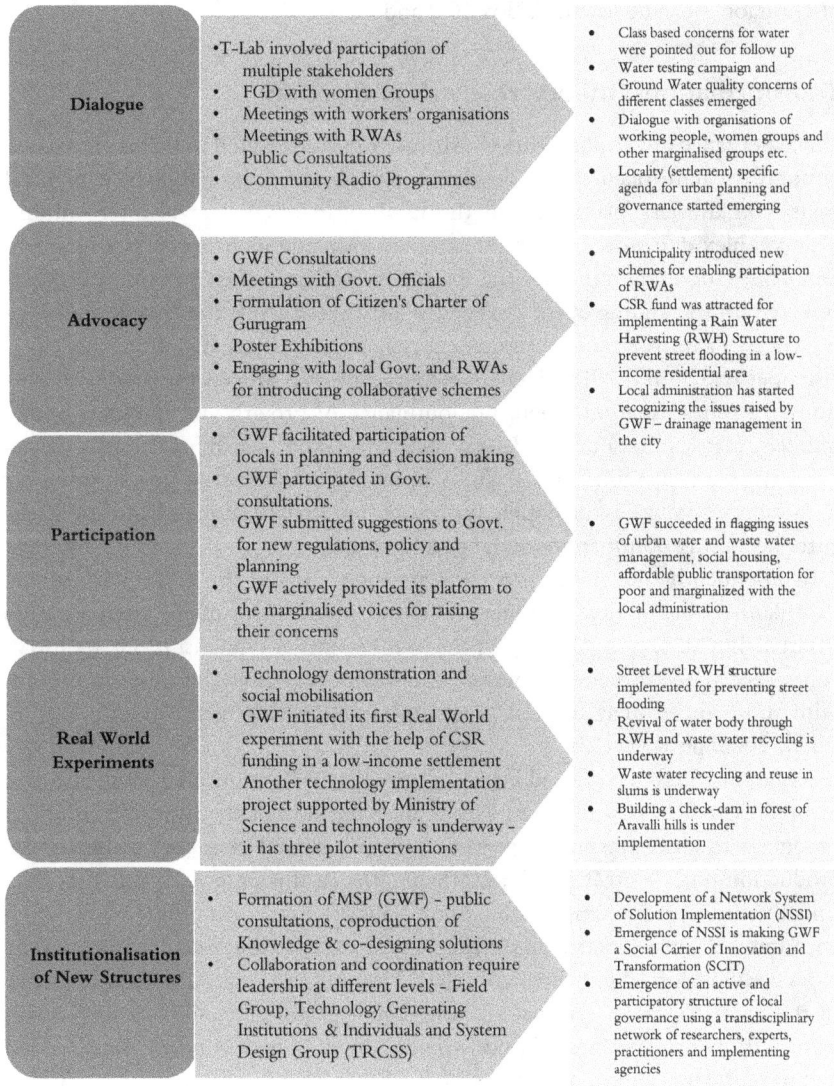

Dialogue	• T-Lab involved participation of multiple stakeholders • FGD with women Groups • Meetings with workers' organisations • Meetings with RWAs • Public Consultations • Community Radio Programmes	• Class based concerns for water were pointed out for follow up • Water testing campaign and Ground Water quality concerns of different classes emerged • Dialogue with organisations of working people, women groups and other marginalised groups etc. • Locality (settlement) specific agenda for urban planning and governance started emerging
Advocacy	• GWF Consultations • Meetings with Govt. Officials • Formulation of Citizen's Charter of Gurugram • Poster Exhibitions • Engaging with local Govt. and RWAs for introducing collaborative schemes	• Municipality introduced new schemes for enabling participation of RWAs • CSR fund was attracted for implementing a Rain Water Harvesting (RWH) Structure to prevent street flooding in a low-income residential area • Local administration has started recognizing the issues raised by GWF – drainage management in the city
Participation	• GWF facilitated participation of locals in planning and decision making • GWF participated in Govt. consultations. • GWF submitted suggestions to Govt. for new regulations, policy and planning • GWF actively provided its platform to the marginalised voices for raising their concerns	• GWF succeeded in flagging issues of urban water and waste water management, social housing, affordable public transportation for poor and marginalized with the local administration
Real World Experiments	• Technology demonstration and social mobilisation • GWF initiated its first Real World experiment with the help of CSR funding in a low-income settlement • Another technology implementation project supported by Ministry of Science and technology is underway – it has three pilot interventions	• Street Level RWH structure implemented for preventing street flooding • Revival of water body through RWH and waste water recycling is underway • Waste water recycling and reuse in slums is underway • Building a check-dam in forest of Aravalli hills is under implementation
Institutionalisation of New Structures	• Formation of MSP (GWF) - public consultations, coproduction of Knowledge & co-designing solutions • Collaboration and coordination require leadership at different levels - Field Group, Technology Generating Institutions & Individuals and System Design Group (TRCSS)	• Development of a Network System of Solution Implementation (NSSI) • Emergence of NSSI is making GWF a Social Carrier of Innovation and Transformation (SCIT) • Emergence of an active and participatory structure of local governance using a transdisciplinary network of researchers, experts, practitioners and implementing agencies

FIGURE 10.2 Designing social mobilisation through GWF: interventions, activities and outcomes.

The South Asia hub of the transformative knowledge network (TKN) decided to begin with its urban interventions in Gurgaon. While this intervention was conceptualised as an experiment designed with the aim of fostering alternate people-centric pathways of water management, it was clear to the team that the focus would ultimately have to be on the challenges of urban transformation (see Box 10.1). Various details about the hub and its work – reconfiguring the ongoing social mobilisation for peoples' participation in respect of urban planning and governance, creating a multi-stakeholder platform for co-production of knowledge and co-design of solutions and transforming the then weakly emergent spaces of public engagement over water conservation, its use and reuse in the city of Gurgaon – can be found in Box 10.2 and Figure 10.2.

Transformations: theory, research and action

The emergence of various forms of urbanisation is attributed to their context and culturally specific occurrence. Yet there exists an overarching influence of global capital on the city planning and the localised neoliberal civic interventions. The complex dynamics of such intertwined local and global processes require a new epistemic understanding; the focus needs to be shifted towards a process-oriented understanding of the concept of 'urban' as against the "fixed, unchanging entity – a universal form, settlement type or bounded spatial unit ('the' city)" (Brenner & Schmid, 2015). Henri Lefebvre calls this process the 'urban revolution' – a transformation where predominance of growth and industrialisation (models, plans, programmes)-driven society is taken over by real estate-driven urbanisation (Lefebvre, 2003, p. 5). A kind of 'post-industrial' revolution is set in motion wherein lies the double process of 'industrialization-urbanization', the latter becoming dominant over the period of time.

Consequently, the urban process is no longer under the control of the urban planners but subject to speculation and profiteering of the entrepreneurs (Merrifield, 2005, pp. 693–694).Of the two 'circuits of capitalism',[1] i.e. industry-commerce and real estate businesses, the role of real estate becomes significant with more investment in land as against industry-commerce (Gottdiener & Budd, 2005, pp. 132–133).

Following Lefebvre, David Harvey (Harvey, 1973) points out that the process of urbanisation has transformed "from an expression of the needs of industrial producers to an expression of power of finance capital over the totality of the production process" (Merrifield, 2005, p. 697). In this process, "capitalists continually shift their investment from one circuit of capital to another" which often encounters disinvestment as an inevitable process. The "built environment of the cities could be forced to become obsolete'" leading to actions like slum clearance in the name of urban renewal (Zukin, 2006, p. 107).The shift in investment pattern from 'primary circuit' (industrial production) to 'secondary circuit' (land and real estate) is an important means of accumulation of wealth and growth of cities.

In this process, reshaping of the built environment in pursuit of profit through creative destruction is responsible for the contradiction that has led to social conflicts and struggles in urban areas (Gotham, 2010, pp. 553–554). Harvey identifies urban space as an active moment – a unit of capital accumulation as well as a site of class struggle where the built environment is the source of profit and loss through property investment that often triggers major urban renewals (Hubbard, 2006, p. 40).

Urbanisation in Gurgaon expresses strong and intimate connections with the secondary circuit of capital accumulation which requires constant priming of urban expansion with the structures of social reproduction of the lives of poor and marginalised working-class migrants. The reasons which explain the sources of unsustainable urban sprawl, the main consequences of urban sprawl for the realisation of goals of economic, social and environmental sustainability and the policies that would be required to make urban water management more sustainable in Gurgaon clearly bring forth the point that urban expansion in Gurgaon originates not just from an overflow of wealth but also equally from an overflow of poverty materialising through massive processes of rural-urban migration, land takeovers, and the more or less unplanned building of urban villages and peri-urban areas that are now popular neighbourhoods where the working classes live without access to public infrastructure required for dignified urban lives.

Opening new spaces for urban expansion, developing and redeveloping the spaces for wealth generation and capital accumulation is a necessity of the capitalist classes investing in Gurgaon. This expansion is continuing only because the mainstream pathways of urbanisation align with the interests of the members of capitalist class operating from within Gurgaon. Take, for example, the DLF Foundation (a philanthropic arm of the DLF Limited – a real estate company), which pioneered the expansion of Gurgaon during the 1980s and 1990s has come up now with its 21st-century flagship initiative, called the 'Gurgaon Rejuvenation Project'– GRP by the DLF (DLF Foundation, 2008). Under the GRP, a capacity building workshop was organised in August 2017 on transforming the Najafgarh Basin (Times News Network, 2017). The Najafgarh Drain is the main drainage system in Gurgaon, carrying most of its sewage towards the Yamuna River in Delhi. The purpose of this workshop was to develop a multi-stakeholder approach for the rejuvenation of the Najafgarh Basin with the long-term vision of developing a roadmap for the development of inland waterways in the Najafgarh drain (DLF Foundation, 2017).

The long-term objective of converting the Najafgarh drain into an inland waterway, seeking low interest, highly profitable "green" funds from the national and international financial organisations, in fact, also revealed quite a lot about the actual interest of leading stakeholder (DLF Foundation) – the real estate speculations in the name of urban rejuvenation.

The GWF understands its interventions as a longer-term process of engagement with the structural power over city planning and development. The elements of structural power comprise finance capital, real estate and IT, land owning castes in urban and peri-urban villages, lack of participation of women in decision making, local vs outsider divides and religious and ethnic divides. The power of neo-liberal ideology and practices over the political and bureaucratic

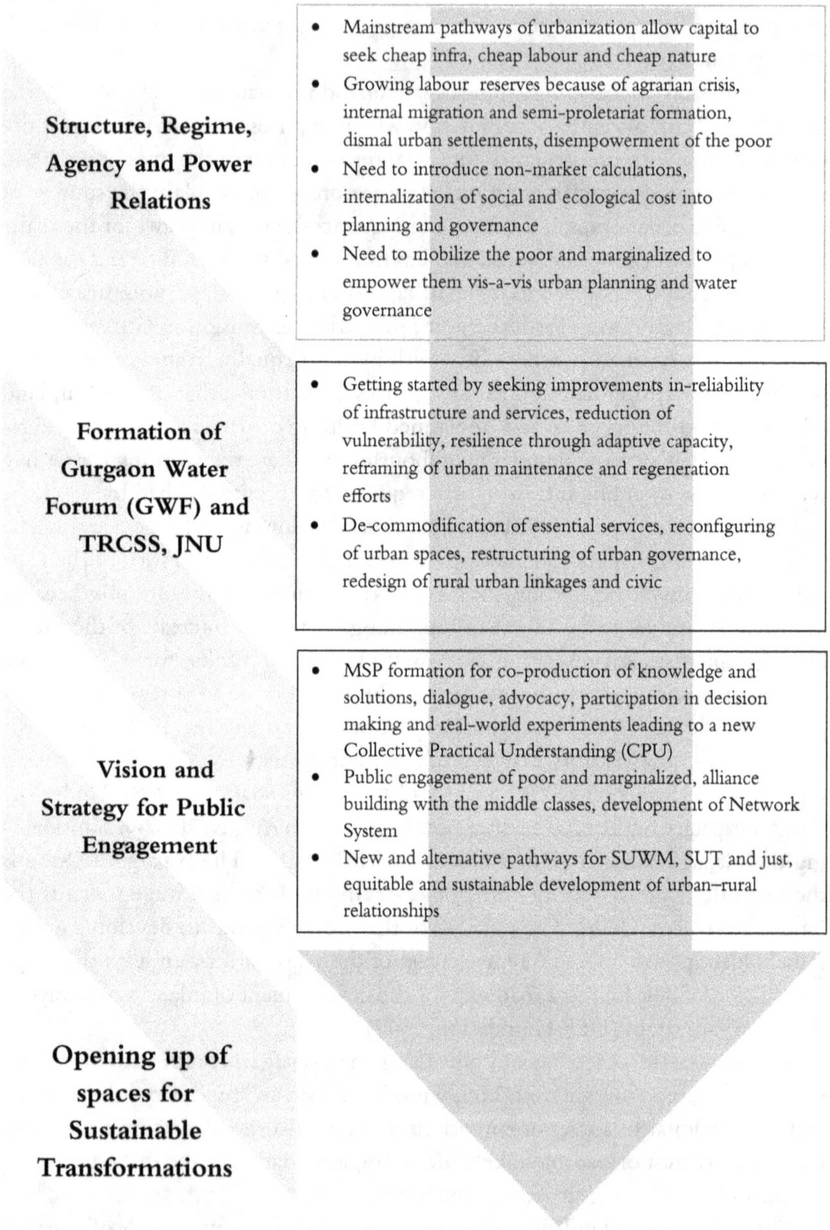

Structure, Regime, Agency and Power Relations

- Mainstream pathways of urbanization allow capital to seek cheap infra, cheap labour and cheap nature
- Growing labour reserves because of agrarian crisis, internal migration and semi-proletariat formation, dismal urban settlements, disempowerment of the poor
- Need to introduce non-market calculations, internalization of social and ecological cost into planning and governance
- Need to mobilize the poor and marginalized to empower them vis-a-vis urban planning and water governance

Formation of Gurgaon Water Forum (GWF) and TRCSS, JNU

- Getting started by seeking improvements in-reliability of infrastructure and services, reduction of vulnerability, resilience through adaptive capacity, reframing of urban maintenance and regeneration efforts
- De-commodification of essential services, reconfiguring of urban spaces, restructuring of urban governance, redesign of rural urban linkages and civic

Vision and Strategy for Public Engagement

- MSP formation for co-production of knowledge and solutions, dialogue, advocacy, participation in decision making and real-world experiments leading to a new Collective Practical Understanding (CPU)
- Public engagement of poor and marginalized, alliance building with the middle classes, development of Network System
- New and alternative pathways for SUWM, SUT and just, equitable and sustainable development of urban–rural relationships

Opening up of spaces for Sustainable Transformations

FIGURE 10.3 Theory of change: engaging with the politics of urban sustainability transitions.

apparatus is currently the reigning regime across the co-evolving domains of business regulations, urban planning and governance, settlement planning, livelihood development, health and education services, urban transportation and access to water and sanitation, resulting in the neglect of environmental and social dimensions. The challenge of empowering the weaker sections lies in changing the agency relationships of middle classes and working people. There is a need to reconfigure the balance of power through reframing the conditions of formation of alliances between the working people and the middle classes.

The GWF uses the power of radical approaches to structural transformation, system transformation and pro-poor enabling approaches to reframe the interventions in urban planning and governance and alliance building. The conceptualisation and implementation of the theories of transformation, change and practice that the South Asia Hub has chosen to adopt to co-design the activities of pro-poor social mobilisation over water in Gurgaon are explained in Box 12.3.

'Transformation' means profound, often long-term changes to the entire system that come about as a result of multiple interacting dynamics involving society, ecology and technology. In this sense, a transformation would involve enabling the poor and marginalised to enhance their access to resources and capabilities for mobilisation of power to innovate and foster a change in the neo-liberal regime. Regime change is needed for creating the conditions for the realisation of ecologically and socially just development through the internalisation of non-market externalities and the participation of working people in the co-design of solutions.

The poor and marginalised working people need to be supported in the efforts to build cross-class alliances for the revitalisation and regeneration of areas in which they reside. There are numerous examples of change in land use overlooking social and ecological considerations. Therefore, the introduction of such externalities in the process of decision making on land use and water use should ensure that capital is made to internalise the social and ecological costs into planning and governance of expansion of urban spaces on which the capital is today much dependent on accumulation.

In this context, as a theory of change, the TRCSS, JNU and its partners have chosen to prioritise the challenge of building cross-class alliances with the objective of realising the introduction of non-market calculations in areas where they live. These interventions should aim to ensure the participation of working people in the co-design activities of social mobilisation through the formation of a multi-stakeholder platform (MSP) – namely Gurgaon Water Forum (GWF) in which the trade unions are an active participant along with the groups involved with the middle classes for a wide range of issues arising out of the problems of urban governance in Gurgaon to maximise the outcomes for the formation of leadership for the activities to be initiated for the formation of structures and institutions to enable the processes of transformation of water management and urban governance (see Box 12.3 for an analytical summary of the GWF activities).

BOX 10.3 THEORY OF TRANSFORMATIONS

The structure, regime and agency relationship are the key to understanding the theory of transformations, moving from abstract to concrete and back to abstract learning through action. For the hub's theory of change, this means:

First, that the Gurgaon Water Forum (GWF) struggles against the neoliberal regime for structural change, democratic identity-based transformation of agency of working people; emphasis on direct action and alliance-building for the transformation of identities.

Second, that transformation requires empowering the marginalised to struggle against mainstream pathways embedded in structures of cheap labour and nature, against the shift from primary to secondary circuit of capital accumulation, against the erosion of urban commons, and against primitive accumulation, authoritarian structures and commodified social reproduction regimes.

Third, a change in the sub-regime of knowledge production is necessary but not enough: contestations matter, radical perspectives have to remain in reckoning. Work on economic and social transformation starts by including a focus on collective practical approaches to livelihoods of the marginalised in the water-related transformative spaces, housing and catchment habitat protection.

Fourth, sustainability transition theory needs to focus on context specific structure, regime and agency relationships; politics of engagement with sub-regimes of planning and governance is by itself not enough.

Fifth, leadership and building of relationships for path construction and spaces for transformations to sustainable urban development needs alignment of structures and institutions to enable longer term changes.

As a multi-stakeholder platform (MSP), the GWF has been proposed and organised for the moment, to serve mainly as a knowledge sharing platform capable of undertaking the co-production of knowledge and co-design of solutions. It works with the help of the individuals and groups collaborating with the GWF and the TRCSS for the benefit of sectional as well as collective interests of the working people in Gurgaon. Long-term stabilisation of the MSP is necessary. With this in mind, the GWF has envisaged the formation of a Network System of Solution Implementation (NSSI). During the project period, the NSSI activities focussed on the mobilisation of the people to erect the scaffolding for a new Social Carrier of Innovation for Transformation (SCIT) to contribute to the development of people-centric framings of the problem and solutions (Edquist & Edqvist, 1979; Smith, et al., 2016). This is illustrated in Figure 10.4. The NSSI structure is designed to accommodate all the relevant participating stakeholders and members of mobilised publics in three subgroups as per their capacities to perform the expected roles and functions. The structure has three types of sub-groups – System Design Groups (SG), Knowledge Generation Groups (KG) and Field Development Groups (FG). The NSSI structure has been formed by drawing on experiences with similar structures tried earlier within the Delhi Science Forum. The NSSI structure was designed to realise a minimum level of political and academic rigour to ensure that the GWF does not collapse after the project is over and the process of implementation of interventions is sustainable also beyond the project period.

The theory of transformations outlined above has led the GWF and TRCSS JNU to be selective in respect of the choice of activities. The focus is currently on the strengthening of the network system of solution implementation (NSSI). The strengthening of NSSI implies gaining as much support as possible from the publicly funded S&T institutions and government agencies. At the moment

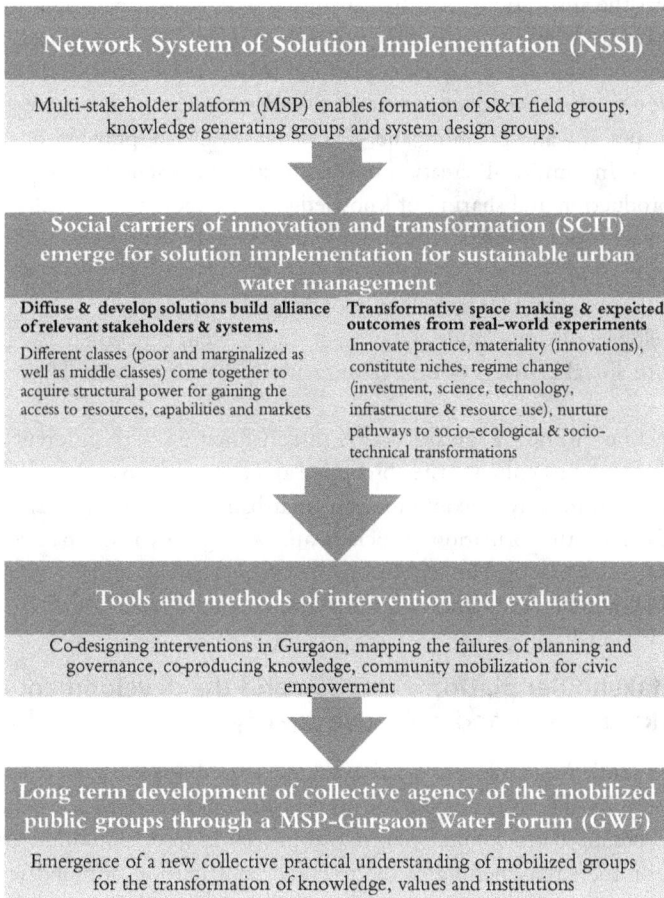

Network System of Solution Implementation (NSSI)

Multi-stakeholder platform (MSP) enables formation of S&T field groups, knowledge generating groups and system design groups.

Social carriers of innovation and transformation (SCIT) emerge for solution implementation for sustainable urban water management

Diffuse & develop solutions build alliance of relevant stakeholders & systems.	Transformative space making & expected outcomes from real-world experiments
Different classes (poor and marginalized as well as middle classes) come together to acquire structural power for gaining the access to resources, capabilities and markets	Innovate practice, materiality (innovations), constitute niches, regime change (investment, science, technology, infrastructure & resource use), nurture pathways to socio-ecological & socio-technical transformations

Tools and methods of intervention and evaluation

Co-designing interventions in Gurgaon, mapping the failures of planning and governance, co-producing knowledge, community mobilization for civic empowerment

Long term development of collective agency of the mobilized public groups through a MSP-Gurgaon Water Forum (GWF)

Emergence of a new collective practical understanding of mobilized groups for the transformation of knowledge, values and institutions

FIGURE 10.4 Network system of solution implementation, social carriers of innovation and transformation and the Gurgaon water forum.

interventions of the mobilised publics associated with the working people as well as the middle classes seek to prioritise the involvement of all of these groups in the activities of dialogue over water, participation in planning and decision making, real-world experimentation and formation of pro-poor social carriers of innovation and transformations.

Research methods

Our methodological approach has been aimed at the formation of Network System of Solution Implementation (NSSI) as a collective agency of the mobilised publics working among the middle classes and the working people of Gurgaon on the issues of urban sustainability. The agency formation has been achieved through the development of their Collective Practical Understanding (CPU) and actions by enhancing knowledge, embedding values and accelerating engagement with the institutions of urban planning and governance. The mobilised groups have been brought together to foster and strive for the formation of a knowledge-based multi-stakeholder platform (MSP) to persist with the proposed repertoire of collective action to create a leadership for public engagement on the key issues of water planning and governance of urban sprawl to be taken up in Gurgaon. In sum, MSP creation in this context is a system building approach for the production and sharing of knowledge using tools of co-production and co-design activities. It includes following stepwise interventions:

i   Creation of a multi-stakeholder knowledge-based platform
ii Develop a collective understanding of the problem concerned
iii Create Social Carriers of Innovation and Transformation (SCIT).

Coproduction of knowledge and action in collaboration with different actors is being accelerated to enhance the absorptive and adaptive capacities of the working people. Ultimately, reconfiguration of urban spaces and governance will have to focus on the formation of socially and ecologically just urban commons. A new collective practical understanding involving changes in the system of mobilisation of knowledge, values and institutions is in progress.

Multi-stakeholder platform creation and the development of networks, alliances and collective agency

In case of South Asia Hub, the T-Lab was understood not as a project but a continuous activity which is not limited to transdisciplinary outreach. The T-Lab was conceptualised as a counter-hegemonic process of intervention. Intervention focussed on the strengthening of the role and contribution of mobilised public groups towards dialogue and advocacy, participation in planning and decision making, real-world experimentation and formation of new institutions for making of pro-poor innovations and transformative spaces for the realisation of sustainable urbanism.

Mobilized Publics	Activities of the GWF	Evolution of NSSI	Stabilisation of the GWF
•Academic and S&T Institutions •Civil Society •Public Administration •NGOs •Others	•Dialogue •Advocacy •Experimentation •Participation in planning & decision making •Institutionalization of new structures of urban transformations	•System Design Group (SG) •Knowledge Generation Group (KG) •Field Development Group (FG)	Social Carriers of Innovation and Transformations (SCIT)

FIGURE 10.5 Evolution of the Gurgaon Water Forum.

In order to realise the contribution of the members of mobilised public groups and achieve a degree of alignment in their contributions to the formation of counter-hegemonic interventions in a sustained way, the South Asia Hub targeted development of a new set of "Social Carriers of Innovation and Transformation (SCIT)". SCIT emerges through the evolution of NSSI. The three major elements of the NSSI (SG, KG, FG) are illustrated in Figure 10.5.

Alignment was sought to encourage the members of the mobilised public groups in the implementation of an NSSI for enabling social mobilisation for sustainable urbanism. In this process, members of the mobilised public groups were encouraged to get actively involved in the development of SG, KG and FG within the larger network of the GWF to achieve a higher level of success in social mobilisation. The network of GWF initiated a number of activities involving members of the mobilised publics. These activities can be broadly categorised as dialogue, advocacy, participation in planning and decision making, experimentation (real-world experiments) and institutionalisation of new structures of social transformation (formation and stabilisation of new institutional structures).

The most significant aspect of this process is the realisation of a collective agency-based-power perspective as a result of alignment among the members of the GWF. More specifically, the power of collective agency of the GWF comes from the contribution of its members in the form of providing leadership roles at the level of SG, KG and FG on the ground through their regular involvement in these activities. The overall contribution of the members of the mobilised public groups participating in the activities of the GWF was categorised and measured in terms of the progress of their contribution in five major stages of the evolution of GWF. The specific stage of their involvement reflects the alignment of their role and contribution towards the development of leadership at the level of FG, KG and SG on a scale of 1–5, as illustrated in Table 10.1.

Out of 140 participants in T Lab 1 (the first T-Lab workshop), we selected those who followed up our initiative partially or up to a greater extent to the time of writing (2020) by contributing in the visions and strategies of the GWF. A chart was prepared mentioning contribution of each of these participants (members)

TABLE 10.1 Stages of the mobilisation of the members of the mobilised public groups

Stages	Contribution of each member in the activities of the GWF
1	Initiation of dialogue
2	Initiation of dialogue and advocacy
3	Initiation of dialogue, advocacy, public participation in planning & decision making
4	Initiation of dialogue, advocacy, public participation in planning & decision making and experimentation started
5	Initiation of dialogue, advocacy, public participation in planning & decision making, experimentation and the formation of a new institution that has started functioning

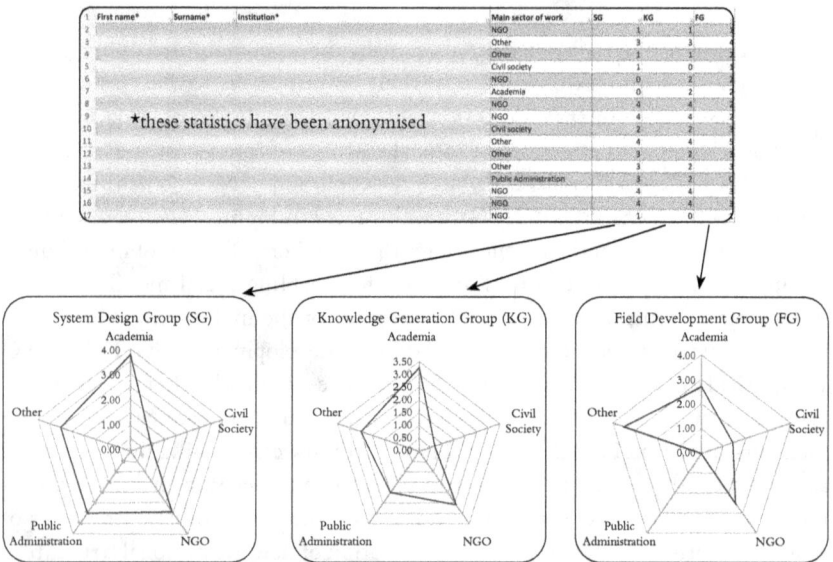

FIGURE 10.6 Measuring the power (collective agency), role and contribution of mobilised publics.

as per stages 1–5 in the realisation of the FG, KG and SG (see the anonymised spreadsheet in Figure 10.6). Later, contributions of different categories of participants were put together in spider charts (see the bottom of Figure 10.6), depicting collective contributions of different groups (shown category-wise: academia, public administration, civil society, NGOS and others) in the realisation of the SG, KG and FG. In this way, the progress towards stabilisation of the GWF (and transformative space formation – see Pereira et al. 2018) has been measured using a scale of 1–5 to indicate the contributions of each mobilised group. Interestingly, not all group members were able to contribute equally in the role of FG, KG and SG, when measured for their involvement in the different stages of activity.

Figure 10.6 shows how members of academia, public administration, NGOs and informal sector, and workers' unions played major roles in the System Design Group. Civil society was less active in the activities of this group. In the Knowledge Generation Group, academia played a major role, while NGOs and informal sector and workers' unions showed willingness to contribute. Public administration was less active as lacking capabilities and civil society was almost reluctant in the process. As far as the Field Development Group is concerned, the informal sector and workers' unions and NGOs played a leading role in the field and helped academia in reaching out to the larger public. Civil society showed limited interest in providing leadership in the field, and public administration was almost absent in the mobilisation of people on the ground.

Key moments in the India T-Lab process

T-Labs are processes where the social mobilisation plans were seeded. Interventions were deliberated upon to enrol the diverse actors with different motivations to participate in the development of interactive innovation spaces. These allowed the TRCSS, JNU to form and mobilise the relevant publics for experimentation with new social-ecological-technological system configurations and sustainability pathways (pathway creation). Innovation for transformative change in the Gurgaon case demanded T-Labs to undertake preparatory work for the context-specific challenges of urban water and waste water management including assessment of mainstream pathways, identification of opportunities for alternative path creation and experimentation. As with the other hubs in the 'Pathways' network, two T-Lab workshops were interspersed with a series of research and engagement activities.

The process of organising the 1st T-Lab workshop started with the research team conducting background research. This background research started much earlier with reviewing the studies on the migration in Gurgaon through the co-design workshop in November 2014 and the subsequent concept note developed by JNU/STEPS Centre in 2015. It was revealed that Gurgaon has seen an influx of migrant workers for employment during the last couple of decades. A study of three peri-urban villages in Gurgaon revealed the poor health and morbidity conditions in related to water and wastewater. Pollution is increasing in the sources of water due to the mixing of untreated sewage, affecting the supply of surface water and causing environmental and health hazards. Heavy concentrations of iron and fluoride are common. The old drainage and sewer system are not capable of bearing the current load of sewage, resulting in frequent water logging and clogging of drains. There exists severe encroachment of natural drainage patterns resulting in frequent urban flooding and destruction of water bodies. The background research highlighted the existence of common and separate challenges facing the people of different classes. We also conducted several field studies to understand the different perspectives and framings held by different classes, using the methods described in the 'Research methods' section of this chapter.

This background research helped us in setting up the agenda for the first T-Lab workshop on February 10–11, 2017, addressing the following broad questions:

1   What kind of public engagement helps realise better the involvement of middle classes, farmers and workers in the processes to be initiated for the promotion of sustainable water management?
2   What kind of policy paradigm needs to be in place to obtain sustainable water management system in a semi-arid region, which is rapidly urbanising and seeking industrialisation through global integration, privatisation and public–private partnerships?
3   What kind of tools and resource materials can help enable the organisation of a platform for dialogue on the problems and challenges of sustainable water management?
4   What kind of contestation enables people to reflect on the conflicts in respect of water availability and use?
5   How far can the participation of people in decision making organised via Panchayati Raj Institutions (PRIs) of local self-governance help to organise sustainable water management?
6   What kind of real-world experimentation is necessary for the promotion of institutional transformation and social carriers of innovation for sustainable water management?
7   How do we understand the role of policy paradigms in the management of transition/transformative change?
8   How should the protagonists of transformative change measure the level of success in the spread of sustainable water management practices?

T-Lab workshop 1

The workshop was open to multiple stakeholders including policy makers, planners, experts, bureaucrats, citizen groups, resident welfare organisations (RWAs), workers' organisations, NGOs, researchers, activists and others. More than 100 people participated. The workshop was aimed at mapping the knowledge, values and institutions of mobilised publics and organising them for the creation of a multi-stakeholder platform for individual and collective actions. The problems identified by the research team were growing dependence of the city on water from distant sources, neglect of protection of local water bodies, lack of systems for water recycling, destruction of natural drainage, Aravali mountain range habitat and catchment areas, replacement of existing freshwater pipelines and sewers to prevent contamination and investment in covering the drains to reduce nuisance.

Deliberations led to the establishment of a multi-stakeholder platform – the Gurgaon Water Forum – agreeing to undertake activities of knowledge creation, utilisation and dissemination. The research team argued that at present the focus of urban planning was on the development of physical infrastructure such as road engineering – highways, flyovers without protecting natural drainage. Urban flooding, they argued, was due to destruction of natural drainage pattern, as a result of urban developmental interventions. By ignoring the carrying capacity of the city, the neo-liberal growth perspective and real estate interests continued to drive the expansion of Gurgaon through the expansion of Dwarka and Kundli Manesar Palwal (KMP) expressways.

In response to the framings of problems by the research team, the critical response at that time came from government officials, who labelled the TRCSS, JNU approach purely academic as opposed to representing possible practical solutions. The concerns raised were rejected and dialogue did not bring changes in the understanding of the dominant stakeholders. Pleas for the need for an integrated water management approach were dismissed. Traffic management was prioritised over drainage as a way to deal with the urban flooding. The mainstream thinking of middle-class RWAs was not very different from that of the administration – that water for Gurgaon would have to come from distant (rather than local) sources.

Following the first T-Lab workshop, the GWF began to focus on collective practical approaches rather than on pushing a shared understanding of the problem space and transformative changes (which proved elusive). Therefore, we prioritised collaborative action with mobilised public groups to develop practical approaches for SUWM. We started on co-production of knowledge, co-design of SUWM solutions and network development for the implementation of SUWM solutions (see Figure 10.3). Priority was given to dialogue with public administration and others in small group meetings focussing on the identification of collective practical approaches, seeking cooperation, assigning of roles, capacity building and alignment. With priority given to moderate/radical perspective on change and the emphasis on equity and ecological soundness, a distinct identity of the GWF has emerged.

In sum, we planned to explore all the possible different strategies for 1) the development of creative entrepreneurial leadership in the city for the implementation of urban planning and participation of the people as a whole in governance, 2) the development of a research network having capabilities and cultures of participation in co-production of knowledge and co-design of sustainability experiments and 3) the development of a system design group at JNU in collaboration with the educational and research institutions and engagement agents for a sustainable city.

Following the first T-Lab workshop, interventions began in the form of the shaping of the legislative framework for urban development planning in Gurgaon. Our participation in the consultation on Gurgaon Municipal Development Authority Bill 2017 was seemingly well received by both governmental agencies and non-governmental organisations. We were able to gather resources from among the different stakeholders including the local government and the

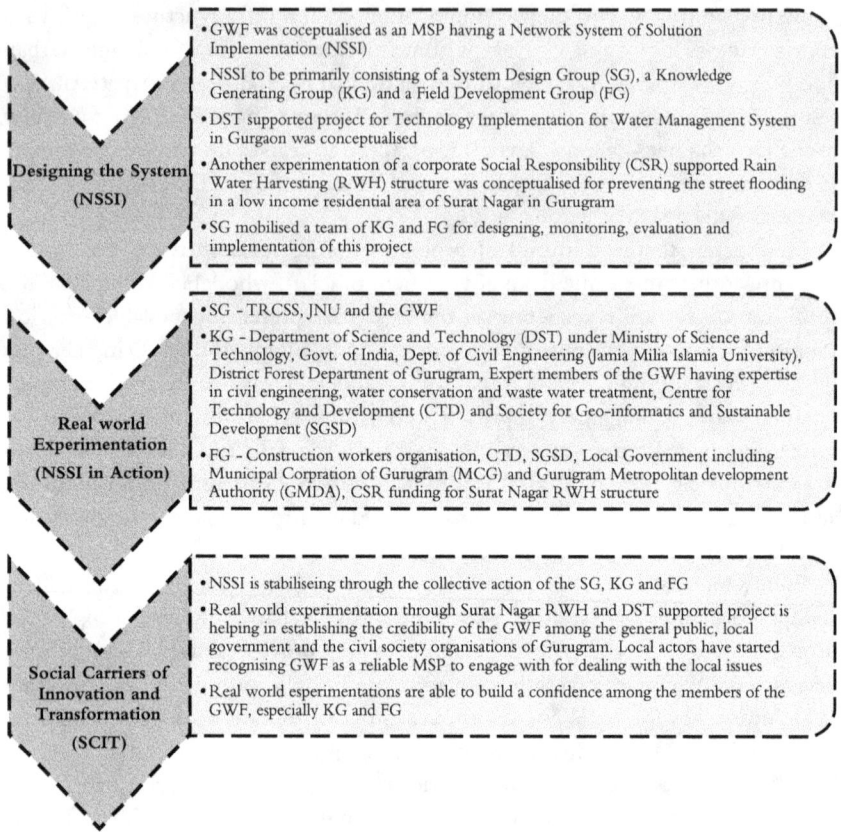

Designing the System (NSSI)

- GWF was coceptualised as an MSP having a Network System of Solution Implementation (NSSI)
- NSSI to be primarily consisting of a System Design Group (SG), a Knowledge Generating Group (KG) and a Field Development Group (FG)
- DST supported project for Technology Implementation for Water Management System in Gurgaon was conceptualised
- Another experimentation of a corporate Social Responsibility (CSR) supported Rain Water Harvesting (RWH) structure was conceptualised for preventing the street flooding in a low income residential area of Surat Nagar in Gurugram
- SG mobilised a team of KG and FG for designing, monitoring, evaluation and implementation of this project

Real world Experimentation (NSSI in Action)

- SG – TRCSS, JNU and the GWF
- KG – Department of Science and Technology (DST) under Ministry of Science and Technology, Govt. of India, Dept. of Civil Engineering (Jamia Milia Islamia University), District Forest Department of Gurugram, Expert members of the GWF having expertise in civil engineering, water conservation and waste water treatment, Centre for Technology and Development (CTD) and Society for Geo-informatics and Sustainable Development (SGSD)
- FG – Construction workers organisation, CTD, SGSD, Local Government including Municipal Corpration of Gurugram (MCG) and Gurugram Metropolitan development Authority (GMDA), CSR funding for Surat Nagar RWH structure

Social Carriers of Innovation and Transformation (SCIT)

- NSSI is stabiliseing through the collective action of the SG, KG and FG
- Real world experimentation through Surat Nagar RWH and DST supported project is helping in establishing the credibility of the GWF among the general public, local government and the civil society organisations of Gurugram. Local actors have started recognising GWF as a reliable MSP to engage with for dealing with the local issues
- Real world esperimentations are able to build a confidence among the members of the GWF, especially KG and FG

FIGURE 10.7 Pathways to sustainability: collective practical approaches, collaborative actions and real-world experimentations.

Municipal Commissioner of Gurgaon (MCG), the main public urban authority, in the form of their goodwill, attention and cooperation.

We subsequently received the consent of MCG for the submission of projects to the Ministry of Science and Technology on the augmentation of water availability, rationalisation of water use, treatment of grey water and prevention of urban flooding. A project eventually got approved by the ministry in July 2019 and – at the time of writing – is under implementation.

Alongside the two universities involved in the submission of projects (Jawaharlal Nehru University and Jamia Millia Islamia), it is possible to claim at least some success for the wider team, including non-governmental organisations, trade union bodies and women's organisations.

The T-Lab, and subsequently the GWF, involved a lot of individuals as well as formally organised groups. Using the resources of a community radio station (a twelve-episode radio programme was aired in the summer of 2017) we were able to mobilise other groups too. Our process started developing and later implementing direct action and real-world experiments. It was our hope that the T-Lab in India would consolidate the multi-stakeholder platform through these processes. Between the two T-Lab workshops this involved strengthening of field group leadership, fostering of knowledge and technology system generating groups and an increase in real-world experimental proposals.

T-Lab Workshop 2

The second T-Lab workshop was organised by the TRCSS, JNU and the GWF a year and half later in Gurgaon on September 29–30, 2018. This consultation workshop was again open to a wide range of stakeholders and some success was certainly evident. This time, significant changes were seen in the framings and approaches of various stakeholders. The public administration had realised that drainage was a high priority area along with the revival of water bodies, water recycling and reuse. Permissions and cooperation for the start of the pilot projects were obtained for collaborative actions on the ground.

Although the RWAs still appeared to be inclined towards long distance water supply sources, they also spoke of the need to conserve water and build local check dams in order to deal with the challenge of urban flooding. Professionals such as town planners supported the idea of carrying capacity; engineers supported the focus on drainage and support for farmers. Trade unions raised the concerns for water logging, water auditing, housing, revival and protection of water bodies and maintenance and repair, capacity building of the workers. The corporate sector too showed interest and participated in the dialogue. The DLF Foundation leadership (the philanthropic arm of one of the developers) was in the audience to participate in the deliberations.

Other outcomes included the stabilisation of GWF, TRCSS, JNU and successful networking with S&T Institutions, academic, and a variety of relevant groups including NGOs, professions, Trade Unions (TUs), civil society groups, experts and practitioners, Resident Welfare Associations (RWAs) confederations, environmental groups, women groups, theatre groups and so on (see Figure 10.8).

The progress we achieved in the second T-Lab workshop was non-linear. Given the multiplicity of the interests and framings of the participating individuals and organisations, feedback loops and reflexivity have played an important role at all stages. Progress between stages has been subject to iterative and recursive processes of learning.

The second T-Lab workshop brought clarity on the challenge of retaining the legitimacy of Gurgaon Water Forum's interventions. In Gurgaon, the T-Lab process started with the ambition of building a robust Network System of Solution Implementation (NSSI) for the SUWM domain. As the project was coming to an end, we had to deal with the challenges of sustaining the ongoing activities and stabilising the structures and process of supporting financially and organisationally the NSSI nucleus created in the course of the project.

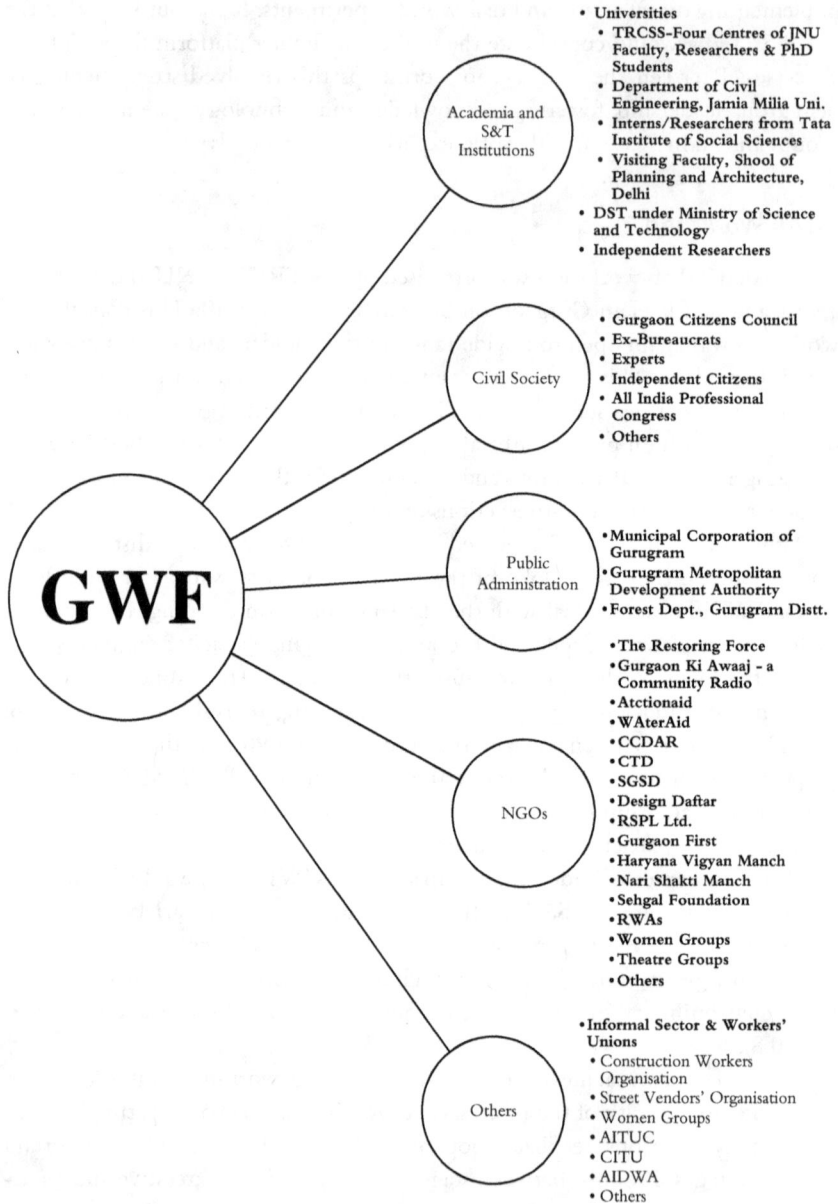

FIGURE 10.8 The Gurgaon water forum: a transdisciplinary network.

Leadership building processes are quite critical to platform formation in Gurgaon. The T-Lab has had to show that as a co-benefit the JNU faculty would
be able to gain meaningfully in respect of the transformation of their research
activity and that the engaged academic activity is also quite rewarding. New

methodological approaches are emerging out of this exercise. There are now many more research students willing to collaborate from within the collaborating centres.

Lessons from the T-Lab process

The first T-Lab workshop was focussed on the minimalist agenda of common activities on the front of water conservation, recycling and so on. The agenda broadened out throughout the project. The leadership has had to keep in mind that to include diverse and heterogeneous actors the processes of "broadening out" (see Chapter 5 in Leach et al. 2010) have had to be implemented without adversely affecting the overall vision and strategy of GWF. To approach this challenge in an effective way, the GWF has pursued the strategy of gaining

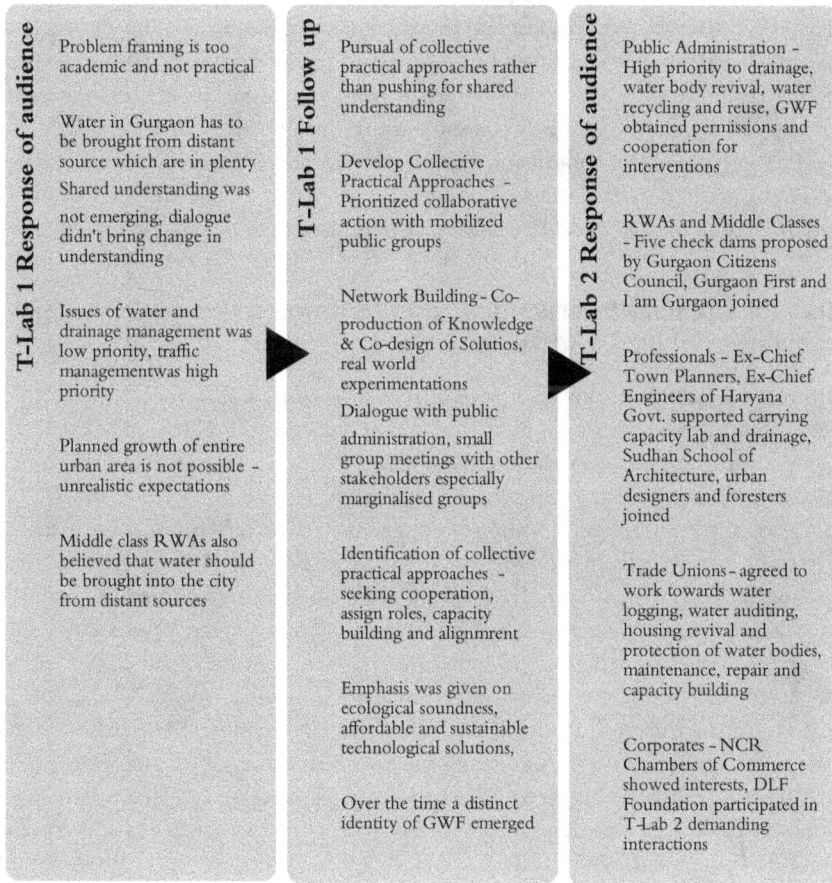

T-Lab 1 Response of audience	T-Lab 1 Follow up	T-Lab 2 Response of audience
Problem framing is too academic and not practical	Pursual of collective practical approaches rather than pushing for shared understanding	Public Administration – High priority to drainage, water body revival, water recycling and reuse, GWF obtained permissions and cooperation for interventions
Water in Gurgaon has to be brought from distant source which are in plenty		
Shared understanding was not emerging, dialogue didn't bring change in understanding	Develop Collective Practical Approaches – Prioritized collaborative action with mobilized public groups	RWAs and Middle Classes – Five check dams proposed by Gurgaon Citizens Council, Gurgaon First and I am Gurgaon joined
Issues of water and drainage management was low priority, traffic managementwas high priority	Network Building - Co-production of Knowledge & Co-design of Solutios, real world experimentations	Professionals – Ex-Chief Town Planners, Ex-Chief Engineers of Haryana Govt. supported carrying capacity lab and drainage, Sudhan School of Architecture, urban designers and foresters joined
Planned growth of entire urban area is not possible – unrealistic expectations	Dialogue with public administration, small group meetings with other stakeholders especially marginalised groups	
Middle class RWAs also believed that water should be brought into the city from distant sources	Identification of collective practical approaches – seeking cooperation, assign roles, capacity building and alignmrent	Trade Unions – agreed to work towards water logging, water auditing, housing revival and protection of water bodies, maintenance, repair and capacity building
	Emphasis was given on ecological soundness, affordable and sustainable technological solutions,	
	Over the time a distinct identity of GWF emerged	Corporates – NCR Chambers of Commerce showed interests, DLF Foundation participated in T-Lab 2 demanding interactions

FIGURE 10.9 T-Labs: challenging dominant pathways of urban water, planning and governance.

the trust and legitimacy from the working-class people and their organisations. With this in mind, real-world experimentation in SUWM was prioritised. Still, it is difficult to claim that we have found an effective solution to the problem of building alliances across mobilised publics

It should be realised that progress remains slow in terms of inserting new demands (such as worker housing) into the agenda building in Gurgaon, however, the GWF has begun efforts to put the idea of "build to rent housing" on the agenda of public administration and policymakers. Further, collaborative action on the agenda of citizenship rights of migrants with the middle classes is yet to be taken up by the GWF. It is a major political issue and will need a carefully worked out strategy if the process of alliance building is to remain unharmed.

In terms of the diversity of alignments within our stakeholder group, while the middle classes (represented through RWAs) have often joined us in both action and deliberations, it has taken more effort and time to mobilise the RWAs. The GWF has limited capacity and insufficient resources to take up the agenda of mobilisation for direct action on the front of urban planning. Efforts are underway to build the capacity of volunteers from among all the classes, but these efforts will have to be intensified if momentum is to be built on the ground.

The experience of mobilising the people for development of collaborative action on water conservation and drainage suggests that it takes time with a non-aligned group of actors and that success is not guaranteed.

Transdisciplinary interventions and re-framing the challenges of urban sustainability

From the beginning, the TRCSS team was convinced that the challenges of reframing must be addressed by the emergent leadership in Gurgaon at the level of transforming the socio-ecological, socio-technical and socio-institutional spaces with a pro-poor approach to innovation. At the same time, the GWF has been able to maintain a sustained engagement with urban residents, administration, experts, planners, policy makers, practitioners, NGOs, civil society groups, workers unions and other stakeholders. Such an engagement with multiple stakeholders, practitioners and implementing agencies has helped the GWF in re-framing the challenges of contemporary urbanisation through the lenses of sustainable urban transformations. Since its inception, the GWF has been fostering formation of transformative spaces and re-framing the debate of urban sustainability through four pathways of social mobilisation and sustainable urban transformation, i.e. reconfiguring urban spaces, reconfiguring urban governance, civic empowerment and new pathways of urban resilience and regeneration as explained in Figure 10.9. Overall, a paradigm shift can be observed in understanding the issues of urban water management in Gurugram.

The collective practical approaches of the GWF have proven the biggest enablers in re-framing the debate of urban water management in Gurgaon. GWF has been trying to implement certain basic elements of the collective action. These elements include the following:

i   Addressing inequality
ii Promoting participation of citizens including marginalised groups
iii Contestations matter (no shared understanding) but agreement on practical solutions is achievable
iv Location specific interventions should be co-designed to enable participation of locals
v   Real-world experiments are necessary to demonstrate success of contestations
vi Participation of not only ordinary citizens but also experts and practitioners who want to collaborate and volunteer
vii The above combine to form an emerging strategy of challenging the power structure.

Informality is quite diverse and highly stratified. In the Indian context, apart from class distinctions, it needs to be captured through the lenses of gender, caste, region, religion, etc. Collective actions also need to recognise the dynamics of human-nature relations. How are these relations progressing? Non-market calculations, the social and ecological cost of human interventions, etc., need to be factored in overall assessment of impacts of human interventions.

The GWF has been able to foster the following collective practical approaches through collaborative action and real-world experiments for initiating the path of sustainable urban water management:

a   Protection of catchment areas, local water bodies, role of Aravalli forest as water sanctuary of future.
b   Replenishment through RWH, recharging wells, protecting water bodies and water footprint auditing.
c   Protecting natural drainage habitat, focussing on drainage to reduce urban flooding and everyday waterlogging.
d   Provided required quantity of potable water for daily use in poor urban settlements.
e   Provided eco-friendly technologies of treatment of brackish and waste water and improving storm water drains across the city.
f   Provisions of dual pipeline, bioremediation, decentralised waste water treatment.
g   Focus on regular clearing of drains.

For initiating collective practical approaches, the GWF started with awareness, dialogue, advocacy and proposals for real-world experiments. These initial activities were followed by the process of co-production of knowledge, co-designing solutions and institutionalisation of NSSI by enrolling different stakeholders into the network. Later, democratising political governance, civic

Perennial waterlogging & seasonal street flooding in low-income and lower castle areas

Vulnerable system & unsustainable practices

Focus on supply side Management

Urban flooding in planned areas too very common during rains

Overexploitation of surface and ground water

Lack of representation of voices of poor and marginalised

Mainstream Pathways (Problem Space)

Vulnerable & Unsustainable

Rising non-priority use

Low priority to reuse, recycling and replenishment

Increasing dependence on underground and distant sources of surface water

Lack of protection of water bodies

Decreasing reliability of water supply system

Inequality in distribution

Paradigm Shift

Re-Framing Mainstream Pathways

- Water conservation practices and revival of waterbodies
- Prevent urban flooding & perennial waterlogging in slums and low-income settlements
- Alternate drainage path, trunk infra for sewage
- Waste water recycling and reuse

Reconfiguring Urban Spaces

Reconfiguring Urban Governance

- Participation in urban planning and decision making
- Participation of locals in urban water management practices
- Equitable distribution of urban water resources

- Public engagement and mobilization - public consultations, citizen science, community radio programmes, meetings, training and rientation programmes
- Building MSP - knowledge sharing, co-production of knowledge and co-designing solutions
- Creation of SCIT

Civic Empowerment

New Pathways of Urban Resilience and Regeneration

- Revival, operation and maintenance of water bodies and watersheds
- Water recycling and reuse to reduce the fresh water demand
- Safe drinking water for all especially in informal settlement
- Avoid mixing of sewage into water supply lines
- Seperate storm water drains to prevent its mixing into sewage systems
- Health and livelihood security for workers involved in waste water management

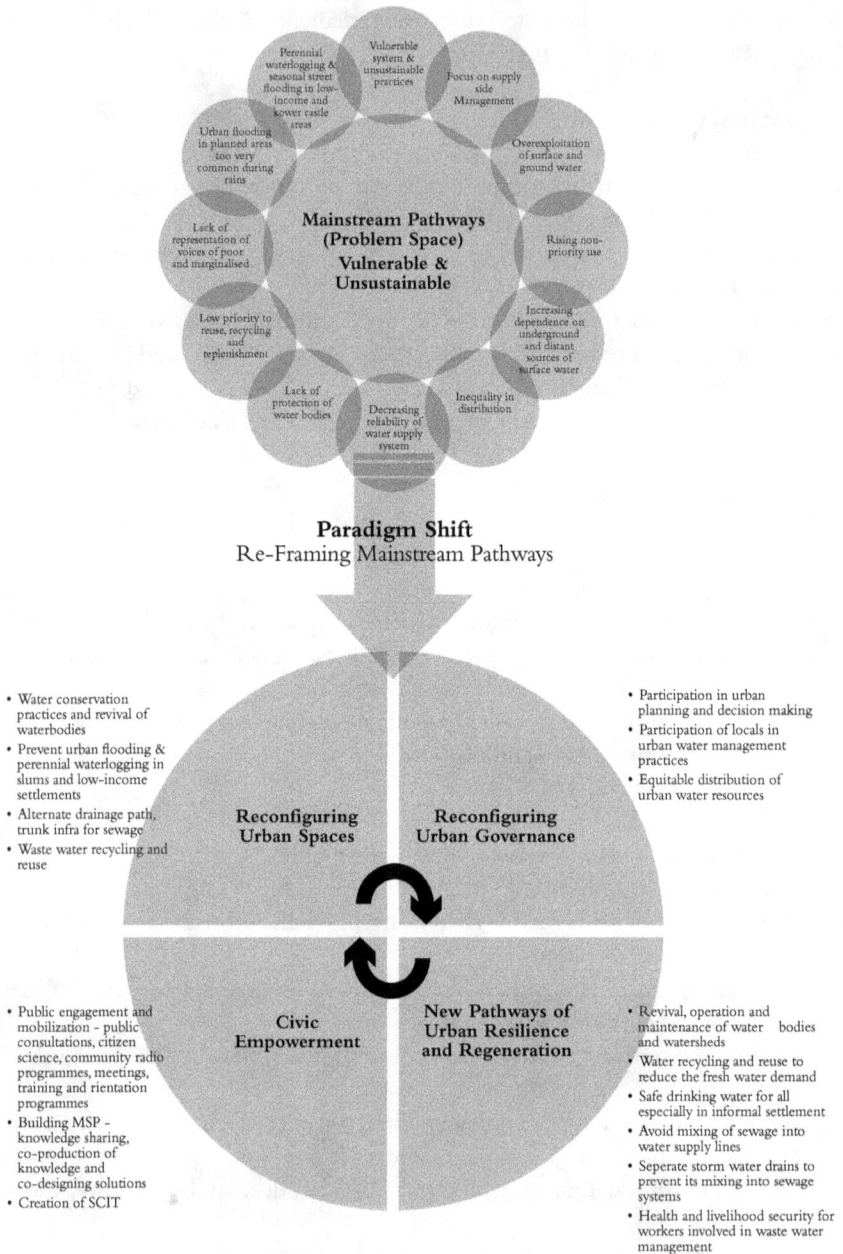

FIGURE 10.10 Transdisciplinary interventions and re-framing the challenges of urban sustainability.

empowerment and construction of new pathways emerged out of the collective engagement of citizens, experts, policy makers and planners.

In order to empower the mobilised publics to engage with the process of urban planning and governance, the GWF and the TRCSS, JNU are also extending the initiative to involve the mobilised publics working at the scale of the national capital region (NCR). The NSSI structure is enabling the GWF and the TRCSS to open up the space for everyday struggles of the working classes in not only the low-income settlement colonies where they live and socially reproduce themselves but also the space for contributing to the struggle for the conservation of habitat and the ecologically and socially just urban water governance in making using the tools of science communication in which Haryana Vigyan Manch (HVM) and the women groups have joined hands with the GWF in Gurgaon. The GWF has been spreading the awareness through community radio programmes among the low-income working classes about water-related concerns. Citizen science initiatives are focussed for the present on water related issues. The GWF is also now focussing on the issues of housing for the urban poor and affordable transportation especially "last mile" connectivity for the working classes including low-income urban residents.

Since the translation of this theory of change involves the development of longer-term strategies of patient, counter-hegemonic interventions with the view to open-up spaces for transformative change that the SASH&KN wants to see in Gurgaon, there are ongoing efforts on the part of the GWF to mobilise the people on a broader platform. For example, the GWF joined hands to influence and impact prior to the elections through the Gurgaon Citizens Charter. This process was able to mobilise to some extent the discourse on urban planning and governance in Gurgaon among civil society organisations.

Insights and contributions from the India hub disciplines, culture and context

Our first insight is that the T-Labs need to be understood as making contributions to social mobilisation for the development of counter hegemonic transformative activity. In the specific context of Gurgaon, the T-Labs focussed on mobilising actors to start resisting neo-liberal reform pathways of development or growth, state disengagement and market-based governance (combined or separately). Social mobilisation (direct action, participation and experimentation) directed at the development of counter hegemonic activity to counter the above approaches to urban development aimed at the development of spaces for transformative changes.

Transformative change requires sustained engagement with the structural causes and with the effects of the underlying dynamics of capitalist pathways, which is increasingly linked to the secondary circuit of capital accumulation in Gurgaon. It was also envisaged that at some point in time the T-Lab would need to focus on the issue of how to interweave the economic and social transformations – related interventions with the sub-regimes of water management and urbanisation.

The mainstream pathways of unsustainable urbanisation in Gurgaon are driven by the combined power of real estate, national and transnational capital and local elites coming from the middle classes and farming communities. The T-Lab process has had to address the issues of structural transformation (s), and the India hub has chosen to find ways of contesting the forces representing transnational and national capital who wield a lot of power on the urban transition at the moment in Gurgaon. In the meanwhile, the GWF continues to focus on fostering the dimensions of sustainability, water resources management and equity (water for all). It is crystal clear that it would not be possible in Gurgaon to tackle the full challenge of sustainable urban water management without countering the real estate and rent-seeking classes.

The dynamics of closing and opening of spaces for new visions of transformation is a political, ideological and socio-cultural process. The MSP needs to add its might and contribute by adding strength to the existing democratic currents. The two challenges of equity and ecological soundness need to be tackled upfront to mobilise the democratic mass. Examining equity and ecological soundness in the domain of water management will allow the GWF to generate credibility for itself. Simultaneous preparations need to be made for the domains of water management, city development and governance of economic and social transformations in an integrated way.

The T-Lab process cannot be planned and implemented on the basis of a static notion of shared understanding (guiding the problem space and the desired transformative changes). The CPU should be the starting point of the T-Lab engagement. For example, there exists now the hegemony of framings such as a belief in growth first, the inevitability of urban change, the need for urban regions to import fresh surface water from Himalayas or the access to rivers like Yamuna and Ganga. The T-Lab methodology needs to target the hegemony of these framings – their hegemony is not permanent and can be contested.

Transformative change requires the multi-stakeholder platform to keep the more radical contestation in its reckoning. The TRCSS, JNU would need to engage with the domains of urban planning, urban design and urban governance through the promotion of legislative and institutional change to promote the participation and role of society in SUWM as well as the policy paradigm related to the planning and governance of economic, social and political transformation.

Intervention should not be limited to the participation in public consultations of local planning authorities, but we need to intervene in the domains of worker housing, legislation for participation of RWAs and local area committees in water conservation, wastewater recycling, SWM and urban planning, design and governance of the urban expansion.

The TRCSS, JNU is building a totally new space for enabling the mobilised publics to contribute in the co-production of knowledge, values and institutions. This process is a continuing activity where the processes of leadership, organisation and system building can be expected to play a critical role in the power dynamics. For success, the T-Lab process would require far more resources, organisation building and leadership. The collaborating mobilised publics will have to upgrade their capabilities and extend the networks. It is necessary to sustain the initiatives that have got going on the ground during the project period. Otherwise it can be easily predicted that the process of T-Lab will come to collapse with the completion of the ISSC project.

The Department of Science and Technology, Govt. of India has recently awarded a technology implementation project to the TRCSS, JNU to be implemented in collaboration with Centre for Technology and Development (CTD) and Society for Geo-Informatics and Sustainable Development (SGSD). GWF was also approached by the private sector to implement a Corporate Social Responsibility (CSR) funded RWH project, which has recently been completed. Other CSR groups are also approaching the GWF for implementing similar projects in Gurgaon. After the second T-Lab the GWF found that more groups are willing to collaborate, including Helping Brains, Haryana Institute of Public Administration, Street Vendors' Association and Sanitation Workers' Union. However, significantly more funds, whether through government or non-governmental sources are necessary to enable the sustenance and development of the GWF.

Finally, there are many more questions which would require answers from the T-Lab process in India. The TRCSS, JNU researchers have the challenge of finding more time to gain the trust of and legitimacy not only from the disciplines but also from the mobilised publics. The T-Lab process is a time-consuming activity.

Note

1 Lefebvre further explains the 'circuits of capitalism'. For him, investments in industrial sector (manufacturing and commerce) represent the 'Primary Circuit of Capitalism' where profit maximization takes place by minimizing the cost of manufacturing, especially the cost of labour. Factories are preferably located close to the areas having cheap housing provisions for its workers. The investment in real estate is called the 'secondary circuit of capital'. The money-flows into real estate through the development of land. It is significant to point out that this kind of investment is not easily convertible into liquid assets. Therefore, when the first circuit declines, the money flows into the secondary circuit resulting in the excessive development of land at the cost of environmental sustainability. In case of the recovery of the 'primary circuit', the reverse flow of money from 'secondary circuit' does not take place quickly. This is because the money invested in built environment can't be easily converted back to cash and the real estate value declines. Consequently, municipal and metropolitan revenue also declines.

References

Arora, S. (2019, February 9). *Centre sought 'water-sensitive' tag in 2016.* Retrieved February 10, 2020, from *The Times of India*: https://timesofindia.indiatimes.com/city/gurgaon/centre-sought-water-sensitive-tag-in-2016/articleshow/67908524.cms

Arora, S. (2019, August 5). *70 societies in Gurugram lay out plan to save water, check pollution.* Retrieved April 10, 2020, from https://timesofindia.indiatimes.com: https://timesofindia.indiatimes.com/city/gurgaon/70-societies-in-gurgaon-lay-out-plan-to-save-water-check-pollution/articleshow/70527676.cms

Brenner, N., & Schmid, C. (2015). Towards a new epistemology of the urban? *City, 19*(2–3), 151–182.

Centre for Science and Environment. (2012). *Gurgaon: The water-waste portrait. in excreta matters – State of India's environment.* New Delhi: Centre for Science and Environment.

Chatterji, T. (2013). The Micro-politics of urban transformation in the context of globalisation: A case study of Gurgaon, India. *Journal of South Asian Studies, 36*(2), 273–287.

Department of Town and Country Planning. (2012, November 09). *Gurgaon-Manesar Urban Complex-2031 AD.* Retrieved January 21, 2020, from Department of Town and Country Planning, Government of Haryana: https://tcpharyana.gov.in/Development_Plan/ColouredCopy/GURUGRAM_FDP_2031.pdf

Dhillon, S. S. (2012, November 15). *Final development plan 2031 AD for Gurgaon-Manesar Urban Complex.* Retrieved February 2020, from https://tcpharyana.gov.in/Development_Plan/Gurgaon/Gurgaon/FDP_2031/FDP_2031_GMUC.pdf

DLF Foundation. (2008). *Gurgaon Rejuvenation Project.* Retrieved February 15, 2020, from DLF Foundation: https://www.dlffoundation.in/grp/mentoring/

DLF Foundation. (2017, August 17). *Capacity Building workshop on Transforming the Najafgarh Basin.* Retrieved March 5, 2020, from DLF Foundation: https://www.dlffoundation.in/najafgarh-basin

DLF Foundation. (n.d.). *Gurgaon Rejuvenation Project.* Retrieved January 10, 2020, from DLF Foundation: https://www.dlffoundation.in/wp-content/uploads/2018/04/brochure_GRP.pdf

DLF Foundation, INTACH and IWP. (2017). *Transforming the Najafgarh Basin: A White Paper.* Retrieved January 5, 2020, from India Water Partnership: https://cwp-india.org/wp-content/uploads/2019/11/White-paper-of-Najafgarh-basin-1.pdf

Edquist, C., & Edqvist, O. (1979). Social carriers of techniques for development. *Journal of Peace Research, 16*(4), 313–331.

Goldstein, S. R. (2016). Planning the Millennium city: The politics of place-making in Gurgaon, India. *International Area Studies Review, 19*(2), 12–27.

Gotham, K. F. (2010). New Urban Sociology. In R. Hutchinson, & R. Hutchinson (Eds.), *Encyclopedia of Urban Studies* (pp. 553–554). London: Sage.

Gottdiener, M., & Budd, L. (2005). *Key Concepts in Urban Studies.* New Delhi: Sage.

Harvey, D. (1973). *Social Justice and the City.* Baltimore: John Hopkins Press.

Harvey, D. (1978). The Urban process under capitalism: A framework for analysis. *International Journal of Urban and Regional Research, 2*(1–4), 101–131.

Hindustan Times. (2017, Month 25). *Gurgaon's water table shrinking by 1–3 metres every years, says CSE.* Retrieved January 21, 2020, from https://www.hindustantimes.com/https://www.hindustantimes.com/gurgaon/gurgaon-s-water-table-shrinking-by-1-3-metres-every-year-says-cse/story-ll7GDE8eRSHFtEjL0LLpVJ.html

HT Correspondent. (2019, March 04). *Central Water Management System among Measures to Improve Supply.* Retrieved March 20, 2020, from https://www.hindustantimes.com:

https://www.hindustantimes.com/gurgaon/central-water-management-system-among-measures-to-improve-supply/story-fypCRJoBtBqciWhF1rFhGM.html

Hubbard, P. (2006). *City*. London and New York: Routledge.

Leach, M., Stirling, A., & Scoones, I. (2010). *Dynamic Sustainabilities: Technologies, Environment, Social Justice*. Abingdon: Routledge.

Lefebvre, H. (2003). *The Urban Revolution*. (R. Bononno, Trans.) Minneapolis & London: University of Minnesota Press.

Malik, V. K., Singh, R. K., & Singh, S. K. (2010). Impact of Urbanization on Groundwater of Gurgaon District, Haryana, India. *International Journal of Rural development and Management Studies*, *5*(1), 45–57.

Merrifield, A. (2005). Metropolitan Birth Pangs: Reflections on Lefebvre's The Urban Revolution. *International Journal of Urban and Regional Research*, *29*(3), 693–702.

Mishra, A., Masoodi, M., Poyil, R., & Tewari, N. (2018). Water demand and waste management with respect to projected urban growth of Gurugram city in Haryana. *Beni-Suef University Journal of Basic and Applied Sciences*, 7(3), 336–343.

National Capital Regional Planning Board. (2020, February 20). Retrieved February 20, 2020, from National Capital Regional Planning Board: http://ncrpb.nic.in/

Rajagopalan, S., & Tabarrok, A. (2014). Lessons from Gurgaon, India's Private City. In D. E. Andersson, & S. Moroni (Eds.), *Cities and Private Planning* (pp. 199–231). Cheltenham and Northampton: Edward Elgar.

Roychowdhury, A., & Puri, S. (2017). *Gurugram: A Framework for Sustainable Development*. New Delhi: Centre for Science and Environment.

Singh, S. (2012, October 30). *Behind Haryana Land Boom, the Midas Touch of Hooda*. Retrieved February 12, 2020, from https://www.thehindu.com: https://www.thehindu.com/news/national/behind-haryana-land-boom-the-midas-touch-of-hooda/article4048394.ece

Smith, A., Fressoli, M., Abrol, D., Arond, E., & Ely, A. (2016). *Grassroots Innovation Movements*. Abingdon: Routledge.

Times News Network. (2017, August 18). *Reviving Najafgarh Basin Key to Stop Flooding in Gurgaon*. Retrieved January 14, 2020, from *The Times of India*: https://timesofindia.indiatimes.com/city/gurgaon/reviving-najafgarh-basin-key-to-stop-flooding-in-gurgaon/articleshow/60110671.cms

Zukin, S. (2006). David Harvey on Cities. In N. Castree, D. Gregory, N. Castree, & D. Gregory (Eds.), *David Harvey: A Critical Reader* (pp. 102–120). Oxford: Blackwell.

SECTION 4

Conclusion

Transformative pathways to sustainability

11

REFRAMING SUSTAINABILITY CHALLENGES

Fiona Marshall, Patrick Van Zwanenberg, Hallie Eakin, Lakshmi Charli-Joseph, Adrian Ely, Anabel Marin, and J. Mario Siqueiros-García

What is 'framing'?

Ideas are powerful. Whether in the form of values, preferences or beliefs about how the physical and social world works, they enable people to make sense of complex socio-physical realities; to identify and prioritise problems, understand why they arise, and articulate the kinds of responses that are desirable and feasible. Ideas, as much as material interests, or command over resources, help to structure and shape collective action.

The concept of framing was described by Goffman (1974) as a cognitive process through which people make sense of events and experiences. In the context of contested sustainability challenges, it is useful to refer to framings as the ideas (in the form of assumptions, interpretations and values) that people bring to a particular issue; shaping how and for whom issues are seen as problematic, and how issues are explained. A particular framing implies a structure and stability to the conceptualisation of an issue (Laws and Rein, 2003), and a focus on the ideas within the frame, to the exclusion of those outside it. For any given issue, there may be multiple contested framings. These framings give rise to empirically observable narratives, or stories, about an issue, problems associated with it, potential consequences and how they can be addressed (Hajer, 1995; Roe, 1994). The interplay between competing narratives is shaped by both power and politics. Powerful institutions have more resources with which to assert the narratives to which they ascribe; specific agendas and social positions are reinforced and enhanced by the dissemination of specific issue frames. Thus, analysis of narratives is useful for revealing underlying framings, and the interplay between narratives can reveal much about the enactment of power.

In the context of research into transformations to sustainability, attention to framings and their associated narratives can provide useful insights into how

DOI: 10.4324/9780429331930-15

system change evolves (see Chapter 3). In transdisciplinary action research, engaging with and influencing framings and narratives with a diversity of actors associated with a specific problem domain can be fundamental to the theory and practice of contributions to transformative change.

Framing and reframing of problem domains and solution strategies played diverse but central roles in the transformative initiatives described in this volume. Framing/reframing in these initiatives was both an element we observed as part of the socio-technical-environmental processes we engaged in, and a tool we mobilised with our partners as part of processes of transformation. In this chapter, we introduce framing as a central concept to our work in transformation, and illustrate how it was manifest in the diversity of projects we were engaged in.

Framing and reframing in STEPS Centre work

Work within the STEPS Centre has an established tradition of seeking to understand different peoples' "framings and their associated narratives concerning the functions and dynamics of particular socio-technical-ecological systems, and the nature of sustainability problems that those systems give rise to" (Leach et al., 2010a). The Centre has examined how different framings lead to sets of narratives about who ought to act on those problems and how, and what count as solutions. It has investigated how certain narratives of sustainability gain attention and are pursued, while others are neglected or ignored (Leach et al., 2010b), exploring the politics involved in choosing and pursuing some variants of sustainability rather than others. The studies demonstrated that, in policy contexts, narratives that appear to reduce uncertainty tend to be favoured and become dominant, even if they are inaccurate, perhaps because they can lead to clearer plans for action (Roe, 1994). They also demonstrated that as strategies develop for interventions based on these dominant narratives, system change develops around them, further marginalising the alternatives (Leach et al. 2010a).

For example, Cavicchi and Ely (2016) describe how dominant narratives framed agricultural, economic and energy challenges in the Emilia Romagna region of Italy, in a way that led to particular pathways of bioenergy development from 2000 onwards. These focussed on large (national/regional)-scale initiatives which responded to industrialisation and energy security concerns to the neglect of smaller scale biogas plants that responded to local needs. They also explored how alternative framings (held by farmers and communities and prioritising the local environment and economy) emerged as a result of material system changes such as increasing environmental impacts of large-scale operations and changes in land prices and became amplified over time.

The ambition of STEPS work has often been to help widen appreciation of alternative framings and pathways to sustainability visions, particularly by helping to make visible the ideas of groups of people who are marginal to formal political processes. In relation to transformation, the premise is that dominant problem and solution frames can lock-in pathways of development and change. This rigidity results in path dependency and the persistence of undesirable and often unjust system states (Stirling et al., 2007; Stirling 2012). The emphasis of the work has not been to promote one particular alternative framing but to bring more options to the table (broadening out the types of knowledge and innovation options that are considered and opening up a range of possibilities for solutions) (ibid).

For example, Randhawa and Marshall (2014) and Randhawa et al. (2020) examined the interplay between contested framings of water and waste management challenges in peri-urban Delhi. They examined the adverse implications of the dominant narratives and their associated policy and interventions from the perspective of local communities; in terms of social fragmentation of basic service provision, environmental health threats and livelihoods. The transdisciplinary research team highlighted possibilities for a reframing of key issues in water and waste management through a sustainability lens. In doing so they helped to bring together the perspectives of groups that had been challenging the dominant narrative on the basis of lack of attention either to social justice or to environmental concerns – but through divergent, rather than convergent framings and strategies. Reframing through a sustainability lens emphasised the complex realities of social-material flows of water and waste. It led to a focus on adaptive, decentralised approaches to waste and water management policy and practice, including possibilities for constructive engagements between the formal and informal sectors and the need for a diversity of technologies and innovation pathways which address social justice and environmental concerns in integrated and complementary ways (Randhawa and Marshall 2014; Randhawa et al. 2020).

In another example of STEPS work, van Zwanenberg et al. (2011) examined the different ways in which international agencies with responsibility for regulating transgenic crops (national regulators in China and Argentina, and local officials in those countries) framed both the *purpose* of transgenic crop regulation and the *object* of control (that is the components of the socio-technical practices that were assumed to require regulation). These framings were then contrasted with small farmers´ experiences of how transgenic seeds are obtained and used, and their understandings of the problems that this entailed. The study revealed how, in both cases, small farmers' circumstances and interests fall at least partially outside of both national and local framings of the problems posed by transgenic crops and of the relevant socio-technical practices. It showed how the actual use of transgenic crops in particular localities in Argentina and China bore little resemblance to how its controlled use is framed in international norms. The study argued that regulations that better address realities on the ground, and that manage to support rather than undermine smaller farmers' livelihoods, imply that national and international understandings of regulatory purposes and the systems requiring control would need to be rethought.

Reframing in the 'Pathways' transformative knowledge network

The 'Pathways' transformative knowledge network (TKN) shared the ambition of earlier STEPS work to understand the evolution of different issue/problem framings and their implications for policy development and practice. The network also retains a focus on potential emergent pathways to sustainability that reflect the framings of previously marginalised groups of people; a manifestation of the centre's core normative commitment to progressive social change. But, while many of the previous STEPS initiatives had sought to work with stakeholders to widen appreciation of possible alternative framings and visions of alternative future pathways of change, the 'Pathways' network sought to push the concept of framing further in the context of efforts of intentional transformation. As a transformative knowledge network we sought to enhance understanding of the dynamics and drivers of sustainability transformations, but also to work as scholar-activists to contribute to transformations in particular contexts, engaging actively as transdisciplinary teams in aspects of the creation and enabling of alternative pathways of change (see Chapters 3 and 4).

Underpinning this approach is a particular type of interdisciplinarity in which diverse stakeholders were 'recognising together how problems are perceived differently – listening and acting' (Allouche et al., 2019). This should be distinguished from a passive listening to the perspectives of others. The teams actively considered how and why sustainability challenges look entirely different depending on the perspective from which they are viewed, recognising the social interactions and politics of knowledge that impact on that perspective.

As we explained in an earlier publication

> The 'Pathways' network involves a wide range of disciplinary perspectives including development studies and science and technology studies. It engages diverse sets of actors in participatory processes to explore alternative framings of problems, and novel ideas for moving towards more just and sustainable configurations of socio-technical-ecological systems. More metaphorically, the Pathways network is honing in on the "wavelength" of the politics of knowledge, and in particular the social interactions that enable alternative, more sustainable directions of change to be realized. This includes both the processes through which possibilities for alternative trajectories of change become recognized, and through which they are able to gain traction.
>
> *(van Zwanenberg et al., 2017)*

As discussed in Chapters 2 and 3 and later in Chapter 12, these activities of the 'Pathways' network can be described in terms of 'enabling' approaches to transformations (Scoones et al., 2020), which tend to challenge incumbent interests and control, emphasising political mobilisation and emancipation.

Team members recognised and reflected on their own roles as scholar activists. The roles rarely involved confrontational approaches in which incumbent interests and control were directly challenged. The range of strategies to enable transformations included the legitimisation of alternative perspectives, enhancement of the agency of marginalised groups and alliance building which led to the recognition across previously divergent interest groups of the potential mutual benefits of realising alternative pathways (Charli-Joseph et al., 2018; Eakin et al., 2019; Marshall et al., 2018; Pereira et al., 2020).

In thinking together across the 'Pathways' network about how possible alternative pathways are recognised and how they gain traction in practice and policy, we have become increasingly interested in processes of **reframing**. Understanding how, for example, a policy community's understanding of a sustainability challenge, and the actors and processes assumed to be central to trying to address that challenge, can be effectively shifted, thereby bringing alternatives into active consideration. Or how communities whose livelihoods are adversely affected by a dominant change trajectory can change their perspective concerning potential drivers of change such that their own collective agency to support transformative processes is recognised and enhanced.

Reframing and articulation of processes of transformative change

Drawing on some of the case studies described earlier in this book, we discuss a number of different ways in which reframing played a role in theories of transformative change across the network, and in the associated T-Lab activities in different contexts.

Theory of change

Each of the 'Pathways' projects began with a problem definition and an articulation of a desired transformative system change. Much of the overall desired system change was beyond the scope and agency of the individual hub projects, but the teams articulated the aims of their projects, in terms of what they would contribute towards processes of transformative system change, and how this would be achieved. This articulation formed the starting point for a theory of change (ToC) for each of the projects, which evolved throughout all phases of a project, and beyond. A ToC describes what needs to change and how, in order to meet the aims of the project, and what assumptions underpin the change processes that are articulated – but it can take many forms (Oberlack et al., 2019; Vogel, 2012). As trajectories of social, technical and environmental change unfold in the complex dynamic contexts in which the 'Pathways' hub teams worked, assumptions were challenged and new possibilities for influence emerged, while others closed down. Thus, revisiting the ToC, helped to support collaborative and iterative processes of reflection and engagement on how change occurs and what influence is feasible in particular contexts; thereby leading to amendments and guiding future interventions and initiatives.

ToC can take many forms, but will often specify how a research team considers which stakeholders' understandings, attitudes, skills and behaviours need to change, and in what way(s), in order to achieve a desired set of outcomes (Vogel, 2012), and furthermore what activities of the project will help enable

TABLE 11.1 Key issues relating to the role of reframing in the 'Pathways' TKN

	Problem definition	Transformative focus of 'Pathways' hub case study	Aim of 'Pathways' hub case study	How reframing plays a part in the 'Pathways' hub theory of change	Strategy
LATIN AMERICAN HUB *Argentina* *The future of seeds (and agriculture) in Argentina*	The risk of further loss of social, ecological and economic diversity in agriculture as a result of the increasing mercantilisation of seeds and the consequent market concentration in world and regional seed markets	An increase in the diversity and availability of plant genetic resources is necessary and will enhance the resilience of food production and producers	To create an experimental space in which coalitions of actors can develop and prototype elements of an alternative seed innovation system that supports the needs and production constraints of small farmers and other producers working within more sustainable agricultural systems, at various scales. Network of support and common vision	Reframing among actors seeking to challenge the dominant trajectory – moving beyond direct challenges to national seed laws to encompass a broader, longer term view of problems and possible solutions Reframing assumptions held by all protagonists that more sustainable agricultural practices cannot address macro development issues.	Explore how 'bridging innovations' (in the form of an open-source seed system) can encourage coalitions between actors who hold different perspectives on agricultural sustainability and seed system functions, and so foster wider, more heterogeneous, support for novel pathway visions of change.

NORTH AMERICAN HUB Mexico *The transformation Lab in the Xochimilco social-ecological system*	A lack of an effective strategy to slow/halt urbanisation of Xochimilco wetland social-ecological system. Efforts to conserve the wetland were failing; despite the clear value of the area to local residents, its cultural and historical symbolism, and its stated ecological significance for the city as a whole.	Actors feel empowered to engage with existing power structures and processes with new energy and constructive strategies	To create a space and process through which a small group of diverse actors could work to discover new possibilities for change-oriented action and identify. alternative development pathways. Enhancing collecting agency	Reframing the problem from one that is out of anyone's control and driven by exogenous stressors degrading the system, to one in which all actors could see their role in and capacity for enacting change.	T-Lab was focussed specifically on building relationships and alliances, forming common values and creating conditions for collective agency out of those relationships.
UK HUB *Transformations towards Sustainable Agri-food Systems in Brighton and Hove*	Limitations to local food supply and environmentally damaging production and consumption practices are contributing to the food system in Brighton and Hove bring unsustainable.	Increased localisation of supply and encouraging innovation for sustainable food production and consumption	To support sustainable agriculture in the local area by bringing practical and policy insights from elsewhere in the country.	Reframing of the local Downland Estate to emphasise environmental value and potential for local food production, rather than framing it as a source of rental income.	Highlight evidence from other initiatives that have focussed on localised supply chain innovation and progressive land use policy, and explore how they could apply in Brighton and Hove with stakeholders.

those changes, and in what ways, and based on what assumptions. The notion of reframing fits well into this approach to a theory of change. In relation to this, as part of the final survey (December 2018), each of the 'Pathways' case study teams were asked to consider the following questions:

a   In what ways and at what levels (individuals or groups at different scales) did a reframing of problems/issues/debates play a role in the theory of change?
b   How do we understand reframing in terms of its potential contribution to a wider process of transformative change?
c   How did the team seek to engage with framing/reframing and what was learnt (about processes and methods)?
d   What, if anything, emerged unplanned as an identified need for reframing as a result of the project process? (reflective of the need to revisit a ToC)

Key issues relating to the role of reframing in the 'Pathways' hubs' theories of transformative change are summarised in Table 11.1. This table begins with a summary of the overall problem definition, followed by the aspects of required system transformation that are the focus of the initiative. This is followed by an articulation of the aim of the transdisciplinary research project itself, the role of reframing within the ToC and the strategy to engage with and influence reframing processes.

Reframing processes

From the illustrations above we can characterise a number of different types of interacting reframing processes and lessons relating to them.

The Argentine case study was concerned with how different actors frame the sustainability challenges associated with market concentration and strict intellectual property rights (IPR) and potential solutions; it demonstrates the role of transdisciplinary research in at least three different types of, mutually reinforcing, reframing processes.

> *Reframing to expand understanding of what constitutes a system and the feedbacks and trade-offs involved.*

This initiative attempted to broaden and enrich existing conversations about IPR and the seed sector, to illuminate the long-term sustainability challenges and therefore open up a dialogue about the importance and significance of alternative pathways. At the start of the project many of the participants in the deliberative process focussed on the immediate conflicts over seed IPR between issues of seed price and access for farmers versus ability of overseas firms to capture innovation rents. The idea was to broaden the problem framing, which had so far focussed on resistance to plans to tighten seed IPR, and incorporate longer term and more hypothetical, but still likely, effects of strict IPRs. These included effects on rural socio-economic and crop diversity, industry structure and economic development, such that the inclusive development and ecological sustainability elements of alternative seed and agricultural systems were apparent. This reframing within the team itself, and the networks of actors with whom the team were engaged, was a precursor to the wider engagement activities that followed. The time horizon in thinking about IPR and the seed sector was an important element in *how* this reframing process was undertaken. Many of the possible problematic implications of strict IPRs that we wanted our team and wider networks to think about are not yet apparent, or there are only indications so far of how they might impact on agricultural systems. Bringing in experience from other countries, where stricter IPRs are more established, was an important means of fostering that longer term and broader perspective.

Reframing of value (what matters and how it matters): building the legitimacy of marginalised knowledge

In the process of conducting the project the desirability of reframing certain issues, which had previously been unanticipated also became apparent. For example, it became apparent that activists campaigning for more diverse, smaller scale and less intensive alternatives generally do not address, or do not have a view about, broader macro level issues – for instance, about how such alternatives could become a means of economic growth, development and diversification, or how exports could be sustained through alternative practices. Partly for this reason, they tend to be ignored, or dismissed as naïve by other actors concerned with the critical macro-economic role of agriculture. So here, the team recognised the importance to "reframe" taken-for-granted assumptions, namely that more sustainable agricultural practice cannot address macro development issues, such as the need to diversify productive activity, or to build new export markets. This reframing process is recognised as a long term objective and based on an ongoing process of alliance building and dialogue which occurs in parallel to the other activities of the team. The nature of this reframing challenge is exemplified in the fact that mainstream policy institutions currently view support for practices such as agro-ecological production primarily as a matter of social welfare policy (to support communities who find themselves marginalised from mainstream economic activity) rather than one of agricultural innovation per se.

Reframing of solutions: the possibilities for divergent interests to come together in alternative pathways

Finally, a key reframing activity stemmed from the team's interest in innovations that could bridge different perspectives on sustainability, demonstrating that there were often mutual benefits of seeking an alternative pathway of change for previously diverse interest groups. The idea was that certain innovations (such as open-source seed licenses) might find sufficient support both among stakeholders concerned primarily with issues such as food sovereignty, local production and small farmers livelihoods, and those concerned primarily with the macro issue of sustaining the role of the agricultural sector, through continued innovation. Might such an innovation prompt stakeholders to appreciate or reinterpret their interests and perspectives in slightly different ways (for example, on the one hand, rural social movements traditionally opposed to any seed IPR whatsoever, but who might see how a protected commons could ensure continued seed access, and on the other hand, domestic seed firms who work within an open-source logic already, but would not be able to compete if patents became more widespread for seeds)? An interesting issue for the research team was how the process of trying to innovate, that is of trying to do new things – or old things in new ways – is by definition a way of thinking about solutions in novel ways, and this also tends to prompt new ways of thinking about issues and problems. Innovation and reframing are thus tightly linked, with causation running in both directions. This type of 'bridging innovation' approach may be particularly effective where there is a possibility to develop alternative pathway visions and to demonstrate the material benefits of them to multiple, kinds of actors and organisations. In developing and engaging an increasing number of people in these bridging innovations (Ely and Marin, 2016), the other reframing objectives are also being simultaneously addressed.

The North American Hub

The Mexico case, focussed on the degradation of the Xochimilco wetland in Mexico City, engaged directly with reframing as a central component of the ToC adopted by the team. In the Mexican T-Lab, reframing was a deliberate strategy to enhance the collective agency of stakeholders, thereby helping to recognise and realise new possibilities for action. While no particular social innovation was imagined for the T-Lab, the team hypothesised that working with diverse actors in the wetland context could lead to alternative framing of the problems they confronted. The ToC embraced the view that reframing could contribute to breaking cognitive pathways and the mental models that limit one's ability to imagine solution possibilities. Such reframing would potentially enhance opportunities for individual and collective agency. Reframing thus was a core component of the engagement strategy, and an explicit and transparent part of the dialogues held with participants in the T-Lab process. Over the course of the two years, reframing was evident in the same core dimensions as identified in the case of Argentina as follows:

> *Reframing Value: Reframing the social-ecological system as a "spiderweb" of shared values and meanings*

As with problem domains characterised by ecological disruptions and environmental degradation, much of the focus in prior efforts to sustain the

Xochimilco wetland had been in terms of collecting environmental data (water quality, biodiversity, land use, etc.), and in documenting the steady advance of informal settlements over the wetland ecosystem. As a result, the dominant framing of the problem focussed on ecological dynamics and "irregular/illegal" (and anonymous) settlers as the primary driver of change; the specific activities, decisions, emotions and relationships of those who lived within and around the wetlands were lacking in this narrative. One of the primary T-Lab activities was to re-situate the individual participants within the Xochimilco system by depicting their actions and their social relations as core dynamics within the broader social-ecological system (i.e. through methods such as Agency Network Analysis, see Charli-Joseph et al., 2018). In collective activities, participants identified the material objects and landmarks that were meaningful to them in the system, and then shifted their focus to make those meanings and values explicit. In this way, they reframed the system not as one of, for example, soils, water, farming implements, fish and tourists but rather one of, for example, autonomy, self-reliance, belonging, beauty, independence. This process situated each actor, regardless of his or her role and activities in the system, as connected through a "spider-web" of shared meanings that then became the basis for a shared identity for the T-Lab group and thus a reframing of the objective for sustainability. Rather than focussing exclusively on sustaining specific material conditions and realities, the group also recognised the importance of sustaining the values and meanings that these material conditions gave rise to.

Reframing of problem and system elements: towards enhanced responsibility, empathy and solidarity.

One of the most significant processes of reframing was in relation to the dominant narrative of what the central problem was that needed to be addressed. The actors in the T-Lab, including the researchers, initially saw the problem as one of ecological degradation caused by urban encroachment by informal and illegal settlements. Through a series of different activities designed to foster reflection and sharing of perspectives, including Q method, open discussions, the "Pathways Game" and other activities (see Ruizpalacios et al., 2019), we noted that the dominant narrative shifted. Participants began to see their own responsibility for the problems they confronted, and saw that the problems were not just external but also internal, related to the attitudes, values and perspectives of their children, the farmers in the wetland, as well as urban residents. We observed the use of phrases in the group such as "We need to change the chip!", referring to the need to change their own narratives about the problem, rather than demanding that others change their behaviour and actions. The September 2017 earthquake, which destroyed many of the informal houses that had encroached on the wetland, also generated a sense of empathy and solidarity. By the end of the T-Lab process, the narratives the participants adopted had more to do with metaphorical "building bridges" across different users of the wetland than blaming external "others" for the lack of progress in solving the critical challenges they faced.

> *Reframing solutions: reframing the role of the researcher as both convener and instigator of solution pathways*

Another critical domain of "reframing" was through the ways in which the different participants in the T-Lab perceived their role, and the role of others, in catalysing change. While the TDR team served the critical role of convener, sponsor and organiser of the T-Lab process, the team stressed from the start the desire for the project to be collaboratively shaped and driven forward. In essence, the transdisciplinary aim of the project required reframing the role of the research team from its traditional role of collecting, collating and disseminating knowledge to one of convening, facilitating and creating spaces for sharing and reflecting understanding. For non-academic participants, this meant embracing a novel conceptualisation of "research" and the role of academic partners. For the researchers, this meant intentionally taking a back seat and letting the interests of the participants direct the evolution of the project, while also being willing to put the specific capacities and skills of academia at the service of the T-Lab group.

The UK Hub

> *Reframing of system elements and boundaries: changing understandings of the city's 'agri-food system'*

The framing of the research, and the discussions and engagements associated with it, evolved as the project progressed. At the co-design workshop, one perspective was that there was no 'agri-food system' in Brighton and Hove, because such an overwhelming proportion of the food consumed by the city is produced elsewhere. This was challenged when the transdisciplinary research team decided to look beyond the city at the surrounding area, broadening the framing of the system to (initially) include a 50km radius in their studies. Later the system boundaries were reframed to extend no further than the Downland Estate, as described below.

> *Reframing the problem focus around centres of responsibility and governance*

While the hub's work started out by identifying a broad problem 'space' (in a non-geographical sense), this changed over the four-year period of engagement and the key reframing aspects of the work emerged only in the late stages.

Initial research interviews following the co-design workshop and the discussions at the first T-Lab workshop began to explore and highlight two areas as key interventions:

- strengthening market linkages via supply chain innovation and
- changes in land use policy to support new entrant agro-ecological farmers

This second area became the primary focus of ongoing research and engagement work in the latter part of the project, on the basis of inputs from local producers and retailers who felt marginalised in mainstream debates. Rather than a blanket 50km radius (which had been used as the sampling field for the earlier interviews) or the Brighton and Lewes Downs Biosphere (a UNESCO-recognised area spanning Brighton and Hove and neighbouring local authority areas and delineated by two rivers), a specific focus on the Downland Estate was adopted. This was the area owned by the Brighton and Hove City Council, thus aligning the research focus with a specific governing actor (or constellation of actors around the local authority). This shift in focus took place against a background of public mobilisation in opposition to the local authority selling off areas of publicly owned farmland (the Downland Estate, which was framed by the local authority at least partially as a source of income through rental or sale to pay for local services amidst dwindling budgets) (Brighton Argus, 2016; 2017).

Reframing value of the Downland Estate around food and ecosystem services

Subsequent research investigated the potential for local agro-ecological food production on the Downland Estate, its relevance to issues of biodiversity conservation and local food poverty, and reframed the publicly owned land on the basis of its environmental value and potential contribution to a sustainable food system. These insights were discussed in depth at the second T-Lab workshop, when mainstream groups (including statutory authorities and local land agents) were brought together with more marginal groups (including landless agricultural producers and community campaigners) to explore innovative approaches to using the Downland Estate. At the time of writing (January 2020), the hub team cannot claim to have seen a broader reframing of the role of the Downland Estate by wider societal actors (in particular the City Council); however there is evidence of other activities that resonate with our work. Elements of the discussions at the second T-Lab workshop are being experimented with by nearby farmers (for example, High Barn Farm in nearby Rottingdean established a crowd-funding campaign in 2019 to set up an agro-ecological community-supported agriculture initiative). Elements of the discussions in the same T-Lab workshop have also been included in community consultations around Brighton and Hove's food system to 2030, with key themes including "better use of land assets" (Brighton & Hove 2030 Vision). The extent to which these will translate to wider systemic change over this same timeframe remains to be seen.

Reframing of solutions: looking beyond project-based interventions to longer-term transformations

In engaging with a wider range of actors, the initial project interest in local food production gave way to a recognition that the Downland Estate, and its multiple benefits, were themselves subject to different understandings and prioritisation. Rather than any particular solution being driven (or even advocated) by the research team, one of the key suggestions that arose in the July 2018 workshop was that a democratic/participatory process was needed to consider the wider role of the Downland Estate, and that a clear vision and political leadership was required to take it forward and implement a new approach to managing the Estate. The workshop also surfaced unanswered questions around a more fine-grained understanding of the potential for food production and a need for continued experimentation around agro-ecological approaches and other forms of innovation (including tenancy agreements, logistics and distribution, business models). Within the broader context of change in UK agriculture following the departure of the UK from the European Union, the research highlighted opportunities for Brighton and Hove "to value and reward its tenant farmers for the environmental contributions they make, and to ensure these are not eroded in the face of growing uncertainties" (Ely and Wach, 2018). Precisely how to do this was a question for the wider community, in which the T-Lab had made an important contribution.

Learning across the TKN: what was reframed, and how?

Through different approaches to reframing, each of the hub initiatives aimed, in various ways, to impact the ways that sustainable development issues were perceived. Through reframing, the initiatives managed to create spaces where assumptions could be questioned, deliberated, and reconstructed. The examples above highlight four distinct, but interacting, processes of reframing: 1) reframing of the nature of a problem, its scope and consequences – involves changes in understanding of what constitutes a system and the synergies and trade-offs involved in different development trajectories, 2) reframing of what is of value in the system and what is valued by whom, 3) reframing of ideas concerning the forms a 'solution' might take and 4) reframing of who does what in relation to transformative change and where agency and responsibility reside.

Across the Pathways network it was clear that if reframing is embraced as a strategy and process of transformative change, there is a need to make explicit the point of departure: i.e. What are the initial frames of problems, relationships and solution pathways? What interests and agendas are associated with such frames, and what responsibilities do they imply? Making such initial framings explicit allows collaborators in an initiative to evaluate how their thinking has changed over time, why, and what this means for their own work moving forward. It also focusses attention on the politics of knowledge and associated power relations, allowing all participants, including researchers, to 'step outside of themselves' and see how their thinking, and the thinking of those around them, is shaped by the interests and agendas of powerful actors.

In all cases, reframing also engaged with the question of "what matters". This was an intentional effort in the Mexican case, resulting in a shift in thinking about the shared underlying values that the wetland system represented to participants. In the Argentine and UK case, reframing entailed recognition of alternative, previously marginalised perspectives and the promotion of these perspectives and activities as valuable elements in the transformations being considered; thereby opening up the types of 'solution' that were possible. Across the TKN the idea of 'putting the solutions into practice' was understood broadly in terms of the means of unlocking the potential for a more plural range of solutions/interventions.

Reframing was also evident in expanding ideas about cause-effect interactions and the agency and responsibility of specific actors. This was particularly evident in Mexico, where the activities and methodology deployed in the transdisciplinary research process were designed to elicit reflection on individual and collective agency, and was instrumental in shifting participants' focus inward to their own actions and capacities, rather than "blaming" others for the challenges they confronted (Eakin et al., 2019).

In all three cases, the core research teams, who acted as both investigators and subjects of investigation (with a diversity of roles encompassing those described by Wittmayer and Shäpke (2014) as change agents, knowledge brokers, reflective scientists, self-reflexive scientists and process facilitators) also reframed their own understanding of what the interaction of researchers and non-academic collaborators could or should be. This was notable in the Mexican case, where many of the participants in the T-Lab had previously experienced interactions with academic partners that had resulted in frustration and low expectations. While such engagements had been less than productive, alternative forms of co-production and collaboration were novel and required reframing what such engagement could be.

In all three of the cases described above, reframing was an emergent outcome of the transdisciplinary research process, occurring concurrently with processes of social learning, discussion and exchange of alternative perspectives on the issues at hand. For example, while reframing was not an explicit part of the ToC articulated in the UK case, as participants in the process learnt of the local government's actions to sell off farmland, the focus of the problem domain shifted and became more focussed. In the Argentinian case, the transdisciplinary research team intentionally introduced insights from other parts of the world where seed property rights were in contention and connected alternative farming and seed breeding practices to the debates at the national and international levels. By revisiting their Theories of Change, the teams could support collaborative and iterative processes of reflection and engagement with non-academic participants on how change occurs and can be influenced in particular contexts. This reflective process allowed the teams to amend and guide subsequent actions, to help enable the potential for synergies to evolve. In the UK case the research focus was amended so much that by three years into the process the team were largely working with a set of issues which had been unanticipated at the outset.

The interplay between reframing, alliance building and innovation

Reframing enables looking at the world in a different way, recognising alternative – often marginalised – perspectives and rethinking core issues of value, responsibility and agency. Reframing can thus be considered a part of social learning processes, and a key part of building alliances across seemingly oppositional groups (Marshall et al. 2018; Page et al. 2016; Pahl-Wostl et al. 2008). As shared values are discovered, and alternative perspectives are evaluated in participatory contexts, conditions can be created for new alliances across disparate groups of actors. Reframing thus works iteratively with alliance building, helping create and reinforce bridging capital. This was observed in the Mexican case, where a growing appreciation among the participants emerged for the livelihood predicaments of both primary producers in the wetland and the informal settlers who were gradually encroaching on the wetland ecosystem. By the end of the process, the participants were discussing what interventions might serve to build figurative bridges to connect the disparate actors in the area. In the UK case, reframing was leading to an initiation of discussions over future land use between landless farmers and community members, and the local statutory authorities and land owners.

The case studies also cast light on the interplay between reframing and innovation, with innovation used to support reframing, and reframing leading to further innovations in support of sustainability transformations. The attention of each of the pathways hubs on novel solutions is in itself a reframing of how to respond to challenges, and how such solutions might be brought into practice (who has agency, what do they need to do to make something new happen, how to convince others that the idea is worth supporting and pursuing, which also involves a kind of reframing process too). This causality runs in both directions, because the effort of trying to do something novel or get a novel practice underway is a vehicle for helping to think in different ways about the problem, or at least directing attention on the need to do so.

For example, the Argentinian hub focussed on 'bridging innovations' that led to reframing and to the building of alliances across diverse interest groups in support of more plural pathways. The open-source tomatoes promoted in this case (see Chapter 6 this volume) attracted a lot of attention within the plant breeding community and the media, which helped to open up a discussion with new actors about what is problematic about a seed industry which is controlled by just a handful of firms. The innovation – the open-source tomatoes promoted through the seed breeding platform – generated and contributed to a longer term process of reframing sustainability problems and their causes.

Trying to do something new also throws into focus particular kinds of problems or barriers to change. Such barriers also need to be thought about in different ways if they are to be overcome, demanding innovation. In the Argentine case, such innovation entailed trying to make collaborative breeding work in maize explicit to address the cognitive barriers faced by both farmers (who assumed their observations of crop performance were too qualitative to be of worth/interest) and breeders (who thought that the traits identified by farmers as desirable were not worthwhile pursuing). The platform helped to challenge those initial assumptions. In Mexico, the participants' recognition that their own attitudes and actions were contributing to processes of cultural and ecological loss lead to innovations in what they considered potential future interventions, shifting their focus from an exclusive focus on the value of "eco-technologies" to a focus on community education and fostering participatory approaches with urban residents.

Conclusions: reframing to address the cognitive locks-ins that resist transformative change

In all of the Pathways hub initiatives, reframing processes, at multiple levels, were understood as a crucial element in addressing the lock-ins that can stand in the way of building alternative pathways to sustainability. This is because dominant ideas form part of the 'glue' that helps to bind the more material, institutional and political elements of established socio-technical-ecological systems together, in mutually dependent ways. Although reconfiguring such systems so as to support alternative pathways of change, is highly challenging, a route into trying to do so lies in shifting the ways in which people think about the problems those systems generate and the kinds of solutions that are possible and desirable. The innovation literature on niche technologies suggests that this is what entrepreneurs and activists trying to develop alternative technologies and practices do; when for example, they try and represent their innovations to, say, investors or policy-makers, as desirable solutions to problems generated by dominant systems (Raven et al. 2016).

Reframing processes, then, are trying to weaken or challenge what we can call cognitive lock-in or ideational path dependency; i.e., the largely unquestioned or unchallenged ways in which sustainability issues and problems are usually thought about. In different ways, all the Pathways hub initiatives were attempting to challenge and broaden the ways in which actors that are implicated in a system, in different ways, think about problems, their causes and how they imagine solutions and processes of change. In this way new sets of ideas may sometimes start to create political realignments or coalitions between actors, prompt recognition of novel policy options, highlight glossed over uncertainties or induce the production of new kinds of knowledge, thus beginning to challenge the logic that helps to reproduce incumbent system structures and practices

The alluring aspect of this is that while cognitive lock-in underpins problematic institutional, political and technological pathways of change, it is something that is amenable to challenge. Unlike the rigidities associated with particular established industrial structure, or physical infrastructure, the ways in which we – policy-makers, citizens, activists and others – collectively think about peoples' roles, their agency, the nature of problems and desired directions of change are amenable to being altered by a trans-disciplinary research process which pays attention to reframing.

References

Allouche, J., Middleton, C. and Gyawali, D. (2019). The Knowledge Nexus and Trans-disciplinarity. In Chapter 4 Allouche, J. Middleton, C. and Gyawali, D. (eds.), *The Water–Food–Energy Nexus*. Abingdon: Routledge.

Cavicchi, B. and Ely, A. (2016). Bioenergy Pathways Framing and reframing sustainable bioenergy pathways: The case of Emilia Romagna. Available at: www.steps-centre.org/publications

Charli-Joseph, L., Siqueiros-García, J. M., Eakin, H., Manuel-Navarrete, D. and Shelton, R. (2018). Promoting agency for social-ecological transformation: a transformation-lab in the Xochimilco social-ecological system. *Ecology and Society*, 23(2). doi:10.5751/ES-10214-230246.

Eakin, H., Shelton, R. E., Siqueiros-García, J. M., Charli-Joseph, L. and Manuel-Navarrete, D. (2019). Loss and social-ecological transformation: pathways of change in Xochimilco, Mexico. *Ecology and Society*, 24(3). doi:10.5751/ES-11030-240315.

Ely, A. and A. Marin (2016). Learning about 'Engaged Excellence' across a transformative knowledge network. *IDS Bulletin* 47(6), 73–86.

Ely, A. and Wach, E. (2018). Endings and beginnings: project-based work within wider transformations, STEPS Centre blog October 3 2018, https://steps-centre.org/blog/endings-and-beginnings-project-based-work-within-wider-transformations/

Goffman, E. (1974). *Frame Analysis: An Essay on the Organization of Experience*. Cambridge, MA: Harvard University Press.

Hajer, M. (1995). *The Politics of Environmental Discourse Ecological Modernization and the Policy Process*. Oxford: Clarendon Press.

Laws, D. and Rein, M. (2003). Reframing practice. In *Deliberative Policy Analysis*. Cambridge University Press. pp. 172–206. doi:10.1017/CBO9780511490934.008.

Leach, M., Scoones, I. and Stirling, A. (2010a) *Dynamic Sustainabilities: Technology, Environment, Social Justice*. London: Earthscan.

Leach, M., Scoones, I. and Stirling, A. (2010b) Governing epidemics in an age of complexity: Narratives, politics and pathways to sustainability. *Global Environmental Change*, 20(3): 369–377. doi:10.1016/j.gloenvcha.2009.11.008.

Marshall, F., Dolley, J. and Priya, R. (2018). Transdisciplinary research as transformative space making for sustainability: Enhancing propoor transformative agency in Periurban contexts. *Ecology and Society*, 23(3). doi: 10.5751/ES-10249-230308.

Oberlack, C., Breu, T., Giger, M., et al. (2019). Theories of change in sustainability science. *GAIA*, 28: 106–111. doi:10.14512/gaia.28.2.8.

Page, G. G., Wise, R. M., Lindenfeld, L., Moug, P., Hodgson, A., Wyborn, C. and Fazey, I. (2016). Co-designing transformation research: Lessons learned from research on deliberate practices for transformation. *Current Opinion in Environmental Sustainability*, 20, 86–92. doi: 10.1016/j.cosust.2016.09.001.

Pahl-Wostl, C., Mostert, E. and Tábara, D. (2008). The growing importance of social learning in water resource management and sustainability science. *Ecology and Society*, 13(1), art. 24.

Pereira, L., Frantzeskaki, N., Hebinck, A., Charli-Joseph, L., Drimie, S., Dyer, M., Eakin, H., Galafassi, D., Karpouzoglou, T., Marshall, F., Moore, M.-L., Olsson, P., Siqueiros-García, J. M., Van Zwanenberg, P. and Vervoort, J. M. (2020). Transformative spaces in the making: Key lessons from nine cases in the Global South, *Sustainability Science*, 15, 161–178.

Randhawa, P. and Marshall, F. (2014). Policy transformations and translations: Lessons for sustainable water management in peri-urban Delhi, India. *Environment and Planning C: Government and Policy*. doi:10.1068/c10204.

Randhawa, P., Marshall, M., Kushwaha, P. and Desai, P. (2020). Pathways for sustainable urban waste management and reduced environmental health risks in India: Winners, losers and alternatives to Waste to Energy in Delhi. *Frontiers in Sustainable Cities*. doi: 10.3389/frsc.2020.00014.

Raven, R., Florian, K., Verhees, B. and Smith, A. (2016). Niche construction and empowerment through socio-political work. A meta-analysis of six low-carbon technology cases. *Environmental Innovation and Societal Transitions*, 18: 164–180. ISSN 2210-4224.

Roe, E. (1994). *Narrative Policy Analysis: Theory and Practice*. Durham: Duke University.

Ruizpalacios, B., Charli-Joseph, L., Eakin, H., Siqueiros-García, J. M., Manuel-Navarrete, D. and Shelton, R. (2019). *El Laboratorio de Transformación en el Sistema Socio-Ecológico de Xochimilco, Ciudad de México: Una guía metodológica. Ciudad de México.* México: LANCIS-IE, UNAM.

Scoones, I., Stirling, A., Abrol, D., Atela, J., Charli-Joseph, L., Eakin, H., Ely, A., Olsson, P., Pereira, L., Priya, R., van Zwanenberg, P. and Yang, L. (2020). Transformations to sustainability: Combining structural, systemic and enabling approaches, *Current Opinion in Environmental Sustainability*, 42, 65–75.

Stirling, A., Leach, M., Mehta, L., Scoones, I., Smith, A., Stagl, S. and Thompson, J. (2007). Empowering designs: Towards more progressive appraisal of sustainability, STEPS Working Paper 3, Brighton: STEPS Centre.

Stirling, A. (2012). From sustainability; through diversity to transformation: Towards more reflexive governance of vulnerability. In Hommels, A., Mesman, J., and Bijker, W. E. (eds.) *Vulnerability in Technological Cultures: New Directions in Research and Governance*. Cambridge, MA, US: MIT Press, pp. 305–332.

Vogel, I. (2012). Review of the use of 'Theory of Change' in international development, (April).

Van Zwanenberg, P., Eakin, H., Turhan, E., Mukute, M. and Marshall, F. (2017). What does transformative research for sustainability look like? https://transformationsto sustainability.org/magazine/transformative-research-sustainability-look-like/

van Zwanenberg, P., Ely, A., Smith, A., et al. (2011). Regulatory harmonization and agricultural biotechnology in Argentina and China: Critical assessment of state-centered and decentered approaches. *Regulation & Governance*, 5(2): 166–186. doi: 10.1111/j.1748-5991.2010.01096.x.

VanKerkhoff, L. and Szlezák, N. (2010). The role of innovative global institutions in linking knowledge and action. *Proceedings of the National Academy of Sciences of the United States of America*, 113(17): 4603–4608. doi:10.1073/pnas.0900541107.

Wittmayer, J. M. and Schäpke, N. (2014). Action, research and participation: Roles of researchers in sustainability transitions. *Sustainability Science*, 9(4): 483–496.

12

EMERGING INSIGHTS AND LESSONS FOR THE FUTURE

Adrian Ely, Anabel Marin, Fiona Marshall, Marina Apgar, Hallie Eakin, Laura Pereira, Lakshmi Charli-Joseph, J Mario Siqueiros-García, Lichao Yang, Victoria Chengo, Dinesh Abrol, Pravin Kushwaha, Edward Hackett, David Manuel-Navarrete, Ritu Priya Mehrotra, Joanes Atela, Kennedy Mbeva, Joel Onyango and Per Olsson

Introduction: the overall ambition and approach of the 'Pathways' TKN

The 'Pathways' transformative knowledge network started off by asking how transformations to sustainability are conceptualised across different theoretical and scholarly traditions, and how this can guide and influence the organisation of transdisciplinary research. We were interested in the role of transdisciplinary research involving new tools and practices and our role as researchers, in both understanding and helping to bring about the kinds of transformative change called for in the 2030 Agenda. In this final chapter we discuss these questions and consider what broader lessons can be drawn regarding the role of research – in particular research that is rooted within the social sciences but extends to incorporate other disciplinary and practice-based inputs – in these transformations.

As discussed in Chapters 1 and 2, we adopted a structured but flexible approach across hubs that allowed for transdisciplinary co-design, theoretical and methodological plurality and co-learning. Research teams in each hub worked with local stakeholders to identify and define the sustainability challenge (problem space) and to design and implement an associated research intervention over subsequent years. We worked with a small number of theoretical anchors (framings, systems and pathways) around which different hubs experimented and innovated. Individual hubs in fact adopted very different theoretical approaches and used the project to ask different questions about processes of transformation and the role of transdisciplinary action research within them (discussed in Chapter 3). However, there were some key elements that were common across all the hubs. They all made a concerted effort to bring out perspectives that might reveal alternative plural pathways, recognising and engaging with asymmetries in

DOI: 10.4324/9780429331930-16

power relations, social differentiation in transformation processes and the politics entailed in understanding and fostering transformation processes.

The transformative knowledge network (TKN) adopted the notion of T-Labs as a methodological anchor (discussed in Chapter 2), building on the wider literature around participatory action research. Experimenting around the T-Labs concept, each of the hubs selected different social science and transdisciplinary methods (discussed in Chapter 4). Chapters 5–10 outlined the research and engagement processes undertaken across different hubs, in which various T-Labs focussed on conducting (or synthesising) research to understand the problem (all hubs), highlighting diverse framings about challenges and solutions (e.g. UK, Mexico, Argentina – see Chapter 11), where necessary helping to create a collective sense of the need for change (e.g. China, India), bridging across different views to build alliances (e.g. India, Kenya, Argentina), or helping to develop some more specific social innovation, prototype or experiment (e.g. Bioleft in Argentina, Gurgaon Water Forum in India).

Within the processes undertaken in each hub, we aimed to collect a minimal amount of comparable data around research and engagement activities (at T-Lab workshops 1 and 2) that was shared across the TKN through the mechanisms described in Chapter 2, and via bi-monthly online calls that continued beyond the lifetime of the project. As well as regular virtual interactions, moments of in-person reflection and exchange across all hubs took place at the outset of the TKN project (Buenos Aires, Argentina, April 2016), at the mid-point (Dundee, Scotland, September 2017), and towards the end (Nairobi, Kenya, October 2019) with representatives of some hubs meeting in person at other times. These in-person meetings were important for developing the friendship, trust and respect that was necessary to learn from diversity. They also offered some scope for in-depth discussion about comparative theory, methods and evaluation, however as discussed elsewhere (Ely et al 2020) time and resources were limited and insights have continued to emerge during the writing of this book.

The extent to which the original ambitions were realised differed across each of the hubs, and has been discussed in the earlier chapters. This chapter focusses on further insights that emerged from the processes of learning across disciplines, cultures and contexts. We organise our reflections on the basis of theoretical insights, methodological insights and learning about the co-learning/evaluation process. We offer tentative conclusions about "transformative pathways to sustainability" and lessons for future internationally networked, social science – led transdisciplinary research for sustainable development.

Theoretical anchors and related insights

As discussed in Chapter 3, the history of collaboration across the network provided us with a number of theoretical "anchors" that could be applied differently in each case. The role of the project was not to test these concepts (derived from work led from the global North) for their applicability in different contexts, but to explore their limitations and put forward alternatives grounded in the contexts in which the research was conducted:

- Systems – defined as "particular configurations of dynamic interacting social, technological and environmental elements" (Leach et al. 2010). The focus on some kind of fundamental system-wide change which will reach desired functions – concerned with enhancing environmental integrity and social justice – underpinned the design of the project and was an important aspect of our conception of transformation. However, the notion of "transformations" was not an anchor with a common definition across all hubs at the outset of the project. Chapter 3 (Table 3.1) discusses the objectives of each hub case study and the underlying theories of transformations that informed their work.
- Pathways – "the particular directions in which interacting social, technological and environmental systems co-evolve over time" (Leach et al. 2010). The concept notes that emerged from co-design workshops identified dominant and alternative pathways. Each of the hubs adopted different lenses through which these were characterised (associating them with concepts such as niches, paths, trajectories, mental models or windows of opportunity), as is evident from Chapters 5–10. The work from the various hubs has led to emerging understandings of how pathways may be/become transformative.
- Framings – defined as "the different ways of understanding or representing a social, technological or natural system and its relevant environment. Among other aspects, this includes the ways system elements are bounded, characterized and prioritized, and meanings and normative values attached to each" (Leach et al. 2010). The co-design workshops and concept notes that emerged from them recognised different system framings, and their fundamental link to debates and challenges associated with sustainability. Chapter 11 considered processes of 're-framing' in transdisciplinary action research and how reframing (of system boundaries, what matters in a system and how, the nature of sustainability challenges and potential solutions) can underpin an appreciation of plural transformation pathways and the potential for realising them.

These anchors helped us to share findings and exchange conceptual interpretations between the hubs. They helped to inform our thinking together about transformations, including the identification and discussion of different approaches to transformations research (structural, systemic and enabling – also discussed in Chapter 3 and in Scoones et al. 2020). Building on these, we highlight examples where one or more of these approaches can form the basis of a transdisciplinary intervention within "solution-oriented" (Feola 2015) "transformational social science" (ISSC 2012).

Structural theories relate primarily to historical analyses of Western sociopolitical systems and draw on concepts such as Marx's (1995) class struggle,

Gramsci's (1971) overturning of established social values/understandings or Polanyi's (1944) notion of the double movement to explain structural reconfigurations at the level of societies. While none of the hubs explicitly cited this literature at the outset of the project, some of the cases in this book point to the importance of structural factors, including those that are pertinent to locally specific conditions, whether of political economy or governance. An example would be the China case, which highlighted attention to workers and the disproportionate burden that green transformations had placed on them. Beyond the status of worker 'subjects' within the Chinese political context, the hukou "household registration" system in China, an important organising structure in the country's urbanisation process, is also relevant. The laid-off workers described in Chapter 8 were primarily land-lost peasants employed in private cement factories before the strict implementation of air-pollution controls. Formally, they had been re-registered as urban residents with urban hukou. However, they had only received basic education, were equipped with limited skills for the urban labour market, and had been forced to leave the agricultural sector (both physically and psychologically). Pollution control policies assumed that technical solutions could result in a more sustainable transformation, but little attention had been paid to the people who were carrying the costs of the resultant changes. Not only was this process of pain made invisible, but the omission of the re-registered urban hukou holders also allowed for a portrayal of China's green economic transition and poverty alleviation as a complete success.

Class was a central organising theme in the T-Lab work in India (Chapter 10), which was "conceptualised as a counter-hegemonic process of intervention". This highlighted intersectionalities between these traditional structural categories and other divisions around caste and gender (with urban–rural migration also playing an important role). Working across these identities, the Gurgaon Water Forum (GWF) (as a multi-stakeholder platform) attempted to build solidarity against the unfettered neoliberal forces shaping unsustainable and inequitable urban development. These elements of structural power comprise finance capital, real estate and IT, land owning castes in urban and peri-urban villages, lack of participation of poor and marginalised people, women workers in decision making, locals versus outsiders and religious and ethnic divides, and adverse integration of formal and informal (economy, urban settlements, planning, etc.).

Drawing on a long heritage, enabled by developments in computer modelling (see Scoones et al. 2007), systemic approaches to understanding transformation draw primarily on more recent theories of socio-technical or social-ecological systems. They are usually based on Cartesian, formal scientific understandings of system dynamics and struggle to accommodate indigenous and situated knowledges or alternative framings. At least in their earlier formulations, socio-technical systemic approaches insufficiently engaged with concepts of power (Meadowcroft 2009; Smith et al. 2010), but have increasingly started to incorporate these critiques into research on sustainability transitions (Avelino et al. 2016). As initially structured, approaches to transformation in the social-ecological literature only superficially addressed issues of agency, power and the implications of differential understandings of system dynamics (Brown 2013; Davidson 2010). There has been a significant effort in recent years to bridge more actor-centric and system-centric approaches to understanding transformative change by highlighting the role of leadership in system-level change (Westley et al. 2013) and by engaging with differential meanings of resilience at different organisational levels and with different societal actors (West et al. 2014; Borie et al. 2019). Challenging framings within and beyond system boundaries, and fostering cognitive shifts towards local collective agency, played a role in a number of the cases.

In the UK hub, which focussed on agri-food systems at a local/regional level (Brighton and Hove), there was a clear recognition from the point of the co-design workshop that the notion of a self-contained agri-food system (scientifically defined in terms of stocks and flows) at this level was questionable, given the high proportion of external inputs of food and energy. While recognising the absence of a closed system, the social-ecological boundaries associated with the Brighton and Lewes Downs Biosphere provided more scope to engage with nearby growers. Towards the end of the project the research was framed around the Downland Estate (seen as a system providing multiple benefits to the city, beyond food, governed by the local authority). This system focus brought various stakeholders together, including more powerful actors with a financial framing and others prioritising biodiversity, access or local food systems, in a process of reimagining the potentials of the Estate for food production and other purposes.

In the work in Mexico (Chapter 9), *chinamperos* as well as residents of irregular settlements of Xochimilco had understandably partial perspectives on the problems facing Xochimilco, viewing the system from their own position, agendas and experiences. As a result, they put forward narratives that lacked an integrated systemic vision of the challenges of the wetland and their roles and influences within it. Changes in the Xochimilco Wetland were largely seen as driven by external forces; solutions were sought that were linear (rather than systemic) and to be applied to very specific needs. The T-Lab process and our work with *chinamperos* and activists concerned about the future of the Xochimilco wetland offered an opportunity to explore the more subjective (affective, experiential) nature of social-ecological systems and how they were perceived and delineated. We reframed the problem at hand by making visible the underlying web of meanings, values and aspirations of the livelihood practices in the region. The wetland "system" was thus reimagined as a product of deeply subjective and personal social relations and identities, rather than geographic attributes, ecological processes and abstract social structures. Through this process, the participants in the T-Lab process in Xochimilco articulated their own roles, relationships and activities in the system, rather than conceptualising the system as somehow external to themselves.

Enabling approaches differ greatly, depending on power relations between researchers and different actors. These approaches focus primarily on individual and collective capacities and agency in provoking transformation. Enabling approaches emphasise what O'Brien and Sygna identify as the "personal" sphere of transformation, in which internal reflection, shifts in individual values and ideas leads to deep, cognitive change and personal commitment to alternative trajectories of action (O'Brien and Synga 2013). Power is explicit in this approach to transformation, given that it emphasises the abilities of different actors, including those in the research team, to mobilise material resources, ideas, knowledge, or technology to instigate change (Scoones et al. 2015). And since power is relational – towards someone and about something/someone – "enabling" is always a social matter (Ahlborg & Nightingale 2018). To some extent, all of our efforts were vested in this approach as those on the research teams engaged with others to explore alternative pathways to change and use our collective agency to pursue such change. This was often intertwined with processes of reframing values, systems, problems or solutions (as discussed in the previous chapter).

In the work in Mexico, our effort was concentrated on building the social scaffolding for the emergence of collective agency. Each participant carried their own social and political history and agenda, which in some cases conflicted with the understandings of other participants. In such a context, working towards building collective agency required acknowledging others as equals, valuable in their own right and as legitimate speakers. As facilitators, the research team had to create a sufficiently safe/"safe-enough" space (Raudsepp-Hearne et al. 2019) for everyone to open up and share their thoughts and feelings towards Xochimilco, regardless of their political views and social position in the community. For example, the research team worked with the other participants to identify what capacities and "powers" each had, and how these powers could be collaboratively mobilised to accomplish more than what any individual could accomplish alone (Ruizpalacios et al. 2019). The team could then see the nascent elements of collective agency emerging, largely through interpersonal trust and frank discussion of values and responsibilities.

The India case (Chapter 10) shows how mobilisation followed from convening groups that spanned different sectors, classes and interests as described above, recognising intersectionalities but trying to overcome them by developing collective practical understanding and collective agency. This was enabled through the process of building a "Network System of Solution Implementation" (NSSI) to evolve alongside the Gurgaon Water Forum on the ground and the Transdisciplinary Research Cluster on Sustainability Studies in the University. In a similar way, Bioleft (in the Argentinean case – Chapter 6) provided an institutional focus for enabling this collective agency – "bridging" across different framings and creating an alliance against the dominant patent-centric pathway. In both these (and other) cases, the resulting alliances enabled action and solution experimentation interspersed with critical reflection. Like the environmental movements described by Temper et al. (2018), these T-Labs adopted "values and ideologies that overtly reject hegemonic economic and political practices" and aimed to "confront and subvert hegemonic power relations". Enabling in this context meant assembling collectives that shared these values and found agency in developing the bridging innovation (Bioleft or Gurgaon Water Forum). This collective agency was further strengthened through broader mobilisation and follow-on projects that extended the scope of its work, as discussed later in the chapter.

Other examples across the TKN attempted to enable transformative pathways via broadening out (Stirling et al. 2007; Ely et al. 2013) the inputs to decision-making or action around different technologies. The Kenyan case (Chapter 7) illustrates the benefits of bringing different groups (with very different framings of energy futures) together to raise awareness of these tensions, and enhance mutual understanding. This represents a different approach to 'bridging', where alliances do not rely on shared opposition to an incumbent pathway, but rather seek to hybridise between established and novel approaches.

In other socio-cultural contexts, the enabling approach was less applicable. China's long history of a repressive authoritarian regime is intrinsically embedded into Chinese political and cultural practice, thus legitimising top-down decision-making and the dominance of the Party-state. People (e.g. the laid-off workers described in Chapter 8) naturally see the Party-state as rulers and themselves as subjects, especially when policies are associated with environmental protection. In this context, despite attempts to create a safe space and reframing sustainability problems and solutions, the enabling approach didn't work and success was limited.

To summarise, the experimental approaches detailed in each hub drew from the broad international body of literature on transformations and various concepts in transdisciplinary and action research domains (see Chapter 3) to pursue efforts towards transformation in their own specific context. This discussion cannot fully explore the disciplinary and cultural entanglements that led to the different strategies that were taken, but the notion of structural, systemic and enabling approaches provides a lens for comparison. Table 12.1 attempts to illustrate whether and how these were applied in each of the hubs.

The work also illustrates how these different approaches interacted with one another. In some of the cases structural perspectives were important in explaining stasis and undesirable outcomes, but also helped new alliances to envisage pathways to transformation. The role that enabling research can play in unsettling structural divisions (e.g. through convening broad networks and building alliances) was particularly evident, e.g. in the GWF, in which middle classes and migrant workers collaborated in opposition to the structural drivers of unplanned urban development. Future research that moves beyond those structural categories that are prominent in the (primarily European) literature to include non-Western categories and social orderings (caste, hukou) offers opportunities to further internationalise our understanding of transformations. Others among the cases presented here bolster the already expansive literature that adopts systemic perspectives to analyse contemporary transitions/transformations, injecting it with an awareness of power and positionality characteristic of 'enabling' approaches. In particular, they contribute new insights about the role of researchers

TABLE 12.1 Application of structural, systemic and enabling perspectives on transformation in each hub

	Structural	Systemic	Enabling
UK		Understanding the Downland Estate as a socio-(technical)-ecological system delivering multiple social and environmental services/sustainabilities.	Bridging different stakeholder groups that view the land as a revenue source or other recognise other values (including those adopting different socio-technical approaches to agriculture) through T-Lab and provision of analysis based on alternative framings enables democratically driven change. This combines with externally driven "landscape" shifts (e.g. Brexit) to create the possibility of a transformative pathway.
Argentina	Understanding the structural nature of the seed industry and resultant (problematic) directions of innovation.	Pioneering a niche innovation (Bioleft) as a novel socio-technical configuration), from which a system transition/transformation may arise.	Experimentation, learning and enrolment of more actors into the network enables gradual niche-cumulation and a potentially transformative pathway.
Kenya		Recognising two socio-technical systems and pathways – centralised (government-controlled) grid infrastructure based primarily on thermal power versus disruptive technology, and changing behaviours associated with alternative pathway of mobile-enabled pay-as-you-go (PAYG) solar home systems.	Working to overcome the tensions between these competing systems, which could provide the basis for transformation. Tensions and contradictions between policies associated with each pathway are addressed by bringing the different stakeholders together.
China	Remaining aware of several structural drivers in a broader context – state power (including environmental interests), development of urbanisation and industrialisation, gender divides. These meant that marginalised groups (e.g. rural women, immigrant workers) suffered as a result of "green transformations".		Bringing these groups together with local officials. This helped to enable a change of perception – we observed changes in local officials' attitudes towards unemployment as a major consequence of air pollution control. However, it is hard to predict whether these changes will generate any impact on local policy-making, which is top-down and authoritarian by tradition.

(Continued)

	Structural	Systemic	Enabling
Mexico	Reflecting on how agents are situated within structures: structures emerge from agency dynamics and at the same time can constrain these dynamics. In particular, structures of formality and informality in rapidly urbanising areas.	Facilitating fuzzy cognitive mapping and eliciting shared values associated with the wetland social–ecological system allowed participants to explore drivers of system change, situate themselves as part of system dynamics, and to identify the aspects of the material world that they associated with deeper cultural and personal value.	Making visible how all the actors who reside and/or work in the wetland are also implicated in its past and future, and identifying the individual and collective capabilities to enable transformative change.
India	Recognising class structures and their implications (e.g. capital/real estate interests lead to unsustainable pathways of development, middle classes benefit from capital but experience some negative implications, mobilised, migrant labour/poorer communities suffer the consequences but are disempowered in policy and action.)	Engaging with the existing system of governance – the policy, planning, regulation and implementation mechanisms; and the knowledge systems that dominate policy and planning discourse. The Transdisciplinary Research Cluster on Sustainability Studies at Jawaharlal Nehru University (academic actors) has emerged as a structure enabling the system of knowledge production to mobilise and organise (co-production of knowledge) and solution implementation (co-designing the solutions) to emerge with the science, technology and society, anchoring and handholding building of the network system of solution implementation.	Bringing together different actors, empowering those who are structurally disadvantaged and bridging divides in the Gurgaon Water Forum. The network system of solution implementation and the social carriers of innovation for transformations enables the possibility of co-production of knowledge and co-designing of context specific solutions against conventionally imported solutions that are not suited to the local context.

in bridging innovations and socio-technical configurations (niches, e.g. Bioleft), the importance of landscape changes (including exogenous events) during the transdisciplinary research process (e.g. citizen mobilisation against land sales) and an appreciation of different framings and re-framings of (socio-technical or social-ecological) systems, (several hubs, as discussed in Chapter 11). Perhaps more than either structural or systemic approaches, the T-Lab processes under-taken by the 'Pathways' TKN have helped to define 'enabling' approaches to transformations and what they look like in different contexts. The different en-abling strategies adopted in each T-Lab (e.g. methods of monitoring network development/broadening out across aligned or non-aligned partners), the pre-liminary work to try to measure and characterise these strategies and insights about how they changed over time are discussed further in the next section.

Transdisciplinary methods and related insights

Chapter 2 described how the project adopted transformation laboratories (T-Labs) as a methodological anchor around which different hubs innovated and experimented. As discussed in detail in Chapter, 4, a T-Lab aims to:

- "Frame the challenge, find change-makers and strengthen their individual and joint capacities to more effectively address the challenge;
- Develop change strategies that test multiple solutions, which could help to solve the challenge;
- Create early prototypes of interventions and build momentum for action. In this case, prototypes could be new business models, services, or kinds of governance that fundamentally change human-environmental interactions and contribute to changes for a better future".

T-Labs, as explored in this volume, opened up spaces for productive collab-oration and interaction between diverse stakeholders, drawing on a range of participatory research methods and engagement strategies to help contribute to sustainability transformations. Seen as a process rather than a methodology, T-Labs have been used in diverse ways to create the kinds of "transformative spaces" in which experimentation with new configurations of social-ecological systems, crucial for transformation, can occur (Pereira et al. 2018; van Zwanen-berg et al. 2018; Marshall et al. 2018; Charli-Joseph et al. 2018). "Transform-ative spaces" has emerged as a concept from diverse cases in the Global South that emphasise the complex realities of what transformation entails from more bottom-up approaches. It is a reflection of navigating histories and differences that have been reinforced through a largely colonial project within which West-ern extractive science remains embedded (Pereira et al. 2020). By opening up and giving space to interpret the idea of transformative change from the perspec-tive of a specific place (rather than a "lab") and build theory and understanding from experiential knowledge (rather than privileging the scientific), an attempt is made to reconfigure the power dynamics away from the researcher and towards the participants. Part of this involves the need to strike a balance between 'safe spaces' (in which marginalised groups can feel confident to voice their concerns) and 'safe-enough' spaces for transformation (which leave room for tension and discomfort, e.g. where dominant narratives are challenged). The operational realities of achieving this balance in T-Labs are extremely context-specific.

T-Labs as transformative spaces are conceived as open-ended processes and developed in this way, however, how to do so remains a difficult area for the action research/research–practice interface. We encountered various problems well-known to those familiar to action research – our research aimed to ensure that marginalised voices were included, however we could not assume that any such partners would have time to engage, and needed to avoid setting expectations of change that we had relatively little agency to galvanise, given the timeframe over which transformations can emerge and the limited time and resources available to the project. In all cases, T-Lab participants were engaging largely on the basis of shared normative commitments and continue to do so in various hubs at the time of writing this chapter, two years after the official end of the project.

Under these circumstances, it was important to consider the roles played by academic researchers (and 'research' more generally) alongside other actors in transformations, over the short and longer term. There are different conceptualisations of the role of researchers in transdisciplinary endeavours, particularly those that are more about process than knowledge production. Witmayer and Shäpke (2014) posit that researchers can play different roles over the course of transdisciplinary research initiatives, and different members of a research team can also serve distinct functions. They identify five such research team roles: as change agent, as knowledge broker, as reflective scientist, as self-reflexive scientist and as process facilitator. In more traditional research projects, researchers often are positioned exclusively as reflective scientists, collecting and analysing data as an external observer, while the other roles are typically more prominent in transdisciplinary work. Across our projects, our research teams combined roles in different ways according to the circumstances and demands of actors with whom we were engaging. Furthermore, our multiple roles changed and evolved as the T-Labs' activities responded to changing conditions.

While T-Labs (as described in Chapter 4) may rely on "participants who are willing to take a leading role" in transformation, this "change agent" role was rarely borne by researchers. In Mexico, e.g. the team served as facilitators and conveners, and brokers of knowledge, but refrained from actively directing the assembled group towards a specific previously defined end, in order to let the agency for change emerge from the convened group as a whole. Self-reflection was a critical part of the project, as the research team pushed back on demands that they provide specific solution pathways yet also recognised that they too had resources and capacities to offer to the group as part of collective efforts towards change. As the Xochimilco T-Lab work developed beyond the lifespan of the project, researchers and other participants established an NGO – Umbela

Transformaciones Sostenibles – inspired by the desire to take forward the kinds of engaged and experimental forms of action research that had been pioneered in the TKN, and to create the institutional form that would best enable this collective action. In India, the Gurgaon Water Forum continued to attract partners, secure additional funding and implement water projects after the formal International Science Council (ISC) grant came to an end, illustrating the longevity and continuing evolution of the NSSI. The GWF was able to initiate the process of institutionalisation of emerging practices and processes of knowledge co-production.

The changing role of the researchers co-evolved with the changing roles (and make-up) of other T-Lab participants. The design of the project (described in Chapter 2) allowed us to trace how engagement with aligned/non-aligned or more/less powerful actors (as described in Marin et al. 2016) changed over time. While attempts to quantify subjective measures of alignment and power were not seen as appropriate by all hub teams, even qualitative reflection about "alignment" yielded interesting insights. Different strategies were identifiable, e.g. in comparison between the UK (Chapter 5) and Argentina (Chapter 6) cases. From the point of the co-design workshop to T-Lab workshop 2, we can see that the UK hub broadened out from a more aligned to a less aligned T-Lab network. It began by engaging primarily with civil society actors, but increasing project momentum meant that the team – acting as knowledge brokers – were able to engage representatives of statutory bodies and the local authority at the second T-Lab workshop. The process facilitator role ended here, but, along with a number of other processes, the T-Lab activities foreshadowed a formal consultation initiated by Brighton and Hove City Council in 2020, that aimed to set out a vision for the future of the City Downland Estate. Here, some members of the research team continued to be knowledge brokers, but engaged as citizens rather than any of the roles described by Witmayer and Shäpke.

The Argentinean hub began with a broader engagement approach (including with non-aligned actors), but later played a change agent role in collaboration with the narrower, aligned network involved in Bioleft (while still engaging with non-aligned, powerful actors through indirect means). Chapter 6 illustrates how the involvement of various groups, aligned in opposition to the dominant pathway but not necessarily in their vision for the future, led to continuous diversity and negotiation of choices, with expectations often generated by particular actions and pathways, rather than an orderly adoption of plans informed by a settled consensus. This came alongside the team's conscious decision to "relinquish some degree of power" (Chapter 6).

Across the hubs, we discussed these changing roles and the questions posed by such open-ended research. Pereira et al. (2019) point to "ethical dilemmas associated with creating a transformative space", which were undoubtedly encountered in many of the hubs, despite the differences in approach that they followed. In all our work, the ethical issues entailed in our interventions were also prominent: who decides what the scope and boundaries of the process should be? Who decides who participates and why? What might be possible unanticipated adverse consequences of implementing a T-Lab process in specific political, economic and social moments? What might be the potential for harm, and who is responsible? In all instances, deliberatively convening a space with the aim of transformation is an act that requires ethical reflection, especially when marginalised voices are included (Pereira et al. 2020). Before embarking on a T-Lab process, expectations need to be managed; and what convening the space could mean for the participants who engage, especially for those who may already be vulnerable, needs to be deliberated on and transparently communicated to all those who take part. The acknowledgement of uncertainty in the process also has implications for how to apply for ethical clearance from universities that are generally less well-equipped to assess such collaborative, messy transformative processes. These ethical issues played out differently in different contexts (which are themselves changing – see, e.g. Yang and Walker 2020). More research and experience would enable a learning community to better ascertain and assess the ethical implications of T-Lab processes and perhaps establish a set of guidelines for setting up such interventions.

Transdisciplinary research and the alliances of actors that it enables are instrumental in navigating the politics of knowledge, and can be influential in addressing the structural biases in knowledge systems that cause cognitive lock-in and resist transformative change (Marshall et al. 2018). These roles in challenging cognitive lock-in, understanding resistance to change and working with diverse stakeholders to reframe elements of sustainability challenges in order to reveal plural pathways for transformation were apparent in all cases. However, the navigation of these multiple roles was a struggle that has been felt across all the cases as teams have attempted to balance their normative commitments, existing and emerging alliances and multiple institutional pressures at local, national and international levels. The TKN's meetings have enabled a sharing of lessons, understanding and support across the hubs about the multiple, changing roles of researchers in these sort of transdisciplinary research processes.

Learning from, through and about transdisciplinary research for transformations

The project aimed to better understand the role transdisciplinary research can play in transformations to sustainability. Accompanying the move from analysis to action was our desire to build understanding of the causal relationships between the research processes we were facilitating and emergent transformational outcomes, or movement towards them. This understanding had to be built through the specificity of the problem areas and the particular stakeholders engaged in each hub context. The theoretical conceptions of transformations applied in the hubs differed (Table 3.1) and were used to select appropriate methods for the T-Labs (Chapters 4–10), which meant that the interventions themselves also necessarily differed greatly.

As well as a high level of diversity across the hubs, the interventions were also built with stakeholders, implying that we could not know or specify what would be done in advance. This emergent and participatory design made it challenging to determine at the outset the specific indicators of intended impact, and so it was not possible to develop a baseline against which to later measure the effects of interventions. In addition, the transformative change we were aiming to evaluate was/is dynamic and unpredictable, and the timeframe long. It was, therefore, highly unlikely that end impact, even if it were to eventually occur, would be discernible during the project lifetime or in the years following (e.g. through to the publication of this volume). Application of simple pre- and post-evaluation methods to measure the net effect of research as an intervention was simply not appropriate.

Our response to the combination of internal diversity and unpredictability was application of complexity-aware evaluation approaches (e.g. Douthwaite et al. 2017; Patton 2010; Apgar et al. 2020). Such approaches argue for regular revisiting of assumptions about how change is unfolding (though real time feedback loops) coupled with the use of goal independent evaluations that capture change as it emerges rather than through tracking predetermined indicators. Evaluating emergent design of interventions to contribute to emergent impact pathways requires, fundamentally, that implementers learn as they go and focus on understanding how change unfolds rather than measuring net effect.

In practice the approach was operationalised through purposefully building moments for critical and evaluative reflection at two levels – (i) within the participatory research processes in each T-Lab and hub and (ii) across them. Reflection within the different hub contexts provided insights in terms of single-loop learning (instrumental learning through theoretically informed action). For example, Agency Network Analysis and Q method were used to explore quantitative differences in perceptions of T-Lab participants as the Xochimilco T-Lab evolved. Alongside qualitative evidence of increased empathy, the theory of change saw these as contributing to collective agency – "one important ingredient towards system transformation" (Chapter 9).

Moments of exchange and reflection within hubs (across academic and non-academic stakeholders) and across teams from other hubs in the network supported double-loop learning (questioning the underlying theories in order to improve them). Double-loop learning can be seen in the shifts in theory of change and strategy in Argentina, from policy engagement towards the action-oriented establishment of Bioleft. Double-loop learning in India involved transdisciplinary co-design with trade unions (Centre of Indian Trade Unions) and science and technology-based voluntary organisations (Society for Geo-informatics), enabling them to change their practice in ways that were more consistent with the longer term interests of working people. Our periodic efforts to report our activities and evolving thinking to each other in the form of blog posts, virtual discussions across multiple time-zones and in-person project meetings provided opportunities to step outside our efforts and take a critical look at the rationales and assumptions we held in each of our separate efforts. Three moments shown in Table 12.2 created opportunities to make explicit and reflect in person upon the assumptions we held about how the T-Lab interventions were supporting process of change, and so to bring together our theoretical work on transformations with our empirical and experiential learning from implementation.

Embedding evaluative thinking into our collaborative research processes within and across hubs enabled learning, yet it also made it difficult to create the space and process to examine causal inference around how change was unfolding as a result of the T-Lab interventions. Opening up space for critically examining evidence of causal inference from within the change process is challenging. Indeed, normative, change-seeking participatory researchers often struggle to evaluate their contribution to change because they are so directly implicated in it. Working across different disciplines and contexts aided the process of reflection by drawing attention to differences in framings and assumptions underlying our efforts, but causality remained elusive.

Our experience aligns with emerging evidence across evaluations of complex research for development programmes (Apgar & Douthwaite, forthcoming; Apgar et al. 2020) on the time it takes, and explicit effort required to refine theories of change through the research process itself. When causal pathways are long and unpredictable, and when the research is participatory in nature, any initial definition of theories of change should be thought of as 'plausible promises' providing a broad direction of travel without prescribing or constraining action. In our case, the initial participatory impact pathways analysis (PIPA) processes enabled an early and prospective view of opportunities for supporting outcomes through contributing to changes in the knowledge, attitudes and practices of specific stakeholders (e.g. shifting demand towards local food in Brighton and Hove). This was helpful to orient strategies for engagement, but as noted in Chapters 5–10, as implementation evolved in context, the teams refined their strategies and so too their assumptions about how they might influence change. It was not till the later stages of the process, through learning and building trust with

TABLE 12.2 Reflective moments and their contribution to evaluation of T-Labs

Reflective moment	Contribution to evaluation of T-Labs
Inception workshop April 2016 Buenos Aires	Informed by co-design workshops in each hub, adapted PIPA processes provided a prospective view of how the T-Lab might influence networks and stakeholders in the system – fed into T-Lab 1 designs (shared between some paired hubs).
T-Lab reflection workshop September 2017, Dundee	Consolidation of early insights and deeper reflection on theories of change, building on initial PIPA – informed some T-Lab 2 activities.
Final workshop October 2018, Nairobi	Reflection on impact and researcher experience as change agent.

stakeholders, that greater specificity on potential causal links between research and outcomes was revealed. Within the growing use of contribution analysis (Ton et al. 2018; Mayne 2008) and realist evaluation (Pawson & Tilly 2001; Punton & Vogel 2020) employed in evaluating research as an intervention, evaluators are grappling with how to identify the 'right level' of theory of change and at what scale along emerging pathways, to be able to investigate causal claims. In reality, it is often not till the end of the research endeavour that we have sufficient understanding of what is even worth evaluating.

An associated challenge to understanding causal inference was the temporality of the change process. In the project timeframe it was not possible to collect robust, observable evidence of transformative change, and so naturally researchers were focussed more on deepening and further opening up opportunities for change as they saw them emerge. Evaluation efforts were therefore proportionate to the scale of the project activities and the resources available. This balance differed across hubs, but in all cases the available time and resources were stretched between commitments to opening up hub-specific transformations and commitments to the overall international TKN-based evaluation/learning enterprise. Individual, institutional, disciplinary and national political cultures all shaped the ways in which we navigated these tensions (reflecting the observations in Chapter 3).

Beyond these instrumental and substantive learning efforts, the project sought triple-loop insights of a "learning about learning" nature (see Argyris & Schön 1996; Tschakert and Dietrich 2010), in this case learning about the learning and collaboration process (Hackett and Eakin 2015 – see Chapter 2). Through insights into transformative spaces including those above, and an examination of the effectiveness of our collaboration (Ely et al. 2020), we have to some extent realised these ambitions. The writing of this volume offers, in itself, a renewed opportunity for this learning about learning, as we evaluate what aspects of the activities we engaged in, and which outcomes we've seen, embody the transformations we are ultimately interested in mobilising, participating in and realising. We are learning from the ways in which different hubs explored specific aspects of what we might understand as 'transformative pathways to sustainability'.

Transformative pathways to sustainability

Taking the above analysis further allows us to explore the notion of "transformative pathways to sustainability", one of the original aims of the project (and the book), as a development of the pathways approach. In our search for a conceptual contribution, we have not articulated an overarching theory of transformative pathways to sustainability, but this should not be seen as a failure. To the contrary, we learnt that there is unlikely to be a single theory of change that works across all disciplines, cultures and contexts, and that the pursuit of such a theory may say more about academic ambitions than it does about the process of change. Instead we draw from the work in different hubs to point to various findings that resonate with, complement or challenge the pathways literature to date.

Pathways are "the particular directions in which interacting social, technological and environmental systems co-evolve over time", but what makes them "transformative" (able to bring about profound change)? What determines the extent to which these profound reconfigurations of interacting social, technological and environmental systems tend towards "sustainability"? What makes them durable or resilient? And what are the roles of research and practice, and the structures of real-world experimentation in helping to bring these about?

In answering such questions, we expanded upon the theoretical "anchors" – reframing, systems-thinking, pathways – discussed above and in the previous chapter. More work is required to explore how these inevitably play roles of differential prominence according to the political, institutional and social conditions where T-Labs are implemented. But elements of the work presented here offer a foundation upon which to build in the future. These could be further examined in future collaborations that apply some of the lessons learnt from the 'Pathways' TKN to new cases, or build upon the rich body of knowledge that has emerged from the network so far.

The structural, systemic and enabling approaches to transformations discussed above can be viewed through the lens of pathways, with each prioritising particular actors, forces, relations or causal mechanisms in their explanation of transformative change. The enabling approach that was common to each of the hubs focussed on fostering transformative agency at the level of individual actors but also across T-Lab networks. Whether through intellectual or affective engagement, several actors witnessed a reframing of sustainability challenges and their capacities to address them. But these became more potent when combined with new relationships and partnerships, reflecting earlier work that has suggested "transformative pathways will often involve transformative alliances among different actors – governments, businesses, academia, and citizens" (Leach et al. 2018). In both these individual and collective senses, the T-Labs played an important role.

While our approaches, activities and the contexts of our separate initiatives differed greatly, we recognise collectively the value of the figurative, social and physical "space" that the T-Labs provided. In each case, the T-Labs simultaneously were providing activities that were directly engaging with, while also providing the reflexive spaces to separate from, ongoing processes of social, ecological and technological transformation. The changing nature of the T-Labs, including the stakeholder categories, alignment and power of the actors involved, and their shifting roles, represents an important 'transformative' aspect of the pathways under construction. The evolving activities, from convening to "establishing a collective sense of the need for change", through to prototyping, developing and testing innovations, represent a microcosm of the kinds of transformation required at the societal level. In some hubs (e.g. Argentina) this evolution was seen as cyclical and iterative. The T-Labs provided a space for both thinking and action, with each informing the other and contributing to innovation and enhanced collective agency. As explained in Chapter 6, "the ability to demonstrate how an initiative works, even if only as a prototype, is a critical source of agency".

The transformative spaces offered by T-Labs thus allowed for the sharing and combination of knowledge and resources (with a view to innovation) in ways that were otherwise rare. At least in some cases, they fostered collaborative imagination and inclusive (and accountable) experimentation. Each of these experiences offers lessons for the design and implementation of Labs as a contribution to transformative pathways in specific contexts. Transformative pathways at societal scales might be characterised by similar cultures of experimentation, drawing on broad knowledge/capabilities and open-ended, non-hierarchical collaborations.

We also recognise the complexity of social transformation and innovation. What might constitute significant change must also be understood in relation to place, culture and political-economic conditions. Whether at the level of individuals, T-Labs or wider processes of transformation – our responsibilities as researchers led us to reflect as much on changes in ourselves as in the systems in which we were intervening. We were required to re-think the role of science and to interrogate the politics of knowledge within social change at a personal level. Transformations research, like the process of co-design (Moser 2016) can be "an agent of transformation itself" and an agent of self-transformation. A number of members of the Pathways network continue to discuss these issues as an aspect of triple-loop learning.

The limited timeframe of the project required attention to what would come afterwards, given the "monthly to decadal" nature of sustainability impacts (Norström et al. 2020). In the Mexico case, T-Labs could be seen as a kind of "cocoon" that participants created to protect themselves while exploring transformation, after which – at some point – it opened up to reconnect to the wider system. With this in mind, the Mexican team were cautious both in the selection of participants and in where interventions would take place (at the university, chinampas, etc.). In the India hub, the NSSI structure was designed to realise a minimum level of political and academic rigour that ensured the GWF did not collapse after the project was over. In all these cases, collective agency may not lead immediately to wider change, but creates a resource – a latent structure or propensity to collaborate – that may be able to respond to future windows of opportunity or moments of need. The T-Lab relationships that aided collaboration following the earthquake in Mexico (Ruizpalacios et al. 2018), or those that have enabled a more coordinated response to the agri-food changes underway in the UK (Ely and Wach 2018), are examples. The arrival of the Covid-19 pandemic (between the completion of the previous chapters and the drafting of this one) posed challenges in every hub, and in many cases, the relationships and networks that had emerged from the previous five years' work supported the immediate responses seen in hubs. Transformative pathways emerging from local levels will play an important role in resetting the 2030 Agenda, alongside top-down efforts (exemplified by the United Nation's call for governments to use the opportunity of Covid to 'build back better' – see UN 2020).

Lessons for internationally networked research on transformations into the future

As a contribution to Future Earth, the Transformations to Sustainability Programme represents one of the few social science-led initiatives applying truly international research effort to the SDGs and wider sustainability challenges. The important leadership of the International Social Science Council (ISSC) in co-ordinating the programme since its genesis should be acknowledged. The role of social science is crucial in understanding – and intervening in – social transformations for sustainability, and this needs to be borne in mind in the design of future research programmes. It is especially important following the merger in 2018 with the traditionally more natural science-led International Council for Scientific Unions (ICSU) to form the International Science Council (ISC).

The findings in this book offer lessons for integrating social and natural sciences with other non-disciplinary specialisms across international networks that are engaging with locally specific sustainability challenges. As is evident from the discussions above and in preceding chapters, the design and implementation of the project tried to balance trade-offs between various objectives at the hub and TKN levels. Moser (2016) described similar phenomena when analysing co-design across a broad range of projects in the same Transformations to Sustainability programme – trade-offs and tensions "between scientific rigor and an open, bottom-up design; codified data and the non-reductive work with parallel narratives; an emphasis on the advancement of science (and theory) for its own sake and the instrumental character of research with practical benefits in specific grounded realities; the immediate needs and wishes of actors and the long-term focus on a more transformative agenda; work at multiple scales with diverse geographies and site-specificity; and, finally, between funder requirements involving multiple innovations creating challenges around feasibility and cost (the opportunity, monetary and environmental costs of global collaboration) and the familiarity and ease of collaboration following more familiar standard procedures". We feel that there is more to learn from our experiences of trying to reconcile these tensions, and from the project's broader strengths and limitations. In considering these, we hope that the triple-loop learning enabled by the Pathways TKN may improve the learning process in future networked transdisciplinary research projects.

A group discussion of "what worked" and "what didn't work", undertaken at the final TKN project workshop in Kenya in 2018, highlighted the flexible approach as a strength citing "respect, learning from diversity across hubs"; "autonomy in the hubs (freedom to find what works for them)"; "legitimate input from the global South" as positives of this approach. At the same time, theoretical and methodological exchanges were suggested to have been limited by the fact that different hubs approached methods very differently. We feel that the use of theoretical and methodological anchors helped us to strike a good balance, but regret that we did not take longer to interrogate these concepts at the outset. Likewise, a structured approach to collaboration that provided a common schedule of research and data collection but allowed hubs to diverge (see Chapter 2) is a pragmatic adaptation that future projects can learn from.

Incorporating online and in-person communication and exchanges into the design of the project was important, however the practical ways in which interactions emerged also showed strengths and weaknesses. The discussion in Kenya, which included senior and junior team members from all hubs, found that the "inception workshop for getting to know each other made a good base – the culture and tone of the project set from the start", mentioned that "having meetings at points throughout the project was great" and stressed the importance of "friendships and networking". Without these enduring friendships, it is highly unlikely that the bi-monthly teleconferences would have continued on so long beyond the end of the project, or that the completion of this book would have been possible. On the subject of virtual communications like the teleconferences, SharePoint, etc., the discussion noted the "technological challenges of virtual, de-centralised information exchange" and, despite experimenting with numerous tools over the time period of the project, concluded that all platforms were "problematic or limited". More broadly, the approach to pairing hubs did not always work due to different approaches/lack of continuity of engagement/'chemistry' and one table thought that "South-South interactions were not fully made use of". This may have been a consequence of time and resources, which were found to be "a constraint to interactions, reflection and learning". Nevertheless, the discussion commended the "commitment from hubs despite challenges faced in their different contexts of work". This has been especially pertinent during 2020–21, when regular interactions continued despite the end of the project and the urgent Covid-19-related challenges being faced by all hubs.

For some, the transdisciplinary nature of the project was their first experience of such work, and the discussion celebrated "knowledge generation and the move from their research to action and impact". Starting with an intention to engage in and be part of a change process offers for some sustainability researchers a radically different positionality which comes with both opportunities and challenges. Reflecting the discussions above, measuring impact was seen as a weakness by some "because of a lack of clear definition of what impact is", although this view was not widely held. More broadly, the TKN members were positive about "establishing a global movement in sustainability, transformative research and action". This movement, in which the Pathways TKN plays a small part, is building momentum and increasingly drawing upon more diverse knowledge and practices. Our TKN has seen the completion of PhDs by students across three hubs (Mexico, Argentina and China) – these and other early career researchers are leading innovators in transdisciplinary research methods and approaches. Incentive structures must recognise this leadership and help to build this momentum. The urgent need to transform science and research further, ensuring that investments deliver on shared global challenges (by bringing about changes at multiple levels) has never been greater.

The discussion in Nairobi also reflected upon the long time-scales over which these changes sometimes take place, and TKN members lamented that "opportunities for follow-on funding have not been successful" and "stakeholders in hubs expect continued support but resources are no longer available". At the time of writing (December 2020), at least three hubs (Argentina, India, Mexico) have been successful in obtaining funds to continue or develop their T-Lab work further, and others (UK, Kenya, China) have seen their engagement continue in other ways. Through Bioleft, the open-source seeds initiative that was launched through the project, a new network of researchers, growers and policy actors is exploring potentially transformative ideas for Argentina's seed system (also initiating collaborative work on maize and tomatoes with the Mexican team). In India, the Gurgaon Water Forum set up during the project continues to be a venue for deliberation on the city's infrastructure. In Mexico, the work in Xochimilco has generated a set of innovations and ideas on research and appraisal methods, which is being taken forward into new initiatives in late 2020 and 2021 that seek to deepen alliances by creating an NGO that institutionalises the collaboration between academic and non-academic T-Lab partners. In the UK, the project outputs are (alongside other resources) feeding into a broad process to develop a "vision for how our downland could be managed over the next 100 years" (BHCC 2020). In Kenya, the new 'African Research & Impact Network' hosted by the African Centre for Technology Studies (ACTS) is taking forward discussions on 'inclusive energy', including through a series of online discussions. The China work in Hebei is being built upon by work on multiple dimensions of poverty, including those linked to green transformations (which have been studied in Datong Coalfield, Shanxi).

Multi-million dollar bids to continue and extend upon the collaboration across the TKN (submitted to UK research councils) have been unsuccessful. This is unfortunate because change of any such scale and depth requires persistence. However, collaborative work involving the UK, India hub and collaborators in China is being funded by the British Academy and the Argentina, UK and Africa hubs are being supported by a new grant from the International Development Research Centre (IDRC). Notwithstanding these encouraging trends, the points raised in the discussion regarding funding highlight important questions for the ISC, Future Earth and other organisations wishing to support networked transdisciplinary research towards the transformative agenda of the Sustainable Development Goals.

When addressing SDG-type challenges, we enter a hybrid space of research and development impact. The sustainability space calls for a focus both on the production of knowledge (often with a focus on actionable or policy-oriented knowledge) and generation of evidence, while also thinking about whether and how we make a contribution to ultimate development outcomes – the desired transformational outcome. As one of the first international projects that has generated evidence about how to accelerate learning and change in this hybrid space, the experience of the TKN in this regard sparked a number of insights that are relevant for the funding, design, implementation and evaluation of future programmes.

Funding

- In general, the funding provided by the T2S programme (now in its second phase) provided better opportunities for new forms of transdisciplinary experimentation than those available in many national or international contexts. More funding of this type, with mechanisms to ensure continued support should be encouraged.
- We would recommend that research funders collaborate with other types of donors (private foundations, impact investors) to improve the ecosystem of support for the kinds of experiments and innovations that emerged from the Pathways TKN.
- Various elements of the T2S programme (e.g. grants led or co-led from a low- or low-middle-income country, emphasis on early career researchers) represent best practice in the field. Resources need to be allocated to building long-term capacity in project management as well as research.
- Bureaucratic challenges of these types of programmes should not be underestimated. International efforts by the Belmont Forum and others to develop infrastructures that address these and reduce transaction costs are of long-term benefit to all.
- Flexibility in contracting modalities should be sought to remove bureaucratic obstacles to learning in real time. Many of the lessons (including those summarised below) require leaders to embrace ambiguity and take risks which are in tension with incentives to communicate simple messages about measurable impact achieved.

Design

- Programme design that incorporates and incentivises interaction across international teams (as in the T2S programme) is to be welcomed. Providing adequate resources to enable face-to-face interaction in the global South is a long-term requirement if ownership is to be shared and power imbalances challenged.
- Rather than aiming solely for academic outputs (e.g. publications) programme design should recognise the enabling elements of transformations, including collective agency, alliances and their role in resisting/destabilising unsustainable incumbents as well as generating alternatives.
- Attention to structural, systemic and enabling approaches towards transformations may be more appropriate in different contexts and at different

times. This book illustrates how programme design may incorporate these as feasible contributions to transformative pathways.

Implementation

- Internationally networked, transdisciplinary research is not well-served by conventional ethical norms (which are often based on "best practice" in Western medical settings). While these play an important role they can hinder transformations and may not be able to recognise the potential risks inherent in actively seeking to co-produce solutions for transformative change.
- Implementation of transdisciplinary research requires more flexibility, addressing changes in knowledge, networks and contextual developments. In this regard, reflexive use of theory of change can help to reconcile tensions between funder and researcher logics.

Evaluation and learning

- Research in the field of transformations to sustainability is not used to evaluating its impact, so there is lots of room for methodological innovation. Some of the work presented here (e.g. India, Mexico and Argentina hubs) offers lessons for how to measure change in networks and enrolment, but these represent a small component of 'transformations'.
- Much of the work in this area needs a broadening of evaluation designs to more theory-based evaluation research that is embedded in how transdisciplinary researchers theorise and learn from their practice. This also needs the funding world to move away from simple, linear and attribution focussed evaluation design. The challenge will be to establish an appropriate balance between catalysing and sustaining change, on the one hand, and studying and evaluating the process, on the other.
- It is important to acknowledge recent progress in supporting design and evaluation of research for development impact, illustrated by IDRC RQ+ (Ofir et al. 2016; Lebel and McLean 2018) and Global Challenges Research Fund (GCRF) foundation evaluation design (Barr et al 2018), which provide some early evidence of a broadening of evaluation approaches and an emphasis on learning. The latter requires nested use of theory of change across scales, e.g. in large international projects such as the GCRF Interdisciplinary Hubs (UKRI 2019).
- Particularly encouraging developments include the reflexive use of theory of change that is promoted through funder guidance to grant holders – this requires grant holders to revisit and update theories of change based on the evidence and learning generated within their projects. This call for adaptive management (see also Ramalingan et al. 2019; Prieto Martin et al. 2020) is in line with much of the learning shared in this book. Deepening impactful

practices will require the whole ecosystem of transdisciplinary research networks to focus on how it enables or hinders learning and reflexivity.

We offer these concluding insights to donors, academics, policy-makers and civil-society organisations who support, develop, implement and evaluate transdisciplinary work on transformations to sustainability. Many of the recommendations above are easily articulated in the pages of a book. However, they are more difficult to action, given the political and institutional structures in which current transdisciplinary sustainability science is embedded. Alongside action-oriented, engaged scientific enquiry and activism, efforts to challenge the power relations that act as a barrier to sustainability need to be seen as an intrinsic element of transformations research. We hope that this book can be seen as a contribution to this ongoing work.

References

Ahlborg, H., & Nightingale, A.J. (2018) Theorizing power in political ecology: the where of power in resource governance projects. *Journal of Political Ecology* 25(1): 381–401. doi: 10.2458/v25i1.22804.

Apgar, M., Snijder, M., Kakri, S., MacLeod, S., Paul, S., Sambo, A., and Ton, G. (2020) *Evaluating CLARISSA: Innovation driven by a participatory learning agenda*, CLARISSA Working Paper 2, Brighton: IDS.

Apgar, M., Hernandez, K., & Ton, G. (2020) Contribution analysis for adaptive management. ODI Briefing Note.

Apgar, M., & Douthwaite, B. (forthcoming) Participatory theory of change: Reflecting on multiple views of how change happens. In *SAGE Handbook of Participatory Research*.

Argyris, C., & Schön, D.A. (1996) *Organizational learning II: Theory, method, and practice.* Redwood City, CA, USA: Addison-Wesley.

Avelino, F., Grin, J., Pel, B., & Jhagroe, S. (2016) The politics of sustainability transitions. *Journal of Environmental Policy & Planning*, 18(5): 557–567. doi: 10.1080/1523908X.2016.1216782.

Barr, J., Simmonds, P., Bryan, B., & Vogel, I. (2018) *Inception Report: GCRF evaluation – Foundation stage, Technopolis Group & Itad.* https://assets.publishing.service.gov.uk/government/uploads/system/uploads/attachment_data/file/800907/GCRF_Foundation_Evaluation_Inception_Report.pdf, accessed 21 February 2021.

BHCC (2020) Protecting our downland for future generations, https://www.brighton-hove.gov.uk/news/2020/protecting-our-downland-future-generations, accessed 17/12/2020.

Borie, M., Ziervogel, G., Taylor, F.E., Millington, J.D.A., Sitas, R., & Pelling, M. (2019) Mapping (for) resilience across city scales: An opportunity to open-up conversations for more inclusive resilience policy? *Environmental Science and Policy* 99: 1–9.

Brandt, P., Ernst, A., Gralla, F., Luederitz, C., Lang, D.J., Newig, J., Reinert, F., Abson, D.J., & von Wehrden, H.A. (2013) Review of transdisciplinary research in sustainability science. *Ecological Economis* 92: 1.

Brown, K. (2013) Global environmental change 1: A social turn for resilience? *Progress in Human Geography* [online first].

Charli-Joseph, L., Siqueiros-García, J.M., Eakin, H., Manuel-Navarrete, D. and Shelton, R. (2018) Promoting agency for social-ecological transformation: A transformation-lab in the Xochimilco social-ecological system. *Ecology and Society* 23(2): 46.

Clarke, A. (1999) *Evaluation research: An introduction to principles, methods and practice.* London: Sage.

Davidson, D.J. (2010) The applicability of the concept of resilience to social systems: Some sources of optimism and nagging doubts. *Society & Natural Resources* 23: 1135–1149.

Douthwaite, B., Mayne, J., McDougall, C. and Paz-Ybarnegaray, R. (2017) Evaluating complex interventions: A theory-driven realist-informed approach. *Evaluation* 23(3): 294–311, doi: 10.1177/1356389017714382 (accessed 28 May 2020).

Hackett, E., & Eakin, H. (2015) ISSC 'Transformations to Sustainability' programme concept note– Water governance challenges, mexico city and phoenix research note from the ASU Water Workshop, 12 December 2014, STEPS Centre and Arizona State University.

ISSC (2012) *Transformative cornerstones of social science research for global change.* Paris: International Social Science Council.

Ely, A., Marin, A., Charli-Joseph, L., Abrol, D., Apgar, M., Atela, J., Ayre, B., Byrne, R., Choudhary, B. K., Chengo, V., Cremaschi, A., Davis, R., Desai, P., Eakin, H., Kushwaha, P., Marshall, F., Mbeva, K., Ndege, N., Ochieng, C., Ockwell, D., Olsson, P., Oxley, N., Pereira, L,. Priya, R., Tigabu, A., Van Zwanenberg, P., & Yang, L. (2020) Structured collaboration across a Transformative Knowledge Network: Learning across disciplines, cultures and contexts? *Sustainability* 12(6): 2499. doi: 10.3390/su12062499.

Ely, A.V., & Wach, E. (2018) Endings and beginnings: Project-based work within wider transformations, https://steps-centre.org/blog/endings-and-beginnings-project-based-work-within-wider-transformations/, accessed 16/12/2020.

Feola, G. (2015) Societal transformation in response to global environmental change: A review of emerging concepts. *Ambio* 44: 376–390.

Folke, C., Hahn, T., Olsson, P., & Norberg, J. (2005) Adaptive governance of social-ecological systems. *Annual Review of Environment and Resources* 30: 441–473.

Gramsci, A. (1971) *Selections from the Prison notebooks of Antonio Gramsci.* New York: International Publishers.

Hackett, E., & Eakin, H. (2015) ISSC 'Transformations to Sustainability' programme concept note– Water governance challenges, Mexico City and Phoenix research note from the ASU water workshop, 12 December 2014, STEPS Centre and Arizona State University, https://steps-centre.org/wp-content/uploads/ISSC-Concept-note_ASU.pdf, accessed 29/9/2020.

Leach, M., Reyers, B., Bai, X., Brondizio, E. S., Cook, C., Díaz, S., Espindola, G., Scobie, M., Stafford-Smith, M., & Subramanian, S. M. (2018) Equity and sustainability in the Anthropocene: a social–ecological systems perspective on their intertwined futures. *Global Sustainability* 1: e13.

Lebel, J., & McLean, R. (2018) A better measure of research from the global south. *Nature* 559: 23–26.

Mayne, J. (2008) *Contribution analysis: An approach to exploring cause and effect,* ILAC Brief 16, Institutional Learning and Change (ILAC) Initiative, https://cgspace.cgiar.org/handle/10568/70124 (accessed 28 May 2020).

Marx, K. (1976) *Capital: A critique of political economy,* Volume 1. Harmondsworth: Penguin.

Marshall, F., Dolley, J., & Priya, R. (2018) Transdisciplinary research as transformative space making for sustainability: Enhancing propoor transformative agency in periurban contexts. *Ecology and Society* 23(3). doi: 10.5751/ES-10249–230308.

Meadowcroft, J. (2009) What about the politics? Sustainable development, transition management, and long-term energy transitions. *Policy Sciences* 42(4): 323.

Moser, S. (2016) Can science on transformation transform science? Lessons from co-design. *Current Opinion in Environmental Sustainability* 20: 106–115.

Norström, A.V., Cvitanovic, C., Löf, M.F., et al. (2020) Principles for knowledge co-production in sustainability research. *National Sustainable.* doi: 10.1038/s41893-019-0448-2.

Ofir, Z., Schwandt, T., Duggan, C., & McLean, R. (2016) *Research quality plus (RQ+): A holistic approach to evaluating research.* Canada: International Development Research Centre.

O'Brien, K., & Sygna, L. (2013) Responding to climate change: The three spheres of transformation. *Proceedings of Transformation in a Changing Climate* (June): 16–23.

Olsson, P., Folke, C., & Berkes, F. (2004) Adaptive co-management for building resilience in social–ecological systems. *Environmental Management* 34: 75–90.

Patton, M.Q. (2010) *Developmental evaluation: Applying complexity concepts to enhance innovation and use.* New York: Guilford Press.

Pawson, R., & Tilley, N. (1997) *Realistic evaluation.* London: Sage Publications.

Pereira, L.M., Karpouzoglou, T., Frantzeskaki, N., & Olsson, P. (2018) Designing transformative spaces for sustainability in social-ecological systems. *Ecology and Society* 23(4): 32.

Pereira, L., Frantzeskaki, N., Hebinck, A., Charli-Joseph, L., Drimie, S., Dyer, M., Eakin, H., Galafassi, D., Karpouzoglou, T., Marshall, F., Lee Moore, M., Olsson, P., Siqueiros-García, J.M., van Zwanenberg, P., & Vervoort, J.M. (2019) Transformative spaces in the making: Key lessons from nine cases in the Global South. *Sustainability Science* 15: 161–178.

Polanyi, K. (1944) *The great transformation: The political and economic origins of our time.* Boston: Beacon Press.

Prieto Martin, P., Apgar, M., & Hernandez, K. (2020) *Adaptive management in SDC: Challenges and opportunities.* Brighton: Institute of Development Studies.

Punton, M., & Vogel, I. (2020) Keeping it real: Using mechanisms to promote use in the realist evaluation of the building capacity to use research evidence program. *New Directions for Evaluation* 2020(167): 87–100.

Ramalingam, B., Wild, L., & Buffardi, A.L. (2019) *Making adaptive rigour work.* Brighton: Institute of Development Studies.

Raudsepp-Hearne, C., Peterson, G.D., Bennett, E.M., Biggs, R., Norstrom, A.V., Pereira, L., Vervoort, J., Iwaniec, D.M., McPhearson, T., Olsson, P., Hichert, T., Falardeau, M., & Aceituno, A.J. (2019) Seeds of good anthropocenes: Developing sustainability scenarios for Northern Europe. *Sustainability Science.* doi: 10.1007/s11625-019-00714-8.

Ruizpalacios, B., Charli-Joseph, L., Eakin, H., Siqueiros-García, J.M., Manuel-Navarrete, D., & Shelton, R. (2019) *The transformation laboratory of the social-ecological system of Xochimilco, Mexico City: Description of the process and methodological guide.* Mexico City: LANCIS-IE, UNAM.

Ruizpalacios, B., Charli-Joseph, L., Eakin, H., Mario Siqueiros-García, J., & Shelton, R. (2018) *Creating bridges through the Pathways to Sustainability game,* https://steps-centre.org/blog/creating-bridges-through-the-pathways-to-sustainability-game/, accessed 16/12/2020.

Scoones, I., Newell, P., & Leach, M. (Eds) (2015) *The politics of Green transformations.* Abingdon: Routledge.

Scoones, I., Stirling, A., Abrol, D., Atela, J., Charli-Joseph, L., Eakin, H., Ely, A., Olsson, P., Pereira, L., Priya, R., van Zwanenberg, P., & Yang, L. (2018) *Transformations to sustainability,* STEPS Working Paper 104. Brighton: STEPS Centre.

Scoones, I., Leach, M., Smith, A., Stagl, S., Stirling, A., & Thompson, J. (2007) *Dynamic systems and the challenge of sustainability*, STEPS Working Paper 1, Brighton: STEPS Centre,

Scoones, I., Stirling, A., Abrol, D., Atela, J., Charli-Joseph, L., Eakin, H., Ely, A., Olsson, P., Pereira, L., Priya, R., van Zwanenberg, P., & Yang, L. (2020) Transformations to sustainability: Combining structural, systemic and enabling approaches. *Current Opinion in Environmental Sustainability*. doi:10.1016/j.cosust.2019.12.004.

Smith, A., Voß, J-P., & Grin, J. (2010) Innovation studies and sustainability transitions: The allure of the multi-level perspective and its challenges. *Research Policy* 39(4): 435–448.

Stirling, A., Leach, M., Mehta, L., Scoones, I., Smith, A., Stagl, S., & Thompson, J. (2007) *Empowering designs: Towards more progressive appraisal of sustainability*, STEPS Working Paper 3, Brighton: STEPS Centre.

Ton, G., Mayne, J., Delahais, T., Morell, J., Befani, B., Apgar, M., & O'Flynn, P. (2019) Contribution analysis and estimating the size of effects: Can we reconcile the possible with the impossible? *CDI Practice Paper*.

Tschakert, P., & Dietrich, K.A. (2010) Anticipatory learning for climate change adaptation and resilience. *Ecology and Society* 15(2): 11.

UKRI (2019) *UKRI GCRF global interdisciplinary research hubs*, https://www.ukri.org/wp-content/uploads/2020/10/UKRI-22102020-GCRF-Hub-booklet-June-2019.pdf, accessed 21 February 2021).

UN (2020) Climate Change and COVID-19: UN urges nations to 'recover better', April 22 https://www.un.org/en/un-coronavirus-communications-team/un-urges-countries-%E2%80%98build-back-better%E2%80%99, accessed 16/12/2020.

Van Zwanenberg, P., Marin, A., & Ely, A. (2016) How *do we end the dominance of rich countries over sustainability science?* STEPS Centre: Brighton, UK. Available online: https://steps-centre.org/blog/how-do-we-end-the-dominance-of-rich-countries-over-sustainability-science/ (accessed on 9 September 2019).

van Zwanenberg, P., Cremaschi, A., Obaya, M., Marin, A., & Lowenstein, V. (2018) Seeking unconventional alliances and bridging innovations in spaces for transformative change: the seed sector and agricultural sustainability in Argentina. *Ecology and Society* 23(3): 11.

West, S., Haider, J., Sinare, H., & Karpouzoglou, T. (2014) *Beyond divides: Prospects for synergy between resilience and pathways approaches to sustainability*, STEPS Working Paper 65, Brighton: STEPS Centre.

Westley, F.R., Tjornbo, O., Schultz, L., Olsson, P., Folke, C., Crona, B., & Bodin, Ö. (2013) A theory of transformative agency in linked social-ecological systems. *Ecology & Society* 18: 1–16.

Wittmayer, J.M., & Schäpke, N. (2014) Action, research and participation: roles of researchers in sustainability transitions. *Sustainability Science* 9(4): 483–496.

Yang, L., & Walker, R. (2020) Poverty, shame and ethics in contemporary China. *Journal of Social Policy* 49(3): 564–581.

INDEX

Note: **Bold** page numbers refer to tables, *italic* page numbers refer to figures and page numbers followed by "n" denote endnotes.